THE CATTELL CONTROVERSY

THE
CATTELL
CONTROVERSY

RACE, SCIENCE, AND IDEOLOGY

WILLIAM H. TUCKER

UNIVERSITY
OF ILLINOIS PRESS
URBANA AND
CHICAGO

© 2009 by the Board of Trustees
of the University of Illinois
All rights reserved
Manufactured in the United States of America
C 5 4 3 2 1

∞ This book is printed on acid-free paper.

Library of Congress Cataloging-in-Publication Data
Tucker, Willim H., 1940–
The Cattell Controversy : race, science, and ideology /
William H. Tucker.
p.   cm.
Includes bibliographical references and index.
ISBN 978-0-252-03400-8 (cloth : alk. paper)
1. Cattell, Raymond B. (Raymond Bernard), 1905–1998—
Political and social views.
2. Racism in psychology.
I. Title.
BF109.C38T93   2009
150.92—dc22   2008034984

To the memory of my mother,
Doris G. Tucker

CONTENTS

PREFACE

Discharged from the U.S. Army only two weeks earlier, in September 1965 I registered for my first college course in psychology, Theories of Personality, taught by Professor Leland ("Bud") Bechtel. In addition to the work of such well-known names as Sigmund Freud, Carl Jung, Alfred Adler, Carl Rogers, Abraham Maslow, and Gordon Allport, Bud introduced me to the factor analytic approach of Raymond B. Cattell. I was captivated by the orderliness of Cattell's notion that human personality could be deconstructed into a set of specific "source traits" and impressed by the sophisticated methodology he had developed to accomplish this goal. Indeed, the realization, beginning with my discovery of Cattell's work, that complex issues in psychology could be studied with quantitative techniques was instrumental in my decision to pursue graduate work as a psychometric fellow, a position sponsored by the Educational Testing Service to support students specializing in psychological measurement.

It was not until two decades later that, while doing research on an anthropological journal founded to provide an outlet for the views of American segregationists and European adherents to Nazi *Rassenhygiene,* I came across Cattell's name as author of one of the articles. Initially thinking that he must have chosen this venue unaware of its background and purpose, little by little I was forced to the conclusion that this was no accident; not only was the content of the article frighteningly consistent with the journal's perspective, but it turned out that Cattell had authored numerous similar publications in the same journal, and there would be more to follow. This surprising discovery eventually led me to the substantial body of work, relatively unknown among mainstream psychologists, in which Cattell outlined the radical, eugenic motivation for his research in personality and social psychology and the ultimate purpose for which he intended the results. It is this literature that is the primary topic of the following pages.

I shall argue that Cattell's ideology, as an informing influence on his science, has implications for the way in which his accomplishments should be viewed and, in particular, for the decision to name him the recipient of a specific honor within the field. At the same time, however, I wish to distinguish between criticism and any desire for proscription. Researchers and theorists have an absolute right to pursue the topic of their choice and to offer interpretations or practical applications as they see fit. But they should not expect to be immune from opposition.

* * *

I don't think it is possible to write a serious book without imposing on others. In any event I certainly have done so, burdening friends and colleagues with drafts of chapters and benefiting from their comments and suggestions. I owe a large debt of gratitude, in particular, to Andrew Winston for his careful reading of a number of chapters, but even more for his encouragement and friendship. Dan Hart, Bill Whitlow, Patrick Markey, and Howard Gillette each read some piece of the manuscript and offered valuable advice. I had a number of discussions about the book's conclusion with Ira Roseman, whose observations helped me to clarify some of my thinking. And I was privileged to be invited by Bill Cross to present portions of the book to the graduate colloquium in social-personality at the City University of New York, the members of which asked provocative questions, leading me to rethink some of the issues. I am also grateful that Barry Mehler, director of the Institute for the Study of Academic Racism, was kind enough to share the contents of his own files on Cattell. As reviewers for the press, both Barry and John Jackson made insightful comments that forced me to sharpen my argument in a number of places. All these people have contributed to whatever strengths may be found in this book; the weaknesses that remain are my responsibility alone.

This is my third book with the University of Illinois Press, and I could not ask for better support. Since I first mentioned the idea for this book to the editor, Joan Catapano, she has encouraged my work on the project. The final draft has benefited greatly from Annette Wenda's meticulous copyediting.

An NEH Fellowship enabled me to complete work on the book, and I am grateful for the award and for the support from Rutgers University that accompanied it.

Shortly after I began work on this manuscript, my mother suffered a stroke and died eight months later, twenty-six days shy of her ninety-fifth birthday. Until the stroke, this strong-willed woman had lived entirely on her own, setting an example of independence in the face of advancing age that I can only hope to emulate. It is to her memory that I have dedicated this book.

THE CATTELL CONTROVERSY

INTRODUCTION
"A FIERCE WIND"

Every college student who has taken a course in personality psychology has heard of Raymond Cattell, the father of trait measurement. Although his name is not particularly familiar to the public—not even to fairly well-read people unless they happen to have majored in psychology as undergraduates—Cattell's enormous body of work has made major contributions to scientific thought about personality, human intelligence, and multivariate methodology. The author of fifty-six books, more than five hundred journal articles and book chapters, and some thirty standardized instruments for assessing personality and intelligence in a professional career that spanned two-thirds of a century before his death in 1998, Cattell must be considered one of the most influential research psychologists ever. A 1968 review of one of his books referred to him at *that* time—when he still had a couple of hundred publications to come—as "America's (and perhaps the world's) most productive psychologist."[1] In a study of "the most eminent psychologists of the 20th century," he ranked sixteenth overall. One component of the ranking process was frequency of citation in the professional literature, a measure on which Cattell placed seventh, just ahead of B. F. Skinner; the top two names on the citation list were Sigmund Freud and Jean Piaget.[2]

Such an impressive record of accomplishment naturally elicited a string of honors and official recognitions to match. Cattell's many awards included such highlights as the 1982 Educational Testing Service Award for "distinguished service to measurement," the 1986 Behavior Genetics Association Annual Dobzhansky Memorial Award for "eminent research in behavior genetics," and the 1997 award for "Distinguished Lifetime Contribution to Evaluation, Measurement, and Statistics" from the American Psychological Association's Division 5 for specialists in that field. Even five years after his death, the Society for Personality Assessment named Cattell the posthumous recipient of its Marguerite Herz Memorial Award for his contributions to measurement. As an additional honor, professional associations established a number of awards in his name. The Society of Multivariate Experimental Psychology, of which he was the founder and first president, presents the Cattell Award annually to a researcher who has made outstanding contributions to this specialized area. And at its annual convention the American Educational Research Association also presents the Raymond B. Cattell Early Career Award to a "scholar who has conducted a distinguished program of cumulative educational research."[3]

In August 1997 the American Psychological Association (APA) announced that Cattell had been selected the recipient of that year's American Psychological Foundation Gold Medal Award for Life Achievement in Psychological Science, which would be presented only weeks later at the annual convention to be held in Chicago; the APF is the APA's nonprofit, philanthropic organization, which recognizes the career accomplishments of members, bestows awards, and provides grants and scholarships. Referring to the exceptional diversity of the honoree's "prodigious, landmark contributions to psychology," the accompanying citation placed Cattell "among a very small handful of people in this century who have most influenced the shape of psychology as a science."[4] The Gold Medal Award—the APA's most prestigious honor and one that had been presented only a dozen times previously—was clearly intended as a capstone to Cattell's remarkable career, and the ninety-two-year-old recipient, now in ill health from a number of serious ailments that would lead to his death only six months later, journeyed from his home in Hawaii to the convention, accompanied by a companion, a fellow scientist, to assist him.

Then, only two days before the scheduled ceremony, the APF distributed a statement at the convention, announcing that "presentation of the Gold Medal Award for Life Achievement in Psychological Science . . . has been postponed due to new information presented to the APF board which requires further study." More specifically, the statement noted:

> Concerns have been expressed during the past two weeks . . . involving the relationship between Dr. Cattell's scientific work and his views on racial segre-

gation. In order to provide full due process to Dr. Cattell, the Foundation will provide a Blue Ribbon Panel of senior research scientists to thoroughly review Dr. Cattell's research and writings and advise the Board on its further actions. The issues to be considered by this panel, and ultimately by the Trustees, include important interests of scientific psychology—the importance of protecting science, including politically unpopular science vs. psychology's opposition to the inappropriate use of science to promote destructive social policy.[5]

The next day the *New York Times* reported on two of Cattell's chief critics, neither of them a psychologist. Professor Barry Mehler, a historian at Ferris State University in Michigan and the director of the Institute for the Study of Academic Racism, had written to the APA claiming that Cattell had a "lifetime commitment to fascist and eugenics causes" and was "openly affiliate[d]" with a particular racist and anti-Semitic ideologue. In addition, according to the *Times,* Abraham Foxman, director of the Anti-Defamation League of B'nai B'rith, had also written to the association to protest the award, arguing that its conferral would give the professional group's "seal of approval to a man who has, whatever his other achievements, exhibited a lifelong commitment to racial supremacy theories." In response, Cattell acknowledged that he believed in eugenics and in fact that he had proposed a religious movement called "Beyondism," of which eugenics was a part, but only on a voluntary basis.[6]

In addition to these highly publicized accusations, two members of the APA—both psychologists who study the use of social science by racist movements—had also contacted the association to express similar concerns about their professional organization's choice of honoree. Ten days before the convention, Andrew Winston, a professor at the University of Guelph in Ontario and a fellow of the APA's Division 26, History of Psychology, wrote to Joseph Matarazzo, the chair of the APF's awards committee—with a copy to Raymond Fowler, the APA's chief executive officer—citing a number of publications that documented Cattell's "life-long commitment to eugenics and racism." Winston's conclusion was firm but nonconfrontational: "Given your own history and deep commitment to human welfare," he wrote to Matarazzo,

> I know that these details must have been unknown to you, and will be distressing to you. Unfortunately, this is not a matter of a person holding private political views while doing commendable scientific work. These views on eugenics are his scientific views, and Cattell believes that his scientific work has provided the foundation for his politics. He has built an organization, the Beyondist Trust, to promote these views. Having studied his writings with some care, I must conclude that the APF award to Cattell will be a moral stain on our discipline and our organization.[7]

I was the other psychologist to bring Cattell's political ideology to the association's attention, having written about his social philosophy in a book published three years earlier. A week before the convention I called Rhea Farberman, the APA's director of communications, and emphasized that I had no intent to tell the awards committee what decision it should make but wanted only to ensure that the committee was fully informed. At her request I sent Farberman the relevant portion of my book along with a cover letter, pointing out that this was not a case of a scientist who, parenthetically, happened to have objectionable political opinions; Cattell's political ideology and his science were inseparable from each other.[8]

The APA's decision to postpone the award produced the sort of outrage that typically accompanies what is judged to be an excess of political correctness. Once again, it seemed to many observers, modern-day heresy was being punished by oxymoronically intolerant liberals, ever eager to suppress any sign of deviation from egalitarian dogma. Calling Cattell a "victim of liberalism," for example, an editorial in the *Augusta (Ga.) Chronicle* declared that the APA had yielded to "some shrill ultra-liberals," who claimed that "*some* Cattell studies are used to support white supremacist views. Well, any group can cite bits and pieces of any data to support its views. A disappointed Cattell flatly says he doesn't support any racist 'eugenics philosophy.' But the intolerant Left could care less." Some members of the profession were also furious with the postponement. In a letter to the association's monthly, Douglas K. Detterman, occupant of a named chair at Case Western Reserve University and an APA fellow, known for his research on intelligence and mental retardation, announced that he had "reluctantly decided to end my nearly 30-year association with APA. I cannot remain a member after the way Raymond Cattell was treated. . . . APA and APF have caused the career of a distinguished scientist to end under a dark cloud."[9]

Although a distinguished Blue Ribbon Panel was indeed appointed in mid-November, it was disbanded only a few weeks later, after Cattell withdrew his name from consideration for the award.[10] The withdrawal was accompanied by his "Open Letter to the APA," in which Cattell avowed his belief in "*equal opportunity for all individuals*" and his passionate opposition to "*racism and discrimination*" as "*antithetical to my life's work.*" The critics, Cattell wrote, had "twisted" his position by taking statements out of context and employing "all the little tricks that journalists use."[11]

On February 2, 1998, Cattell died. Along with the eulogies from friends and family members, tributes and remembrances (many of them available online)[12] poured in from the legion of devoted researchers who had apprenticed in Cattell's lab over the years, especially during his most productive period at the University of Illinois; many of these persons had gone on to highly productive careers of their own and become well-known contributors to the field, often collaborating with their mentor. Naturally, a primary theme in their fond recollections was the recognition of Cattell as "one of the giants of twentieth century psychology,"[13] the field's "master strategist,"[14] and one of "the greatest and most prolific contributors to the science of human personality."[15] Almost everyone who had worked with him, even for a short time, regarded Cattell with a mixture of awe and gratitude for his brilliance, his prodigious work ethic, and his ability to inspire others. A University of Munich professor who had spent a year with Cattell as a visiting research associate three decades earlier recalled that "it was one of the most inspiring and productive periods in my life," adding, "I bow down before one of the most eminent psychologists of our century." But in addition to this appreciation of his scientific genius, there was also great affection for Cattell as a person and genuine admiration for his engaging personal style—his good manners, sense of humor, and ability to treat everyone with respect, no matter their status or background. He was both "a gentle man and a gentleman," observed two former collaborators in a jointly written tribute.[16] "As a result of Dr. Cattell's example," wrote one contributor, whose sole interaction with the deceased scientist had occurred a quarter century earlier "as a lowly undergraduate" working briefly in his lab, "I now try to treat younger people in the manner that Dr. Cattell treated me. . . . Dr. Cattell had a significant impact on my life, and I will always be extremely grateful." More than just an extraordinary scientist, Cattell was regarded as a truly great human being by many of the people who came in contact with him. One of the three speakers at Cattell's funeral in Hawaii, Richard Gorsuch—a longtime friend and associate who had done his doctoral research in Cattell's lab and was also a Christian minister, known for his contributions not only to multivariate methodology but also to the scientific study of religion—no doubt expressed a widely shared sentiment when he began his eulogy by declaring, "'When a fierce wind blows, a great man has died.' A fierce wind blew here early Monday morning, February 2nd."[17]

Perhaps understandably, however, in view of the events in the last six months of Cattell's life, the praise and reverence in some of these remembrances were tinged with a degree of bitterness over the feeling that this heroic figure had been foully traduced at exactly the moment when he should have enjoyed his greatest triumph. One psychologist referred to "the failure of the APA to separate [Cattell's] scholarly contributions from sanctimonious disparagement by lesser scientists." Two other researchers complained that "few psychologists have engendered greater execration,

and none . . . has been so publicly humiliated by the organization representing American psychology" as this exceptional scientist and human being.[18]
No one among these many scientists who had honed their research skills
in Cattell's lab could reconcile their fond recollections of a wise and decent
mentor with the image of a segregationist or racist.

As someone who believes that there is demonstrable substance to the latter
half of this seemingly incongruous combination, I am no less troubled than
Cattell's supporters by the contradiction between appealing personality and
repugnant ideology. This book is my attempt to explain how one of the most
eminent research psychologists of the twentieth century was at the same time
a proponent of a belief system that not only rationalized but actively encouraged practices in conflict with both constitutional guarantees of equality and
generally accepted notions of human rights. It is not a biography—I have
conducted no interviews nor examined any personal papers or archives—but
rather a study of the relationship between science and politics in the work
of this extraordinary individual, demonstrating that his impressive body of
accomplishments in the former domain was always intended to serve the
goals of the latter.

Having played a role, however small, in the events leading to the postponement of Cattell's award, obviously I do not approach this topic as a completely
objective observer. However, for what it's worth, my own opinion has itself
changed considerably over time: at first an admirer of Cattell for his undeniably significant scientific contributions, I was initially reluctant to accept his
ideological writing at face value, certain that he could not really mean what
the words seemed to say. It was only gradually, as I read more and more work
by both Cattell and those whom he acknowledged as intellectual traveling
companions, that I found charitable interpretations no longer tenable. It might
be argued that this transition too is reason to suspect bias on my part, converts
being justifiably known for displaying the most extreme enmity against the
position they have relinquished. But in any event, it is my intent to describe
Cattell's thought, both scientific and ideological, as fairly and accurately as
my admittedly imperfect ability will allow. It is, of course, for the reader to
judge whether I have been successful in this endeavor.

* * *

Raymond Bernard Cattell's life spanned almost the entire twentieth century.
He was born into a solidly middle-class English family in 1905, a full decade
before it was possible to make a transcontinental phone call, and died in
1998, when most academics began their day by connecting to an electronic
network that placed them instantly in touch with millions of people and

billions of pages of information throughout the world. At the beginning of his professional career, a single factor analytic study—the complex statistical procedure in which Cattell specialized—required a cadre of research assistants laboring sometimes for the better part of a year with a mechanical calculator; by the time of his death, although it might take an hour or two to enter the data, the actual analysis could be executed in a matter of seconds on a laptop computer. Of primarily Scottish ancestry on his father's side, the previous two generations of Cattells had been "engineer designers" running their own business. His mother's family, the Fields, had been English country landowners, reluctantly forced to enter what Cattell called "the industrial game" as a way to retain the squire's status, but whose heart remained in "timbered houses [and] thoroughbred horses." Ever interested in the relative intellectual merits of different genetic backgrounds, later in his life Cattell administered IQ tests to his parents, discovering that his father's score was "only 120 against my mother's 150"—a result he judged quite consistent with "the relative occupational records of the Fields and the Cattells," the former having produced five doctors among their offspring.[19]

According to Cattell's own account, most of his childhood was spent in an idyllic setting on the coast of Devonshire. Learning to sail at only seven years old and much preferring exploration of the coast to any enjoyment that "could be found in a leather ball," Cattell developed a lifelong love for the water and, as a young man, published a book on a series of voyages through the area he had first sailed during his youth.[20] In addition to natural beauty, South Devon was also rich with historical associations, to which Cattell was surprisingly sensitive at an early age. Growing up within visiting distance of Plymouth, where the Mayflower Compact had been written, and Dartmouth, from which Richard the Lionhearted had set off for the Crusades, even as a child he developed a sense not only that his native land had played a significant role in events far beyond its own shores but that "middle-class Victorian England was in some respects a high point from which civilization was capable of falling away." Intellectually mature far beyond his years, at age ten Cattell was reading H. G. Wells, Jules Verne, and Arthur Conan Doyle.[21]

Two discordant notes intruded on this otherwise ideal childhood. His own precocity, according to Cattell, created a conflict with his older brother, especially in an educational environment that promoted students by ability rather than age. Again keenly aware of differences in intellectual ability, Cattell characterized his older sibling as a "strong and warm" individual who could "have made a mark on the world" if only his intelligence had equaled his personality. Although his more powerful brother could not be "overcome," he "could be outwitted." The problem was eventually resolved when Cattell's parents moved his older brother from the highly "selective" school that both boys attended to a less demanding public institution. World War I, which began as Cattell entered his second decade, was also a sobering experience. The trainloads of wounded returning from the front left him with "an abiding sense of seriousness" and a realization "of the brevity of life and the need to accomplish while one might."[22]

Quickly recognized as a talented student, Cattell attended London University, graduating at nineteen with first-class honors—the equivalent of magna cum laude—in chemistry and physics. However, his experience in the city, in such sharp contrast to the "Eden in the West" of his youth, further intensified the sense of social concern that had first been aroused by the war. Moved by the extremes of wealth and poverty, Cattell abandoned "what were essentially boyish interests" in the hard sciences and dedicated himself to the elevation of human beings, concluding that "to get beyond human irrationalities one had to study the workings of the mind itself."[23]

By coincidence, just as his interests were heading in this more socially oriented direction, Cattell happened to attend a lecture by Cyril Burt—later to become the first psychologist ever knighted—on the work of Sir Francis Galton, founder of the eugenics movement and one of the first persons to attempt a scientific study of individual differences in intelligence.[24] Learning of this plan to improve intellectual ability through control of the breeding process confirmed Cattell's own transition. He packed away the flasks and test tubes and "walked over to Charles Spearman's laboratory to explore the promise of psychology . . . [as] the source of rational hopes for human progress," his attention now focused on the idealistic goal of striving for "a rising intelligence in a more gracious community life of creatively occupied citizens." Motivated by eugenical goals, he decided to devote himself to psychological research, a career choice that provided the young Cattell what he later described as "exactly what I had to have—a means of contributing more fundamental solutions to social problems, along with the intellectually esthetic fascination of pursuing a science." Cattell was ever mindful of the former objective as well as the latter. Long after he had earned well-deserved recognition for his scientific accomplishments, he emphasized that his "concern to bring social scientific research to remedy the irrationalities of politics and to arrest . . . degenerative, e.g., dysgenic, trends in social life remain[ed] as great as ever."[25]

Although psychology was a relatively new science, and the object of ridicule in some quarters, fortunately for Cattell, Spearman, a highly respected pioneer in the study of human abilities, held a chair in the discipline at London's

University College, and Cattell spent the next five years obtaining his doctorate under this prominent scientist. Looking forward to a research career, he then had to face the practical problem of how to make a living, only to find that there were precious few positions available, a shortage made all the more difficult by the economic depression then at its most severe. Forced to survive by accepting a series of "'fringe' jobs in psychology" over the next five years,[26] Cattell nevertheless managed to keep some research activity going, although he now turned primarily to Burt as a mentor, Spearman having left for the United States. Always indefatigable, at the same time he also finished a book that he had begun writing as a graduate student, designed to "awaken the public to the importance of psychology"—the first of many works during his career describing Cattell's view of social science's practical application to human problems.[27] By accepting a newly created position as director of a school psychological service and child guidance clinic in the city of Leicester, he enjoyed a few years of occupational stability but chafed at the administrative and clinical duties, later acknowledging that he felt like "a charlatan" in the latter role and complaining that his experience in the position had cost him "some of the most potentially vigorous research years" of his life.[28] During the last two years of this appointment, he was named a Darwin Fellow by the British Eugenics Society, which provided him with a grant to conduct research on the decline in intelligence in England. In keeping with the beliefs of the previous two generations of eugenicists, the resulting study found a strong inverse relation between intelligence and family size, leading Cattell to predict that, unless drastic measures were taken, there would be a disastrous increase in the proportion of "dull and defective" people with a consequent decrease in the number of gifted; the nation, he warned, would be swamped by "sub-men."[29]

Almost a decade after earning his doctorate, Cattell still saw little prospect of a full-time research post. There were only a dozen or so academic positions in psychology in the entire country, and most of their occupants were "discouragingly hale and hearty." In addition, his wife, an artist whom he had married in 1930, had left him four years later, no longer willing to put up with "neglect as well as straitened circumstances." In late 1937 E. L. Thorndike, a prominent educational psychologist at Columbia University in New York, came to Cattell's rescue, offering him a position as a research associate. Although the eugenics movement in the United States—which in the teens and twenties had exercised considerable influence on thought among the well educated and could point to a number of policy achievements—had now lost its intellectual cachet, Thorndike was one of the few academics still holding fast to its tenets at the time.[30] He would soon publish *Human Nature and the Social Order,* a 963-page tome that argued bluntly for a system of mathematical weights to be applied differentially to each person's desires: in this social calculus a superior individual's wants would count for 2,000, an average person's for 100, and an idiot's for 1. It was after reading Cattell's report for the British Eugenics Society that Thorndike invited him to join the research group at Columbia. Although leaving his beloved England "was like the wrench of a tooth extraction" for Cattell, he accepted the appointment, consoling himself with the thought that it was only temporary.[31] In fact, he would spend the next sixty years, the rest of his life, in the United States.

Cattell's experience at Columbia was not very productive; he conducted little research and was "continually depressed." However, he did manage to publish a refinement of his views on psychology's practical significance, arguing that science could provide the basis for morality and even for a system of religious beliefs—his first detailed description of a religion derived from science, a notion that Cattell promoted for the rest of his life.[32] He dedicated this book to William McDougall, who had just died. An internationally known psychologist at the time and cofounder of the British Psychological Society, who had also emigrated to the United States for the last two decades of his career, McDougall was the third major influence—along with Spearman and Burt—on Cattell's thought, especially on his social ideology.

After a little more than a year in Thorndike's lab—long enough for him to marry a Columbia University student and divorce for a second time[33]— Cattell received what appeared to be his first truly desirable opportunity: the G. Stanley Hall professorship of genetic (that is, developmental) psychology at Clark University in Worcester, Massachusetts. It is impossible to discuss the history of psychology in the United States without paying considerable attention to both G. Stanley Hall and Clark. Hall obtained his doctorate at Harvard under William James in 1878 before studying with Wilhelm Wundt, who had created the world's first psychological laboratory at the University of Leipzig. Returning to the United States, he played an instrumental role in almost every significant event in the growth of psychology as a social science. In 1883 Hall established the discipline's first experimental laboratory in North America at Johns Hopkins, which awarded the first U.S. doctorate in psychology to one of his students, and went on to found the *American Journal of Psychology.* Selected also to be the first president of Clark University, naturally he placed special emphasis on the Psychology Department, which hosted the first meeting of the American Psychological Association, at which Hall was named the organization's first president. The department again received international attention in 1909 when it sponsored a symposium in psychoanalysis that featured appearances by Carl Jung and Sigmund

Freud, the latter giving his only speech ever in the United States.[34] From the 1890s to the 1920s Clark remained an international center for the study of psychology, its university press publishing most of the field's professional journals as well as many important books.

Despite its illustrious history, however, Clark turned out to be yet another disappointment for Cattell. First of all, the prestigious-sounding professorship was available only because a new president at the university was much less supportive of the Psychology Department, which had become an unappealing place to work, and as a result its most eminent members had found positions elsewhere. According to Yale professor of psychology Seymour Sarason, who was working on his doctorate at Clark when Cattell was a faculty member, the department was "small and undistinguished" at the time "and had trouble attracting graduate students." In addition, Cattell was expected to teach, yet another encroachment on the time he would have preferred to spend on research and one that he resented no less than he had the demands of administrative and clinical work at Leicester. No believer in the teacher-scholar model, Cattell later argued fervently that it was a needless distraction, a waste of "man hours," for a "talented researcher" to provide instruction to students, "which many equally intelligent but less creative academics could do just as well." Moreover, he maintained, the teacher and the "true scientist" were "poles asunder in psychological type," the former being no more suited to the "'showman' demonstrations" required in the classroom than "a woman with child is fitted to engage in acrobatics."[35] Clearly considering himself to belong on one side of this rigid dichotomy, he was not pleased to be burdened at Clark with the responsibility of the other.

Three years later Cattell moved again, this time to the Psychology Department at Harvard, where he was able to devote more time to serious research on personality structure, his major interest. But he found to his dismay that he and Gordon Allport—the department's renowned personality theorist, who two decades earlier had taught the first course in North America on that topic—"spoke a different language," approaching the subject in such disparate ways that undergraduate psychology majors were required "to dissolve oil in water and to perfect feats of methodological reconciliation which no faculty member could perform."[36]

It was World War II that finally changed Cattell's professional life forever, when he was invited through the Adjutant General's Office to participate in a group of researchers with expertise in psychological measurement working on assessment issues and personnel selection. Left entirely to his own devices, he was able to immerse himself in the creation and administration of objective personality tests. Eagerly anticipating the "rich harvest" of data that would supply a "feast of curiosity," Cattell seemed almost disappointed when the conflict ended and the organization that had sponsored his work was disbanded: "Alas . . . the banquet was snatched away. Peace was declared." But just at that moment Herbert Woodrow, a recent president of the APA and a professor at the University of Illinois, was looking for someone with the kind of expertise in multivariate analysis that was Cattell's specialty. Having read one of Cattell's recent publications, Woodrow invited him to occupy a newly created research professorship at the university, exactly the sort of academic position he had been seeking for a decade and a half: "adequate resources and equipment"; ample clerical assistance; generous grant support that became available after establishment of the National Institute of Mental Health (NIMH) in 1946; beginning in 1952, use of the Illiac, the first computer ever built and owned by an educational institution; and, most important of all, no obligation to teach or engage in any of the other typical faculty governance activities.[37] "Life began at forty," Cattell later wrote. "At last . . . I was truly able to organize my life around research."[38]

Remaining at Illinois until his retirement twenty-eight years later, Cattell established a reputation as one of the world's most productive research psychologists, and the Laboratory of Personality Assessment and Group Behavior, which he directed, became arguably the world's most important center for multivariate studies of personality. His yearly publication record could often pass for the entire career of many less talented academics. In the 1968 *Annual Review of Psychology*, the author of the chapter "Personality Structure" digressed from his main theme to make the following remarkable observation:

> Although literature reviews should properly be concerned with research and not researchers, Cattell occupies such a unique position in the field of personality structure that his work demands separate consideration. In the period under review [May 1964–May 1967], Cattell has published four books, 12 chapters and 40 articles; a total of almost four thousand pages that must somehow be summarized. In addition, he has found time to launch a new journal and edit a massive handbook. This alone would warrant separate consideration, but there is more. The appearance of so many major works and especially the publication of his *Collected Papers* has once again forced an evaluation of a body of literature so vast, uneven, and demanding that many American workers have simply tended to ignore it.[39]

This extraordinary productivity was due in part to the hundreds of young scholars who served as graduate research assistants or doctoral associates in Cattell's lab, typically four of the former and two of the latter every year.[40] Even after leaving Illinois and becoming outstanding scientists in their own right, many of them continued the association with their mentor, essentially acting as disciples whose own research extended his approach both in methodology and in substance. Reflecting on their assistance at the end of his time at Illinois, Cattell was not so "sentimental" as to claim that all of them had demonstrated real intellectual potential and named only those he thought had become truly "productive"—a list that still included seventy-seven people.[41]

Another contributing factor, not only to Cattell's research program but also to the stability of his personal life, was his third marriage—in 1946, to Alberta Karen Schuettler, a mathematician whom he had met when she was a student at Radcliffe. Applying her own considerable quantitative skills to measurement issues, along with Cattell she cofounded the Institute for Personality and Ability Testing, established in 1949 to publish, market, and provide technical support for the many assessment instruments derived from his research. (IPAT remains an active corporation, which has expanded the range of its consulting services but, based on Cattell's tests, continues to specialize primarily in personnel-related tasks, such as employee screening, selection, evaluation, and guidance.)[42] Karen Cattell served as IPAT's director and chairperson, a position she maintained until 1992, even though, in 1980, this marriage too ended in divorce.

A final factor enhancing the status and productivity of Cattell's lab was his role in organizing the Society of Multivariate Experimental Psychology, an association of researchers specializing in multivariate quantitative methods and their application to substantive issues in psychology. SMEP became a reality in 1960, after "three years during which," Cattell acknowledged, "I did not do so much research but campaigned for my conception" of how this group should be formulated.[43] True to Cattell's vision and indicative of his personal style, which could be quite intellectually snobbish, SMEP—unlike most professional associations, which not only are open to anyone with the appropriate educational credentials but often solicit membership—was structured to be both small and highly selective, its size limited to sixty "well-chosen" members (later increased to sixty-five). To avoid "distinguished deadwood," all members had to retire at age sixty-five (although they could be reelected if able to demonstrate that they were continuing to engage in high-quality research), and anyone who did not give a paper at one of the annual meetings for three years in a row was automatically converted to "inactive status."[44] When there was a vacancy, new members were accepted through a nomination and election process only after their "full bibliographies" were circulated. As a result of this intense competition, "very gradually the Society got the substantive, empirical, 'discovering' types," and "through its ranks," declared Cattell, with little exaggeration, "have passed the most brilliant hundred or more in the field." Cattell himself served as the organization's president for its first two years, and a number of the subsequent presidents developed their multivariate skills in his lab. Six years after founding SMEP, Cattell was also instrumental in the creation of the society's professional journal, *Multivariate Behavioral Research*, designed in his view as an outlet for studies conducted by members and other specialists that were not being published in substantive journals because editors and readers lacked the technical sophistication to understand them. In 1984 the journal devoted a double issue to a special collection of essays describing the many different areas of Cattell's research and evaluating its impact in each case.[45] Cattell's role as the inspiration for and founder of SMEP further confirmed his reputation as the leading figure in the country at the time—and perhaps in the world—in the field of multivariate analysis.

Retiring from the University of Illinois in 1973, Cattell moved to Boulder, Colorado, where he spent the next few years conducting research at his Institute for Research on Morality and Adjustment, an independent organization he had founded to conduct basic research on specific problems, such as the increase in crime. However, he had difficulty obtaining funding for the institute, leading him to complain that foundations and granting agencies dispersed money to "unproven researchers with expert grantsmanship techniques" rather than to "people of proven investigatory capacity."[46] In addition, the altitude and severe winters in Colorado aggravated a heart condition, forcing him to seek an environment less threatening to his health. For the last two decades of his life, Cattell functioned as an adjunct professor at the University of Hawaii at Manoa—its abundant coastline a nostalgic reminder of his beloved Devonshire—where he continued to direct graduate students, analyze previously collected data, and produce a steady stream of books and articles.[47] After his fourth marriage, once again he was assisted by an academically talented wife—Heather Birkett, a clinical psychologist who coauthored a number of studies with Cattell and wrote a book published by IPAT on the instruments for personality-trait measurement constructed by her husband.[48]

Although while at Illinois he had produced occasional articles on the scientifically derived moral philosophy motivating much of his research and then authored a substantial book on the subject shortly before retiring from the university,[49] it was during his time at Hawaii that Cattell devoted more energy to refining and promulgating the ideology that he had first formulated as a graduate student six decades earlier. In addition to writing more extensively on his worldview, he joined the advisory board of the *Mankind Quarterly*, a controversial journal founded by segregationists and Nazi sympathizers as an outlet for their views on race and eugenics, and published some of his own conclusions about these topics in its pages.[50] As a last attempt to perpetuate his thinking, and in the hope that his own essentially religious principles would eventually influence policy, in 1993 Cattell established the Beyondist Foundation, which issued an eponymically titled newsletter intended to pursue the specific eugenical objectives derived from his belief system.

Despite this incredibly productive career, there was long a sense among the "Cattellians" that their mentor had not been accorded the degree of recognition to which his accomplishments rightfully entitled him. Indeed, the double edition of *Multivariate Behavioral Research* devoted to a discussion of his research was largely an attempt to understand why Cattell's work had not exerted a greater impact on thinking in the field—why it was, as the *Annual Review of Psychology* chapter "Personality Structure" had pointed out in 1968, that "many American workers have simply tended to ignore" a "body of literature so vast." One possible explanation for this neglect had to do with Cattell's professional persona. Even his most devoted supporters acknowledged that Cattell was a polarizing figure in psychology for many reasons that had nothing to do with his sociopolitical views, which, in any event, were not well known to many scientists intimately familiar with his research. As two of his friends acknowledged after his death, a part of Cattell's public persona was "not calculated 'to win friends and influence people.'"[51]

First of all, his characterization of his own work was relentlessly grandiose; as John Horn, a particularly close friend and protégé who edited the dedicated volume of *Multivariate Behavioral Research,* observed, Cattell's "immodesty [was] . . . breathtaking." With himself clearly in mind, Cattell once explained that a career in science appealed to those "gifted mortals" with a "mature personality" interested in "the benefits in health and fulfillment which science can bring to wayward and ignorant mankind."[52] In response to any hesitation of the field to recognize the significance of his "inspired" and "courageous" work, Cattell regularly invoked the most flattering comparisons: there had been a similar delay, he pointed out, in appreciating the conclusions of Copernicus, Galileo, Pasteur, and Mendel, and Newton too had to bear criticism from his inferiors.[53]

Of course, grandiosity alone might have been a venial offense, no more than a tolerable quirk and not without a certain charm emanating from a mind as fertile and productive as Cattell's, had it not been combined with an arrogance bordering on contempt. In addition to communicating the details of his research, Cattell seemed to view professional publications as an opportunity to remind disciplinary colleagues not just of his brilliance but of their mediocrity as well. Much more common among English academics than among their American counterparts, perhaps this tendency was influenced in part by Cattell's mentor and model, Cyril Burt, who was also notorious for his personal attacks in print on intellectual adversaries.[54] In any event, in contrast to the gracious demeanor he apparently exhibited toward his colleagues and research assistants, Cattell's writing seemed to delight in belittling and insulting most of his fellow researchers. In language uncommon for scientific journals, Cattell began one article after another with a gratuitous swipe at the rest of the field, expressing his irritation at other scientists' inability or unwillingness to adopt his methods and disparaging their efforts at "superficial 'research'"—the sarcastic quotation marks enclosing the noun a particularly sharp verbal elbow in their ribs—as an utter waste of time. (In retrospect, this style now seems like a precursor of the Internet phenomenon, in which participants in a discussion respond to opposing viewpoints with a harshness they would be very unlikely to employ face-to-face.) According to two of his most loyal friends and supporters, a coeditor of one of his major publications "had to soften the tone of Cattell's introduction to the volume, else as the co-editor stated, 'He would have lost half his potential readers.'" Even the reviewer who called him "America's . . . most productive psychologist" and psychology's "master strategist" was distressed by Cattell's "penchant for addressing snide innuendos at other psychologists," describing their work in such terms as "'magpie research,' . . . 'pedestrian,' 'bankrupt,' . . . 'sadly misguided,' . . . 'delusions'" and their instruments as "'gadget measures, 'toys,' 'parlor games,' and 'museum pieces.'"[55] As the review suggested, Cattell was especially harsh on attempts at trait measurement that differed from his own approach. *His* research used scientifically designed instruments; in one of his favorite epithets, others relied on "gadgets."[56] The traditional bivariate, controlled design for studying human behavior preferred by the majority of research psychologists was as "useless," he regularly declared, as "trying to eat soup with a fork."[57] Particularly ironic, given these constant expressions of contempt, was Cattell's complaint that *he* had to endure "snide" and "vituperative" comments, as well as outright "hostility," from those unwilling to "face the real intricacies inherent in psychology."[58]

Nor was Cattell reluctant to announce the reason that so many of his fellow scientists' efforts were completely wrongheaded: their education, and perhaps their abilities, were inadequate to the task. Psychology, he often complained, was attracting too many "refugees" from mathematics and the physical sciences, people who "strive to make up by the warmth of their hearts for the emptiness of their heads,"[59] "a half-trained intellectual proletariat" with "an aversion to skilled calculation." His own factor analytic methodology—the only one, he never tired of repeating, that could possibly advance knowledge in the field—required "more statistical finesse . . . than the typical Ph.D. student [in psychology] can muster."[60] The problem, Cattell declared numerous times, was that "psychology is too difficult for psychologists," and the trouble, he bluntly observed, "lies in the mediocrity of the researchers and teachers."[61]

No doubt because he had so little respect for most other researchers, Cattell often really didn't know much about their ideas; as his friend Horn acknowledged, "Cattell's understanding of the work of others is often superficial." When a new edition of his well-regarded book on intelligence was published sixteen years after the original, for example, it was reviewed by the prominent Berkeley educational psychologist Arthur Jensen, who praised the work's "wealth of thought-provoking information" and referred to Cattell's "amazingly rich and far-reaching intellect," calling his "erudition . . . legendary." At the same time, however, the review noted that, aside from the numerous references to Cattell's own publications, there was no mention of "any of the significant developments in this field" over the previous decade and a half, "a period of greater progress in intelligence research than at any previous time in the past 50 years"; indeed, Jensen pointed out, the book did not contain a single reference to any article that had appeared in the leading journal in the field.[62] On one occasion this neglect on Cattell's part had practical consequences when a grant committee for the National Institute of Mental Health rejected his proposal for funding on the grounds that it had disregarded the work of other scientists. Although Cattell had enjoyed substantial funding for years from the NIMH and other government sources, he was nevertheless irate—and unrepentant: he saw no more value in considering other schools of thought "than workers on the early steam engine could incorporate the latest developments in the stage coach." In fact, he called for "research on research" in order to prove to granting institutions that "the man is more important than the design,"[63] a principle the application of which would conveniently award support to Cattell even if his proposal was not ranked as high as that of other scientists.

A final source of irritation for many other scientists was Cattell's prose style, which, again according to the reviewer who had lavished praise on him, was "almost bound to infuriate" readers. Or as another reviewer of one of his books aptly noted, "Cattell, the writer, is hardly the equal of Cattell, the psychologist."[64] A minor reason for this widespread annoyance was his extensive use of neologisms: the proliferation in Cattell's writing of terms such as *exviant, cortertia, dissofrustance, premsia, threctia,* and many others seemed an attempt to create an entirely new language for the field, inevitably estranging some colleagues who did not share it and making communication with other researchers unnecessarily complicated. Indeed, in one edited volume on personality change intended for other professionals, the editor felt it necessary to direct readers to an appended glossary "for those unfamiliar with the terms employed by Cattell and his associates."[65]

But the more significant problem with Cattell's writing was its sacrifice of clarity for productivity. *New York Times* editor Max Frankel reportedly emphasized to his staff that there was no such thing as "good writing"—only "good rewriting."[66] Cattell rarely rewrote, apparently regarding the task as yet another encumbrance—like teaching, administration, or even "excessive family cares"—on time better spent concentrating on research. Naturally, this reluctance to bother with revisions helped lead to such a prodigious output. Eschewing both typewriter and, later, the computer, Cattell wrote, according to those closest to him, faster than most people could read.[67] He also dictated much of his writing, often bringing to the lab a set of tapes for the clerical staff to transcribe, a task they were not able to complete before he brought in the next day's set.[68] But there was a cost: the publication of these unedited drafts sometimes seemed not so much prolific as incontinent, producing frequent complaints that it was a chore to read Cattell's prolix writing, not only from critics but also from supporters; one ardent admirer of his work neverthe-less characterized Cattell's prose as "an alphabet soup so thick a parenthesis drowns." In a typical example of his assault on the English language, Cattell explained, in an article on motivational traits, "The derivation of the innately preferred response pattern from the displaced ergic pattern is probably going to be attacked through the study of relative rigidities, taking the discovered common *goal* of the attitudes in the pattern as the undisplaced point of refer-ence." Even his friend Horn acknowledged that "large segments of his writing are often disjointed."[69]

Well aware of the ill feeling generated by Cattell's contentious style, some of his followers harbored the belief that the APF Gold Medal Award was "delayed until his 92nd year" because it was only then that the retirement or death of the many scientists he had offended throughout his career finally allowed Cattell's "younger disciples," who had now reached positions of influence, to nominate him successfully. Indeed, there had been at least one previous unsuccessful attempt, twenty-two years earlier, to gain this honor for him.[70] In addition to helping fill out the brief profile of Cattell above, I raise this issue—of the characteristics that so repelled many other psychologists—in order to emphasize that it played no role whatsoever in the opposition to the award. (As Howard Gardner has shown, great minds have often been connected to difficult personalities, but the irritation caused by the latter has rarely prevented recognition of the brilliance exhibited by the former.)[71]

The "Cattell controversy" that is the subject of this book is concerned not with his intellectual arrogance, belittlement of other scientists, or inability to communicate clearly but with his ideology and its relationship to his science. Although, as I shall argue later, Cattell himself viewed these domains as inextricably interwoven, his work in the latter area motivated largely by its instrumental value for his goals in the former, I shall begin with a detailed description of his scientific accomplishments unencumbered as far as possible by their ideological associations in order to suggest the basis for the APF's initial decision to make him a recipient of the discipline's highest award.

FACTOR ANALYSIS
AND ITS DISCONTENTS
CATTELLIAN SCIENCE

Harold Bloom, the well-known literary critic and staunch defender of the traditional canon, maintains that Shakespeare invented human personality. More than three centuries would pass from the Bard's time, however, before science—more specifically, the newly created field concerned with human behavior—began systematic attempts to understand how his invention worked. Indeed, although psychology became a recognized science in the late nineteenth century, decades were still to elapse before researchers in the field turned their attention to the study of personality. Even as late as 1919 a speaker, commenting to an audience of social workers on the difficulty of finding a textbook on the topic, declared, "The study of personality does not exist, either as a science or an art, written down."[1]

One reason that it took so long for psychologists to discover personality was their initial focus on its predecessor as the core element of human nature: character. As historian of science Ian Nicholson points out in *Inventing Personality: Gordon Allport and the Science of Selfhood*—his aptly titled book on the role of the "patron saint of personality" in the development of the field—the

Victorian era's focus on character was appropriate to a cultural landscape that emphasized "hard work over leisure, courage over popularity, self-sacrifice over self-aggrandizement, and moral conviction over intellectual ability."[2] But as the predominantly agrarian American society experienced the relatively sudden and dramatic changes of industrialization and urbanization, a different psychological discourse more appropriate to this new context emerged, replacing the morally freighted construct of character with the more modernist conception of personality. In the former approach selfhood was achieved through surrender to an ethical standard informed by an external framework, whereas in the latter it was achieved through realization of a set of characteristics emanating from within the self. The new approach was thus consistent with the priorities of an increasingly industrialized society, in which employers and administrators were interested in personality traits such as dominance, sociability, and aggressiveness, rather than the qualities of character.

Yet even after its establishment as a recognized field of study, personality did not assume the central focus that it would appear to merit. Although psychology tends to be a highly fragmented discipline, subdivided into a host of specialties often isolated from each other, personality is arguably its broadest single topic. Only the study of personality stands at the intersection of clinical psychology, abnormal behavior, human development, motivation, emotions, learning, social relations, and the relationship between genetic and environmental influences, overlapping with each of these behavioral areas and having significant implications for a thorough understanding of any of them. To say that personality is truly at the heart of psychology is no exaggeration. It is thus particularly puzzling that, through its many editions from 1957 to 1997, the most widely used text on the topic has called personality the "dissident" in the development of the discipline, "never . . . deeply embedded in the mainstream of academic psychology."[3] This is a strange paradox: the core subject matter of the field—what should be its substantive mainstream—lies perhaps not outside its scholarly mainstream but certainly far from its center.

The explanation for this apparent contradiction can be found in what Lee Cronbach, in his 1957 presidential address to the American Psychological Association, famously called "the two disciplines of scientific psychology."[4] "Experimental psychology" seeks to discover general laws—to identify the variables that make different people behave alike. Supposedly patterned after the approach that has proved so effective in the physical sciences,[5] *this* discipline of psychology attempts to study behavior under controlled conditions, in which one or sometimes more so-called independent variables are systematically manipulated in order to observe the effect on some "dependent" variable. Such tight control of the experimental situation allows the researcher to conduct rigorous tests and draw conclusions about causation, determining, for example, whether an appeal based on fear is more effective in attempting to change behavior than an appeal based on reason, whether one lengthy period of practice or a number of shorter periods are more effective in learning some skill, or whether children act more aggressively after viewing a violent movie than after a nonviolent one. This method regards the differences from one person to another in the same condition of the study as "noise"—what statisticians call "error variance"—obscuring the effect of the independent variable in much the same way as static can obscure the signal on a radio, and researchers purposely design experiments in ways that will minimize such individual difference variation; the only variation of interest to experimentalists is that created by the different conditions to which subjects have been exposed.

In contrast, "correlational" or "differential" psychology seeks to understand why in the same situation people behave differently from each other, viewing these individual differences not as an annoyance blurring the effect under investigation but as the principal object of interest. Instead of studying the factors that, say, affect learning for people in general, the differential approach seeks to explain why some people learn faster than others. In place of the rigid control afforded by the experimental approach, *this* discipline of psychology substitutes the naturalism of more lifelike situations, gathering data of much greater complexity and using multivariate statistical techniques to make sense of the results. Where experimental psychology focuses on the variation among conditions—or, as they are often called, "treatments"—differential psychology focuses on the variation among persons. Although it is possible to investigate questions about personality through the experimental method, naturally the field is much more firmly anchored in the correlational techniques appropriate to the investigation of individual differences.

Both these approaches to studying behavior were developed around the dawn of the twentieth century. Whereas experimental psychology was expanding at the time to include more and more substantive areas, the differential approach focused almost exclusively on intellectual ability and was often referred to as "genetic" psychology—an allusion not to the latest subfield of biology but to use of the "genetic method," which traced the development of the individual.[6] Almost from the moment of its introduction in the mid-1910s, the "mental test"—in the sense of an instrument for measuring intellectual ability—became differential psychology's principal method as well as its major substance. (Actually, the term *mental test* had been coined twenty years earlier by James McKeen Cattell—one of the first

American research psychologists and no relation to Raymond Cattell—who used it to refer to such psychophysical measurements as tests of reaction time and sensory discrimination.) Although lip service was paid to the importance of assessing other personal traits, researchers focused obsessively on intelligence, no doubt gratified by the public recognition, influence, and prestige they suddenly enjoyed, as their conclusions played a prominent role in the nation's discussions over immigration and the putative threat of the "feebleminded." After spending the first ten pages of a twelve-page article in a popular magazine in 1923 discussing intelligence, well-known Harvard psychologist Robert M. Yerkes acknowledged the significance of "temperamental traits" but observed that "little progress has been made" toward assessing them. This neglect of other characteristics by scientists did not mean, however, that the human personality was still being ignored by psychology at the time. But it did leave professional interest in the topic mainly in the hands of clinicians and psychoanalysts, whose conclusions were based not on empirical assessments but on their experience and intuitions working with patients, leading Gordon Allport to complain that "the bulk of all literature on the psychology of personality is written from this one [Freudian] point of view." Paul R. McHugh, occupant of a named chair and director of the Department of Psychiatry and Behavioral Medicine at the Johns Hopkins University School of Medicine, refers to this "tendency . . . to rely upon feelings for evidence" and to claim knowledge without proof as "romanticism," and although McHugh was concerned with the conflict between "romanticists" and "empiricists" that took place in psychotherapy in the 1970s and '80s, his description of the former is an equally appropriate characterization of the pronouncements made by their forerunners half a century earlier, many of them having been trained in the Freudian tradition. It was not until the latter half of the 1930s that academic theorists formalized the study of personality in classic works by researchers such as Allport, Ross Stagner, and Henry Murray and his associates.[7] But having attracted the attention of academic researchers late in the discipline's scientific development and relying mainly on nonexperimental techniques, personality remained peripheral to the mainstream for some time.

Just around the time that Allport and Murray were defining the field, Cattell began his own interest in the study of personality, after being mentored in London by Charles Spearman and Cyril Burt. These prominent researchers were two of the three most important scientists—Louis Leon Thurstone at the University of Chicago was the third—in the development of the multivariate statistical procedure called "factor analysis." Factor analysis is a data reduction technique: it begins with a large number of variables and attempts to account for the relations between them by postulating a smaller number of underlying hypothetical constructs or factors; Cattell often called them "functional unities."[8] Although the method is now used in many different fields, most of the technical details involved in factor analysis were developed by psychologists studying the structure of intelligence. In fact, there are some important results in matrix algebra, the mathematical field on which the technique is based, that were first published in psychological journals.[9]

The concept behind factor analysis is straightforward, involving the identification of groups of variables that tend to cluster together; if some variables tend to appear and disappear as a group, it suggests that they are not independent of each other but may be manifestations of some more basic construct. The cornerstone of the process is the correlation coefficient, a statistic describing the degree of relationship between two variables on a scale from 0.0 to 1.0 or 0.0 to -1.0, depending on whether they both tend to increase at the same time or one tends to increase as the other decreases; the larger the value of the correlation coefficient (either positive or negative), the stronger the relationship between the two variables. Height and weight, for example, have a correlation of approximately +.5, meaning that taller persons tend to be heavier, although the medium size of this correlation suggests that there are many exceptions to this general trend—people who are short and heavy or tall and thin. All the correlations between every possible pair of variables can be displayed in a correlation matrix, an example of which appears in table 1. Each of the seven letters denotes a variable, and each numerical entry indicates the correlation between that cell's row and column variables. It is not necessary to complete the lower left half of the table, which would be a mirror image of the upper right; that is, the correlation between, say, variables p and r is the same, whether p is the row and r the column or vice versa. Although there are seven variables in the table, the correlations between them clearly form two distinct groups: variables p, q, r, and s all have very high correlations with each other, as do variables t, u, and v with each other, but none of the former has a sizable correlation with any of the latter. This pattern suggests that the correlations might be "explained" by two underlying factors, the nature of which could be determined by seeing what the variables in each group had in common with each other. If, for example, the first four variables were all tests involving reading and vocabulary, then a factor involving verbal ability would be an obvious interpretation.

The technical details of this procedure are somewhat more complex. The underlying assumption of the factor analysis model is that an individual's score on any particular variable can be expressed as a linear combination of the factors in what Cattell referred to as the "specification equation":[10]

Table 1. Correlation matrix

	p	q	r	s	t	u	v
p		.85	.75	.90	.15	.20	.10
q			.95	.80	.18	.12	.16
r				.88	.05	.10	.14
s					.20	.08	.15
t						.78	.84
u							.92
v							

$x_{ji} = a_{j1}F_{1i} + a_{j2}F_{2i} + a_{j3}F_{3i} + a_{j4}F_{4i} + \ldots + a_{jn}F_n + a_{js}U_{si}$. In other words, presuming that the variables are all ability tests of some type, a person's score on test j is determined by a sum of products: the extent to which performance on that test requires the first factor (a_{j1}), multiplied by the person's ability on the first factor (F_{1i}); plus the extent to which performance on test j requires the second factor (a_{j2}), multiplied by the person's ability on the second factor (F_{2i}); plus a similar product for each additional "common" factor; plus a final component consisting of the extent to which test j requires a specific factor (a_{js}), one required only by that test and no other, multiplied by the person's ability on that "unique" factor (U_{si}).[11] Thus, the specification equation is like a recipe: it indicates how much to weight (the *a* coefficients) each of the "ingredients" (the factors), which then combine to produce the exact performance or behavior. Suppose, for example, that the events in the Olympic decathlon have three common factors—speed, strength, and endurance. Then the score for competitor i on, say, the pole vault (test j) might be determined by the sum of four products: a measure of his ability to run fast (F_{1i}), weighted by the degree to which the pole vault requires speed (a_{j1}); a measure of his strength (F_{2i}), weighted by the degree to which the pole vault requires strength (a_{j2}); a measure of his endurance (F_{3i}), weighted by the degree to which the pole vault requires endurance (a_{j3}); and a measure of his ability at the unique skill involved in the pole vault but in none of the other events (U_{si}), weighted by the degree to which the pole vault requires that skill (a_{js}).

At the start of a factor analysis, however, the number and nature of these underlying constructs are unknown, and the problem is to take the observed data—scores on the variables and the resulting correlation matrix that indicates the relationship between every possible pair—and from this information "extract" the factors and decide on their meaning. The "solution" to a factor analysis—that is, the numerical result of the procedure—is itself a matrix like the one in table 2, in which the rows are the variables or tests and the columns are the hypothetical factors. Each entry in this matrix, called a factor "loading," is the *a* coefficient in the specification equation and indicates the degree to which a specific test requires or depends on a particular factor; like a correlation, a factor loading takes on a value between 0.0 and plus or minus 1.0. The mathematics of the procedure produces this factor matrix but does not identify the name or nature of the factors, a task that requires an interpretation based on the pattern of loadings—that is, by deciding what the variables with large loadings on a specific factor have in common. In table 2, for example, variables *p*, *r*, and *s* have high loadings on factor *I*. If those three variables are cognitive measures involving verbal tasks, then the factor might plausibly be defined as verbal ability. Similarly, the interpretation of factor *II* would depend on the content of variables *q* and *t*, and the interpretation of factor *III* on the content of variables *u* and *v*. Of course, the values in table 2 are hypothetical examples, constructed to illustrate the logic of factor analysis; real data are never so clear and simple.

An additional complexity in the process of factor analysis is the fact that the solution—that is, the matrix of factor loadings—is not unique; like a single equation with two unknowns, an infinite number of factor matrices can provide an equally acceptable solution from a purely mathematical point of view.[12] The reason for these multiple possible solutions is that the factor loadings for each variable are formally identical to the coordinates in a space whose dimensionality is equal to the number of factors but whose axes can be placed arbitrarily. Thus, although the relationship of the points to each other is fixed, each possible "rotation" of the axes produces a differ-ent set of coordinates or loadings. (It is as if the hands of a clock were fixed at a particular angle to each other—for example, 45°, with the minute hand behind the hour hand—but the clock face with the numbers on it could be rotated to any possible position, making it impossible to know whether it was reading 3:00, or approximately 11:44, or one of the many other possibilities.) Researchers must decide which of the resulting orientations is the "correct" one—obviously not in a mathematical sense, which provides no basis for

Table 2. Matrix of factor loadings

Variable	Factor I	Factor II	Factor III
p	.80	.00	.00
q	.00	.85	.00
r	.75	.00	.00
s	.60	.00	.00
t	.00	.70	.00
u	.00	.00	.65
v	.00	.00	.75

preferring one possibility over another, but in the sense that it yields some psychologically meaningful interpretation of the factors.

In the study of intellectual ability, for example, long the most important area of application for factor analysis, some scholars have insisted that the "correct" rotation for the factors extracted from a battery of cognitive tests places the first axis through the center of the points, thus defining a factor that accounts for the maximum variation possible. Whenever the variables are tests of some kind—mental or physical—the first factor produced by this strategy is typically characterized by relatively large loadings for each variable, especially if all the correlations are positive, and is thus interpretable as some sort of general ability. Researchers in intelligence call this factor g, for "general intelligence," which they interpret, from the large loadings on many variables, as an ability required to some degree by every one of the tests in the battery. Indeed, in a famous paper recognized as originating the field of factor analysis, Charles Spearman, under whom Cattell obtained his doctorate, proposed that general intelligence was the *only* factor that various measures of cognitive ability had in common; underlying any test in Spearman's theory were thus only two components: general intellectual ability and whatever ability was unique to that particular test.[13]

At the opposite extreme, it is also possible to rotate the factor matrix to a position more similar to that in table 2, one that yields exceptionally large loadings for a few variables and very low loadings for all the others. This strategy, first proposed by Louis Leon Thurstone at the University of Chicago, attempts to produce a pattern of loadings usually referred to as "simple structure," which makes interpretation of the factors much easier because each one is determined entirely by a small number of variables with high loadings; whatever those few variables have in common defines the factor. Using this approach, Thurstone concluded that there were from seven to nine factors—"primary mental abilities," he called them—underlying performance on cognitive tests.[14]

In areas that do not involve the measurement of abilities, including most of the studies conducted by Cattell, the goal—often not easily attained—is to rotate the axes in search of a simple structure. Indeed, Cattell maintained that there is always "*one* rotation position to be found which makes especially good sense" because it matches some meaningful entity with which the researcher "is familiar on *other* and general scientific grounds—some influence which he has reason to believe is a functional unity in nature." Only this "*one* position in the rotation . . . corresponds to the real factors," according to Cattell, "and all the other positions are mathematical transformations" of this real one, like the shadows on the wall seen by the prisoners in Plato's cave.[15]

Finally, it is also possible to let the factors be correlated with each other—that is, instead of requiring the reference axes to be perpendicular to each other, to allow them to intersect at an acute angle. For example, it might be the case that factors for speed and strength can be extracted from the correlations of performance on the ten events in the decathlon, but the competitors who are faster also tend to be stronger. When an analysis produces a number of these "oblique" factors, a "second order" factor analysis can be conducted, one that begins not with the correlations between the original variables but with the correlations between the "first order" factors and seeks to identify a yet smaller set of factors underlying them. Thurstone's set of primary mental abilities, for example, could themselves be factor analyzed, resulting in more basic dimensions of intelligence; or an analysis of the decathlon factors of speed, strength, and endurance might produce a second-order factor of general athletic ability.

Trained first by Spearman, who pioneered the development of factor analysis, and then guided by Cyril Burt, who also made major contributions to the process,[16] Cattell, perhaps more than anyone else in the first half of the twentieth century, saw the potential in the technique as much more than a tool for studying the components of the intellect. Indeed, his extraordinarily productive career was largely constructed around the application of factor analysis to a host of psychological domains previously untouched by such multivariate methodology. Firmly convinced that factor analysis was not just *a* useful technique but the only valid method for studying many facets of human behavior, Cattell bristled at the notion that correlational research was not considered experimental by psychology's narrow definition of the latter. "An experiment is an analysis of carefully observed data, controlled or uncontrolled," he declared, "and most real life data are uncontrolled."[17] Referring to his more traditional experimentalist colleagues dismissively as "brass instrument psychologists,"[18] Cattell often placed quotes around the phrase "experimental psychology,"[19] as a reminder of the sterility of their attempts to understand human behavior through controlled laboratory settings in contrast with his own "in situ" studies; psychologists in the United States, he insisted, had been "trained in the half-truth that . . . science consists of controlled experiment," and unless they adopted his methodology, they had no more hope of understanding personality "than Galileo's critics could hope to see Jupiter's moons, when they refused to put an eye to his telescope."[20] Many of Cattell's research articles began with a pronouncement that some field of psychology—and sometimes even some other academic discipline—would never find anything of value unless it followed his example: "Psychoanalysis will become a science when it becomes a branch of factor analysis"; "counseling is a branch of science in which no real progress will be made" until it too turned to multivariate methods; researchers in social psychology had to "restrain themselves from superficial 'research' until a correct foundation for the meaningful description and measurement has been achieved" through factor analysis; and as long as it resisted "the methods used in the true sciences," it was "unlikely that history" would earn "acceptance as one of the social sciences."[21] Factor analysis became Cattell's hammer, and almost every problem in social science looked to him like a protruding nail.

The Building Blocks of Personality

When Cattell first turned his attention to the study of personality, the field was characterized largely by two approaches. On the one hand, clinical practitioners, often trained in the Freudian tradition, offered penetrating insights into the human psyche that were, however, limited by a concentration on the abnormal and unstable and by an almost total absence of that sine qua non of science: measurements. On the other hand, more quantitatively oriented scientists noted that people often behaved consistently in different situations—by, for example, being friendly, aggressive, generous, altruistic, or shy—and explained this consistency as a consequence of properties within the person called "traits": friendliness, aggressiveness, generosity, altruism, and shyness. Assuming that these characteristics were continuous dimensions on which individual differences could be represented, scales could then be constructed and each person assessed to determine the relative amount of a trait that he or she possessed. But the problem for trait theorists, unsurprisingly, was the difficulty in coming to some agreement on the number and nature of these basic personality constructs, and soon there was a bewildering array of ad hoc traits and scales, based largely on hunch and supposition.[22] With his usual mixture of disdain and sarcasm, Cattell dismissed many of these tests as lacking in the "honesty of science" and using methods "unimaginatively copied from aptitude testing, or possibly from bookkeeping or plumbing." In response to the chaotic proliferation of constructs and tests, "some psychologists," he claimed, had "reached such a stage of desperation that they were ready to fix traits if necessary by fiat, by setting up a commission to say what the important traits are and how they should be defined."[23]

To Cattell, factor analysis seemed the ideal method to resolve this confusion by identifying the basic dimensions of personality, the small number of "source" traits that would constitute not only its fundamental categories, like the Linnaean taxonomy was for biology, but also its building blocks, like the elements in the periodic table were for chemistry. The designation of a person's rating on each of these basic traits—the "amount" of the trait he or she possessed—would thus provide the ultimate description of an individual human personality. In addition, in Cattell's conceptualization, it would enable precise prediction of behavior in a specified context. Indeed, his definition of *personality* was "that which tells what a man will do when placed in a given situation." The specification equation in the factor analysis of intelligence had assumed that a person's performance on some test could be predicted as a combination of his or her ability on each factor, common and unique, weighted by the extent to which the test involved that factor. Similarly, Cattell saw the factor analysis of personality as a way to predict how someone will behave in a particular situation based on the person's rating on each of the fundamental traits and on some trait specific only to that situation, weighted for each trait by the extent to which it was required by that situation.[24] If, for example, performance in a debate has a weight of .6 on general intelligence, .3 on practicality, .8 on ego strength, and .2 on some specific "debating" trait, then it would be possible to predict someone's relative standing as a debater by inserting his or her rating on each of these four traits into the specification equation. Nor did this approach mean that Cattell rejected the value of clinical insights; rather, he believed they could be confirmed, if in fact valid, by factor analytic results. The factor analysis of personality thus presented an opportunity, he believed, to combine Spearman and Freud.

The question was how to begin: what sort of data should be collected to create the correlation matrix from which factors of personality could be extracted? The variables in the factor analysis of intelligence had been cognitive tests of different kinds, but nothing quite so obvious presented itself as a starting point for a similar study of personality. There had been earlier attempts to tackle this problem, but with no systematic rationale to inform the choice of variables, they inevitably seemed to be an arbitrary set of characteristics. In 1932 Cattell himself had made the first effort at such a study, assembling a grab bag of traits from the work of other researchers and clinicians. The next dozen years brought little improvement. One study of "neurotic and delinquent" children collected data on their "main traits of character . . . as expressed by the [eleven] primary emotional reactions": anger, sociability, joy, tenderness, fear, and a half dozen others. Another used teachers' ratings of ten characteristics of schoolchildren, including bodily activity, excitability, initiative, and self-consciousness. A study of pupils at a Catholic parochial school began with thirty-four variables, among them—perhaps unsurprisingly—obedience, respectfulness, religiousness, neatness, and orderliness; almost half the variables in this case involved the absence of a trait—for example, "lack of cheerfulness," "lack of humor," and "lack of forwardness."[25] Yet other investigations included such idiosyncratic traits as a "pleasant voice," a "smiling countenance,"[26] and "impulsive kindness," which was to be distinguished from "tendency to do kindnesses on principle."[27] Perhaps the best effort of this sort was conducted by University of Chicago psychologist Louis Leon Thurstone, a pioneer in the use of factor analysis, who asked each subject to think of someone he or she knew well and rate that person on sixty common adjectives. In addition, most of these earlier attempts used ratings by authority figures, which were of questionable reliability, may have been based on superficial knowledge of the subjects, and in any event introduced the biases of the adults; describing one child as "gloomy and morose," for example, a teacher suggested that the boy was "worn out with secret masturbation."[28] Aside from the Thurstone study, the only other exception to this reliance on authority and also the only analysis to report statistics on the reliability[29] of the variables was a study using a self-assessment personality inventory, yielding scores on only four scales, such as neurotic tendency and introversion-extraversion—in other words, the sort of traits that might be the outcome of a factor analysis, but not its starting point.[30]

Cattell took a bold approach to this problem. Instead of beginning with any preconceived notions about which characteristics should be of interest, he started with all of them—every personality trait in the English language. In the late nineteenth century Francis Galton, in the course of developing the concepts of eugenics, had turned to the thesaurus to gain an idea of the number of "conspicuous aspects" of the human personality but gave up when he realized that there were more than a thousand. In 1936, however, Gordon Allport and Henry Odbert at the Harvard Psychological Laboratory were more perseverative, compiling from *Webster's New Unabridged International Dictionary* a list of more than 4,000 traits, or about 1 percent of all the words in the language—everything from "abandoned, abject, abrupt and absent-minded" to "zealous, zestful, and zetetic" (the last adjective meaning "seeking; proceeding by inquiry").[31] This list provided the starting point for Cattell's efforts.

His first task was to reduce this huge set to a more manageable number. Quite apart from the impossibility of collecting data on so many traits, it was the precomputer era, and the calculations necessary to create just the correlation matrix for a large number of variables would have been staggering;[32] the much greater computational labor to conduct a factor analysis on such a matrix was completely out of the question. The process of reduction was carried out in two steps. First, in order to eliminate redundancy two research assistants, one of whom was actually a literature student, independently classified the traits into groups of synonyms; there were, for example, 48 synonyms for "talkative." As a part of this step, opposites were incorporated into a synonym group, so that some traits were defined on a bipolar spectrum, such as "talkative . . . taciturn." With little disagreement between the two judges, this step narrowed the list to about 160 traits, to which were added a small number of terms for abilities and interests, bringing the total to 171.[33] Although this "Complete Personality Sphere," as Cattell called it, was obviously a substantial reduction from the original set of some 4,000, it was still much too large for factor analysis.

The second step in the condensation process involved the collection of data on the reduced list of variables. Cattell obtained ratings on whether each of a large sample of adults was above or below average on each of the 171 traits; if the trait was bipolar, then the rater judged whether the person was closer to one end of the spectrum or the other. The correlation coefficient between every pair of traits was then computed—14,535 in all—a daunting task that was made only slightly less onerous by the fact that there were just two possible values for each variable; to inspect the results Cattell had to lay the correlation matrix out on a table fourteen feet square. With a logic similar to that underlying factor analysis, though using a much simplified procedure, his goal was to find clusters of traits that could be considered a single variable because all the traits in the cluster were highly correlated with each other. The first such cluster, for example, was composed of 8 traits—argumentative, arrogant, assertive, autocratic, boastful, conceited, exhibitionistic, and headstrong; Cattell titled the cluster "assertive, egotistic."[34] This step further reduced the number of variables to a final set of 60, but produced a problem that has plagued much of Cattell's subsequent multivariate research: what to name each of these clusters, especially when some of them brought together seemingly disparate characteristics. Cattell himself seemed to be aware of this difficulty, noting that he had given the clusters "provisional titles," which he considered in many cases "unsatisfactory, since language lacks terms for the broad qualities revealed by the clustering." What name might be appropriate, for example, for the cluster composed of these 6 traits: austere, independent, polished, reliable, thoughtful, and wise? Cattell chose to call it "gentlemanly, philosophical." Or the cluster combining affected, debonair, exhibitionistic, flattering, and talkative, which he named "foppish, sycophantic."[35] In any event, this was a major achievement—within a few months to condense all the trait-descriptive terms in the English language to a basic five dozen—and he intended that data collected on these 60 variables should be the input to a factor analysis that would identify a smaller, even more fundamental set of characteristics defining the human personality.

But now Cattell faced a second problem: *how* to collect data on such variables. Again he planned an innovative strategy: he would conduct three different kinds of studies, based on three different methods of assessment. Measurements could be based on subjects' behavior in real-life situations, producing what he originally called BR-data ("behavior rating") but later renamed as L-data ("life record"). Ideally, Cattell had hoped to obtain this sort of information through objective measurements not dependent on a rater's judgment, such as school grades and number of automobile accidents, but he acknowledged that in practice it was much more common to rely on "secondhand" data in the form of ratings by someone who knew the subject well.[36]

A second medium was Q-data ("questionnaire"), which included a subject's responses on instruments designed to measure attitudes, opinions, and personality traits. Although he made use of such devices in the interest of completeness, Cattell was wary of their susceptibility to subjects' self-delusions or their desire to impress the researcher by creating a false but favorable image of themselves.[37] Indeed, he disliked the very term *questionnaire*, which in his view did not convey the subjectivity of such instruments, and coined the word *opinionnaire* as a more appropriate substitute.[38]

Finally, he thought it particularly important to collect T-data ("test") from objective tests, miniature situations in which the subject must react without knowing what aspect of his or her behavior is being assessed.[39] Even before the war Cattell had experimented with such methods, obtaining results that were so impressive as to stretch the bounds of credibility. For example, he administered a test in which a strip of paper moved past a small window, presenting to subjects a succession of lines and patterns, with the instructions to mark all horizontal and vertical lines but no slanting ones. From this "Cursive Miniature Situation" Cattell claimed to derive scores on personal characteristics such as "leadership" and "cautiousness-timidity" that had close to perfect correlation with independent measures of these traits.[40] Then, as part of his research on personnel assessment during the war, he developed hundreds of brief "objective" tests, each one designed for the measurement of some aspect of behavior thought to be associated with a specific personality trait.[41] Included in this category of data were projective tests based on various Freudian mechanisms.[42]

In the late 1940s Cattell announced plans to conduct a series of landmark studies: the first really meaningful factor analyses of personality. As input he intended to collect data on the sixty trait variables derived from the list of four thousand total possibilities. If in the resulting correlation matrix, some of these variables showed a tendency to co-occur systematically, appearing and disappearing as a group, then it would suggest that they were not independent but rather "surface" manifestations of some more fundamental human trait; the nature of that trait could then be determined by looking at the variables that defined it. Of particular significance, each study was to be based on one of the three different types of data—everyday life behavior, self-report questionnaires, and objective tests. Cattell hoped to demonstrate that data from these three methods would produce identical underlying factors. If such a result could be obtained, it would provide very impressive evidence that the factors were not "mere mathematical conveniences but real, functionally unitary *source traits*," the building blocks of human personality.[43] In addition, from a practical point of view, it would form the basis for construction of a questionnaire to measure these fundamental "source traits," which could be published and marketed by the Institute for Personality and Ability Testing, the organization founded by Cattell in 1949. Shakespeare may have invented human personality, but Cattell was determined to discover its topography.

However, a difficulty arose immediately. "Through lack of funds for so extensive an undertaking," it was not possible to use all sixty clusters, and they had to be reduced to a yet smaller set. To do so Cattell eliminated the "less reliable" clusters and consolidated others with overlap between them, thus condensing the list to thirty-five.[44] Beyond a rather vague description of how this latest reduction was carried out, he offered few details of the procedure. But now each cluster was defined by between six and twelve different traits, and the correlations between the pairs of traits that composed a cluster tended to be lower—sometimes no more than .40—meaning that the clusters were even more heterogeneous and harder to describe with a simple phrase or title. Indeed, although Cattell began a number of his subsequent factor analyses with these thirty-five variables, their names sometimes changed so substantially from one study to the next that it was difficult to identify them as the same list.[45] As Berkeley personality psychologist Oliver John observed decades later, the variables were "multifaceted and lacked coherence," leading John to conclude that "evaluation of . . . [the] 35–variable list . . . depends on one's trust in Cattell's theoretical savvy and innovative genius, but cannot rest on the replicability of his empirical procedures."[46]

The first three studies in this series were all conducted using BR-data, obtained in each case by having persons rated on each of the thirty-five traits by intimate acquaintances or, in one instance, by judges "trained . . . to study more average people."[47] In each study Cattell found eleven or twelve factors necessary to account for the correlations between the thirty-five variables and then sought to rotate each of the factor axes to a position that would permit some sensible interpretation of the factor's meaning. Without the assistance of computers, such rotation at the time was an extremely painstaking process with a considerable element of subjective judgment, as much art as science, that consumed an enormous amount of time—in one of these studies "taking the equivalent of one person's full time for a year." As Cattell had hoped, there was considerable duplication in the results of the three studies: seven of the factors appeared all three times, six appeared twice, and only one factor appeared in but a single study. Thus, there were fourteen factors overall, to which he assigned the letters *A* through *N*. Just as some degree of linguistic creativity had been necessary to construct titles for the trait clusters, it was not an easy matter to decide what to call many of the factors, especially those that were defined by a number of seemingly disparate traits. The high loadings on one factor, for example, came from the following bipolar traits: "gregarious, sociable vs. self-contained"; "marked vs. slight interest in the opposite sex"; "somewhat unscrupulous vs. conscientious"; "composed v. shy, bashful"; "adventurous, bold vs. cautious, retiring, timid"; and "frivolous vs. responsible." Cattell named this factor "Charitable, Adventurous Cyclothymia vs. Withdrawn, Heboid Schizothymia." In the process of interpretation Cattell made ample use of his knowledge of obscure foreign terms, calling one factor, for example, "Spiessburger Concernedness vs. Bohemian Intellectualism"; *Spiessbürger* is a derisive German word for a petit bourgeois, someone with conformist middle-class values. Though unmentioned in his discussion, a number of the factors displayed no large loadings for any of the traits. For example, none of the seven traits in one study or the five traits in another that defined the Spiessburger-Bohemian factor displayed a loading as large as .40.[48] And for another factor, which Cattell labeled "Rhathymic, Adjusted Surgency vs. Schizoid Desurgency" (essentially, "trusting versus suspicious"), the highest loading was .22—on the bipolar trait "cheerful, enthusiastic, witty vs. unhappy, frustrated, dour."[49] In the face of such small, and, in the latter case, really inconsequential values, it was a considerable stretch to suggest that the factors defined by them had any meaning whatsoever.

After concluding that these studies relying on BR-data had indicated the existence of a number of basic personality factors, Cattell then hoped to confirm their validity by demonstrating that the same factors emerged from data gathered by both "objective tests" and questionnaires—from T-data and Q-data. In the former medium, in addition to administering twenty of the tests he had developed earlier, he created another twenty-eight instruments, which were designed not to measure the original thirty-five variables but to represent the "essence" of the factors he had already identified in the BR-data.[50] That is, a study, the purpose of which was to investigate whether a result obtained previously would occur with a different type of data, was conducted largely with tests specifically constructed to produce that result. But even with these acknowledged intentions, sometimes it was difficult to see any obvious relationship between the tests and the factors they were intended to define, and very little evidence beyond intuition was provided in support of such an association. The factor "Cyclothymia-Schizothymia," for example, had been identified in all three of the behavior-rating studies, defined by variables such as "ready to cooperate vs. obstructive"; "good-natured, easygoing vs. spiteful, grasping, critical"; and "attentive to people vs.

cool, aloof."[51] In one of the objective tests designed to produce a high loading on this factor, the subject was asked to decide whether each of a series of jokes was "good" or "poor"; a high ratio of the former to the latter was scored toward the cyclothymic end of the spectrum under the perhaps reasonable assumption that good-natured, cooperative persons are more inclined to find humor.[52] Less intuitively persuasive was the test intended to produce a high loading for the factor "Positive Character Integration vs. Immature Dependent Character," which had also been identified in all three studies by variables such as "persevering, determined vs. quitting, fickle"; "responsible vs. frivolous"; and "emotionally stable vs. changeable."[53] In this case a subject indicated agreement or disagreement with a series of opinion statements and then, after an interpolated activity, was asked to recall his or her response to each statement under the assumption that a person lacking well-integrated character will have an unconscious tendency to recall only consonant opinions. Whatever the validity of these ad hoc measures, the results of the study were at very best inconclusive. The eleven factors extracted from the objective tests were not clearly defined, few of them seemed to replicate those found in the behavior-rating studies, and Cattell concluded that "no judgment" could be made about the correspondence of the source traits derived from the two domains without further research.[54] Even this agnostic conclusion was an unduly favorable interpretation, and shortly thereafter he acknowledged that few of the factors from T-data "line up directly" with those from the other two media.[55] In all his subsequent research Cattell would treat the factors derived from test data separately from other personality traits.

Although Cattell had concerns that Q-data—from personality questionnaires, interest scales, and attitude measures—were too easily falsified to have any real meaning, nevertheless he believed it important to conduct a factor analysis in this medium too for the sake of "scientific completeness," especially if the subjects were university students, "baring their souls for science," and thus more likely than the "semi-literate masses" to produce data of "comparatively high validity and reliability." The ostensible purpose of this study, like the studies of BR- and T-data that had preceded it, was to demonstrate that the "primary source traits or dimensions of personality will in general reveal themselves with equal facility in the three possible media of observation."[56] To accomplish such a goal Cattell could have constructed a questionnaire paralleling the instrument used in the behavior-rating studies—that is, one asking subjects to rate themselves on each of the thirty-five trait variables that he had worked so hard to derive. Or, if he wanted to stack the deck, as he had done to some extent in the objective test study, he could have created items designed to represent the factors already identified by behavior ratings. Instead, however, he suddenly changed the orientation of the research, crafting a questionnaire intended to identify not the basic personality factors that had been his focus but factors that had been discovered in previous questionnaire studies of three different areas: personal adjustment, interests, and attitudes. Indeed, almost every one of the eighty items in this instrument was written to match one of these previously discovered factors.[57] Cattell thought it possible that the factors underlying interests and attitudes were "outcroppings, at the intellectual level, of primary personality factors"; on the other hand, he also thought it possible that they were "reflections of more local culture patterns or of intellectual structures more specific than the basic personality dimensions." But his discussion of the nineteen factors that emerged in this analysis made no attempt to determine whether they supported either of these possibilities, concentrating completely on the extent to which they replicated the results of previous researchers. Then in the article's last sentence Cattell declared, without evidence or elaboration, that fifteen of these nineteen factors had been "matched in a further study with rating and objective test factors and . . . standardized in a full length questionnaire for general use in personality measurement."[58] If true, this really *would* have been impressive evidence for the claim to have discovered personality's building blocks.

However, when this "further study" appeared, comparing the factors derived in each of the three domains, it demonstrated nothing close to such a remarkable outcome. Altogether in this line of research, forty-four factors had been extracted: fourteen from behavior ratings, eleven from objective tests, and nineteen from questionnaires. Yet even after a number of favorable interpretations in deciding whether there was correspondence in a factor from one type of data to another, only three factors appeared across all three types of data, and another six appeared in two of the modalities, leaving twenty-three factors that appeared only once. Even this modest result turned out to be suspect. The master's thesis by Cattell's student David Saunders, cited to support the equivalence of the few questionnaire factors that supposedly did match those from the behavior ratings, in fact demonstrated quite the opposite: as a colleague of Cattell's at the University of Illinois, Wesley Becker, pointed out, Saunders had found correlations of .01 and .02 between two of these pairs.[59] (To which Cattell responded, strangely, that a correlation "far short of perfection" between the questionnaire and behavior-rating factors should not be considered "disproof" of "what are apparently equivalents in the two media.") Although this series of studies was certainly the most ambitious attempt yet conducted to establish the fundamental dimensions of human personality, it fell far short of the goal, and Cattell had to recognize that "only one conclusion is possible, i.e., except for two or three instances, the known personality factors, contrary to our hypothesis, are not outcrops of the same factors in different media." In particular, he observed, it was "the questionnaire factors that lie most in a space of their own," that is, that do not match the factors derived from the other media.[60]

Yet at the same time that Cattell acknowledged this disappointing result, he was also using it as the basis of the twin achievements with which he is most famously associated: the claim to have discovered the fundamental elements of the human personality and the construction of a device to measure them. The first edition of the *Sixteen Personality Factor Questionnaire* was published in 1950 by IPAT and quickly became one of the most well-known and widely used instruments of its type. As its name suggested, the 184-item questionnaire promised to identify and measure the sixteen basic traits of the human personality, each trait being assessed by either ten or thirteen items.[61] The first eleven of these sixteen factors were selected from the fourteen that had emerged in the behavior-rating data; because Cattell maintained the letters he had assigned the factors in the original study, these factors were labeled *A* through *N*, omitting *D*, *J*, and *K*, which were dropped from the final set of sixteen. The twelfth factor, labeled *O*—"Anxious Insecurity vs. Placid Self-Confidence—appeared out of the blue. It had not been mentioned in any of the studies on which the questionnaire was putatively based, and Cattell later explained, cryptically, that it was "not . . . a confirmed factor but only . . . an indicated factor," which had been found in an unpublished study cited in an obscure document available from the Educational Testing Service.[62] Nevertheless, it became one of the sixteen basic traits. Because the final four factors had appeared only in the questionnaire data, they were labeled Q_1 through Q_4.

It was difficult to find the logic in many of the decisions leading to the selection of these particular sixteen factors. Factor *C*, for example—"Emotional Stability or Ego Strength vs. Dissatisfied Emotionality"—was included even though it had appeared in only two of the three behavior-rating studies and in neither the objective tests nor the questionnaire data.[63] In contrast, factor *K*—"Trained, Socialized, Cultured Mind vs. Boorishness"—was omitted from the final list despite having emerged in all three behavior-rating studies. Nor was it any easier to understand the rationale for including the mysterious factor *O* or why the specific four factors had been selected from the questionnaire data, only one of which had a marginal similarity to a factor from one of the other domains, when there were eleven other questionnaire factors that had also appeared only in that medium. No doubt with these many arbitrary decisions in mind, Berkeley personality psychologist Oliver John later commented, "Everything considered, it is difficult to avoid the conclusion that Cattell's . . . factors primarily represent those traits that he himself considered the most important."[64]

Nevertheless, over time Cattell's claims about the original studies became bolder and bolder. By 1957 the questionnaire factors, which he had declared largely "in a space of their own" only seven years earlier, were now said to be almost "completely mutually matched" to the behavior-rating factors, the only exceptions being the four previously acknowledged as unique to questionnaire data and labeled accordingly—Q_1 through Q_4. The only behavior-rating factors that had not also appeared in questionnaire data, he now claimed, were those he had omitted from the Sixteen Personality Factor instrument—D, J, and K.[65]

In addition, two decades after the research, Cattell's description of his procedure introduced substantial improvements that had not actually occurred. In 1973, summarizing the development of the Sixteen Personality Factor Questionnaire for a popular audience, he began by claiming that the original behavior rating studies had been conducted using a list of 171 traits—a number that had, of course, been reduced first to 60 and then to 35 before any ratings took place. Then, according to Cattell, he had waited for years to "assign . . . descriptive names" to the resulting factors while he explored their meaning and "established . . . beyond doubt that they were really mental factors"; not until then was he "quite certain that we had found the building blocks of personality." In fact, not only had he named the factors immediately upon analyzing the data, but he had created the instrument based on the results almost simultaneously: the factor study of the questionnaire data, the study matching the factors in the three media, and the Sixteen Personality Factor Questionnaire were all published in 1950. Moreover, he declared that the "most of [the questionnaire factors] turned out to correspond exactly to the factors that the raters had identified earlier."[66] Not only was this claim contradicted by both his original conclusion and by his student's data cited by Becker, but in the few cases in which there was some correspondence the confident adverb in this observation was hardly warranted by the traits that had actually contributed to the factors. For example, factor F—"Surgency vs. Desurgency"—had been defined in the behavior ratings by such traits as "energetic, alert vs. languid, slow"; and "talkative vs. silent, introspective." The "exactly" matching questionnaire factor, labeled "Relaxed Independence or Rhathymia," was defined by "not [being] annoyed by unintentionally disagreeable acts" and a preference for "the type of job that offers constant change, travel and variety."

More than a half century later, the Sixteen Personality Factor Questionnaire has gone through five editions and, translated into more than thirty-five languages and dialects, is used throughout the world; it has also been adapted for use at different age levels, resulting in parallel testing forms for adolescents (twelve to eighteen years old), older children (eight to twelve), and younger children (six to eight). However, the traits that it assesses are still those derived from the research conducted in the late 1940s.[67] The names of a number of the traits have been modified from those given in the original studies, but these nominal alterations have not resulted from any change in their conceptualization. In some cases the trait names were made more intelligible. "Spiessburger Concernedness vs. Bohemian Intellectualism," for example, became "Hysteric Unconcern (or 'Bohemianism') vs. Practical Concernedness" in the first edition of the questionnaire and in later editions "Abstractedness"—"practical, grounded, down-to-earth vs. abstracted, imaginative, idea-oriented." Much to the exasperation of other researchers, however, Cattell converted many of the original traits to unintelligible neologisms—either acronyms, such as *parmia* (parasympathetic predominance) and *premsia* (protected emotional sensitivity) or words with classical roots, such as *affectia* and *exvia*—in order, as he put it, "to escape from the trailing miasmas of misunderstanding that come with 'popular' meaning."[68] However, he tended to confine such exotic terms to the professional literature. "Parmia vs. threctia" and "premsia vs. harria" in works intended for other scholars were labeled, respectively, "timid vs. adventuresome" and "tough-minded vs. sensitive" in the questionnaire and in treatments designed for a broader audience.[69] However, none of this tinkering suggested any doubt on his part that these sixteen factors constituted the building blocks of personality. Indeed, Cattell continued to insist that "one of the first tasks" for new students of personality "should be to learn the names and natures of these 16 PF source traits," much as "medical students learn hundreds of new names [and] . . . chemists know over 100 elements."[70]

Having discovered what he was certain were the basic source traits of personality—not just those assessed by the *Sixteen Personality Factor Questionnaire* but also the other factors that had been identified only in Q- and T-data—Cattell was eager to impose some sort of order on the chaos in the field. He called for the discipline to establish a "Universal Index" of factors that would assign a standardized number recognized by all of psychology to each trait he had identified in each of the three data domains, as well as to others that had been discovered by intelligence researchers from cognitive tests. Cattell's first suggestion for such a system proposed that an international committee of prominent scientists set out standards for factor verification and determine when new research findings qualified for inclusion on the list he had already compiled; he even named the persons he thought should serve on such a committee.[71] But when this ambitious proposal was ignored by most of the field, Cattell continued to use the system himself, referring to it in a passive voice conveniently lacking an agent, as a "practice [that] has arisen of identifying . . . [factors] . . . by U.I. numbers." However, rather

than reducing what Cattell called "the Babel of misunderstanding in communication," the universal indexing system only exacerbated the problem
when many other psychologists were unwilling to treat his list of traits as
psychology's periodic table or to use the idiosyncratic names he had assigned
to them.[72] A typical research article discussing the role of traits such as U.I.
25, "tensidia," and U.I. 30, "dissofrustance," in distinguishing psychotics from
normals was probably intelligible only to other Cattellians, who knew that
the former indicated a psychotic tendency and the latter an "apparent . . .
tendency to dissociate under frustration." The failure of other psychologists
to recognize the wisdom of his methods and the importance of his nomen-
clatural insights was galling to Cattell, who compared their shortsightedness
to "what the seekers of the philosopher's stone and the elixir of life had to say
about Dalton, Priestly, and Lavoisier." But for vindication he looked to the
future, foreseeing a time when his efforts would be recognized as similar to
those "in which chemistry grew out of alchemy."[73]

Although, in concept, universal indexing was intended to apply to the
factors from all three domains, in practice Cattell used it almost exclusively
for those derived from T-data, referring to the behavior-rating factors by
the letters from A to O and those from questionnaire data as Q factors with
numerical subscripts. In the "objective test" domain, however, he referred
to the factors that had emerged from his research as U.I. 16 through U.I. 33
(later expanded to U.I. 35), reserving the first fifteen index numbers in this
medium for ability variables such as "Associative Memory," "Mechanical
Knowledge," "Verbal Knowledge," and "Word Fluency."[74]

To assess the traits that had emerged from T-data Cattell developed the
Objective-Analytic (O-A) Test Battery.[75] Although it did not claim to measure
traits as fundamental to personality as the basic sixteen, this instrument
constituted a truly novel approach to assessment; when the battery first appeared, H. J. Eysenck, also a world-famous personality researcher, declared
that "nothing like it exists at the moment." Like the method that had been
used to identify such factors originally, the O-A battery was composed of
a number of performance tests for each trait, measuring behavior in actual
situations rather than relying on responses to questions and thus supposedly "unfakable and freed of . . . subjective motivational distortions," because the subject had no knowledge of what was being assessed. Different
versions of the instrument were constructed to measure varying numbers
of traits up to all eighteen. However, as one reviewer of a version designed
to measure only ten traits complained, the battery was "long and tedious,"
requiring some four to five hours for complete administration, in addition
to which the validities—the extent to which the trait scores correlated with

real-life behavior—were no better than those for self-report measures. In addition, some of the tests seemed quite counterintuitive. For example, one test measured the amount of time necessary for a subject's pulse to return to normal after immersion of an arm in ice water as an indication of U.I. 24—"Anxiety"—but the faster the rebound, the *more* anxiety he or she was assumed to experience.[76] Although it played an important role in Cattell's own research program, the O-A battery never achieved the widespread recognition of his famous sixteen-factor questionnaire.

Although Cattell's notion of sixteen basic traits underlying normal personality is still well known in psychology and his resulting questionnaire marketed by IPAT is used frequently in personnel work, mainstream thinking has long since rejected his numerical conclusions. Over four or five decades marked by changes in methodology from laborious hand calculation to computerized factor solutions, there have been numerous attempts by researchers other than Cattell and his associates to replicate the factor structure discovered in his studies. All have failed.[77] One of these attempts gathered data on thirty of the same thirty-five variables used by Cattell,[78] and two of them reanalyzed the original set of correlations from two of his behavior-ratings studies, one of these reanalyses finding numerous errors in his work.[79] From Cattell's point of view there was a simple explanation for this inability to replicate his results: no one outside his own lab did factor analysis correctly. Because of the judgmental component involved in much of the process—especially in rotation—there were, he emphasized, "hundreds of ways of going wrong in a complex procedure like factor analysis, and only one that gives the truth," and Cattell was certain that he alone had found it. But instead of his sixteen factors, there is now almost unanimous agreement in the field of personality research on the "Five-Factor" model—the so-called "Big Five," a result that first emerged from the unsuccessful efforts to replicate Cattell's findings.[80] Not everyone agrees on the exact definition of the factors, although there is substantial support for the "OCEAN" interpretation proposed by Paul Costa and Robert McCrae, researchers at the National Institute on Aging: openness to experience, conscientiousness, extraversion, agreeableness, and neuroticism.[81] But the number of factors has provoked little dispute.

Despite the scholarly consensus in its favor, to Cattell the Big Five was "a scientific nightmare," which he considered almost a personal attack—a "heresy ... partly directed against the 16PF test." It was possible to arrive at a smaller number of factors, he allowed, but only through a second-order analysis—a factor analysis of the correlations between the sixteen basic traits—and even though the five-factor theorists had not conducted any such analysis, "the 'general opinion,'" according to Cattell, was "that the five are second order factors."

That is, he claimed that these other researchers had arrived at their five-factor conclusion "by doing first order . . . factorings and arbitrarily stopping at what [they] think should be the number of second orders." In addition, he declared, "the true second orders have been known to be *eight* for more than twenty years."[82] Actually, over the years Cattell had made periodic pronouncements of the correct number of second-order factors, always certain of his conclusion and untroubled by the fact that it differed from his previous ones. In 1946, in a somewhat confusing analysis, he had apparently found five second-order factors;[83] in 1957, six; in 1959, two "substantial factors," implying perhaps that there were others of less substance; in 1980, seven; and in 1995, only months after publishing his fulmination against "the fallacy of five factors," Cattell described the development of the latest edition of his *Sixteen Personality Factor Questionnaire*, noting that a second-order analysis had produced five interpretable factors (there was a sixth, but it was not interpretable).[84] Indeed, the Web site for Cattell's Institute for Personality and Ability Testing claims that its founder "derived five Global [that is, second-order] Factors of personality in the 1960s and is considered by many to be the 'father of the Big 5,'" although it goes on to note, unsurprisingly, that using all sixteen scales from the questionnaire "predict[s] actual behavior better than the Big 5."[85]

However, it would be misleading to evaluate Cattell's significance to an understanding of personality traits solely in terms of the debate over the number of factors. Whatever the research may suggest is the "correct" answer, Cattell is acknowledged by everyone in this field as its pioneer, the scientist whose work brought the study of traits into the modern era and made it possible even to raise the question. Researchers who disagree with Cattell's conclusion have nevertheless regarded his research as the standard to which all subsequent work had to be compared and invariably begin their own studies by acknowledging his role as the field's founder and expressing homage for his achievements. One of the canonical studies in support of the five-factor model, for example, observes, "One cannot undertake work in this field without consideration of the monumental work of Cattell"; another of his critics calls his research program "unrivalled" in "scope and intention."[86] Despite Cattell's opposition to the five-factor model, IPAT's acknowledgment of his role as its true parent is hardly inflated: even though he refused to acknowledge paternity, the Big Five was indisputably his illegitimate child.

Understanding and Applying Traits

For Cattell, deciding on a taxonomic structure for personality was merely the first step on a very long journey. The identification of source traits, both the basic sixteen and the additional factors from T-data, was the beginning of an ambitious agenda that would combine theory-based research and practical application. The scientific challenge was to understand how each trait developed over time from childhood to old age, whether it was found in different cultures, and—most important, in his view—the extent to which its "major origin" was "in genetic or environmental sources."[87] Cattell's lab conducted numerous studies on the first two of these issues, claiming that the same sixteen personality factors could be identified at different ages, from six to sixty,[88] and that, when the questionnaire was translated, they appeared in diverse national cultures—among them, Germany, Chile, Japan, New Zealand, France, and India; as Cattell concluded, "It seems that basic human nature is the same world-wide."[89] Although naturally there was substantial criticism of these claims from personality researchers who disagreed with Cattell's model,[90] even a few of the critics agreed on the value of his innovation in the third area—the development of a new method for estimating the heritability of a trait; Hans Eysenck, who dismissed the sixteen-factor theory as "of limited interest" because no one outside of Cattell's circle had ever replicated his findings, called his "system of genetic analysis . . . possibly his best and most enduring contribution to methodology."[91]

The concept of heritability is misunderstood by most of the lay public and more than a few scientists. Heritability is commonly and inaccurately confused with genetic determination, when in fact the two terms are considerably different from each other.[92] As the phrase implies, a genetically determined trait, such as the number of fingers on a human hand, is genetically programmed to have the same value in almost every environment. *Heritability,* in contrast, is a technical term from the field of population genetics, referring to the proportion or percentage of variation in a trait from one person to another that is associated with variation in their genes. Since the degree of variation is measured by a statistic called "variance," heritability is thus the ratio of genetic variance to observed variance in a trait. As a consequence, despite the fact that the number of fingers on a hand is genetically determined, its heritability is low because the differences between persons on this trait have very little association with differences in their genes—the rare genetic mutation notwithstanding—and more to do with environmental events such as combat injuries, accidents with chain saws, and frostbite or other medical conditions necessitating amputation. Genetic determination applies to an individual, whereas heritability applies only to groups; it is nonsense to refer to the heritability of a trait for a specific person. Moreover, because its value is affected by changes in the degree of environmental variation, heritability is not a constant—a fixed percentage—but a variable, which is inevitably high when environmental conditions are the same for everyone but can decrease with extensive environmental differences experienced by different members of a group. The heritability of, say, lung cancer in a community is high if everyone smokes or if no one smokes, but it is low if some people do and others don't. What a large value of heritability does indicate, however, is that, in the existing environmental conditions, genes are substantially involved in the differences from one person to another in a trait.

The problem in attempting to estimate the value of heritability for a complex human trait such as an aspect of personality is that its variance cannot be easily partitioned into a genetic and an environmental component, which are, after all, theoretical constructs and thus not empirically measurable. Indeed, because of this difficulty some of the world's leading geneticists have maintained that "'heritability' does not even exist in the human . . . context" and that attempts to estimate its value are meaningless.[93] Other scientists disagree and have developed models for heritability that have typically begun with kinship correlations on a trait—between identical twins, fraternal twins, parent and child, and so forth. However, to get from these correlations to the proportion of observed variance that is genetic, every one of these methods depends on a host of simplifying assumptions necessary to eliminate some of the many unknowns, which always outnumber the observable variables. In the most well-known design, the correlation between the scores of separated identical twins on some trait is used as an estimate of its heritability, but even this simplest of models depends on a number of assumptions.[94]

Although Cattell had done some heritability studies in the 1930s relying on the traditional methods, in 1953 he published his own highly original approach to estimation: Multiple Abstract Variance Analysis (MAVA).[95] Instead of the correlational procedure with its set of assumptions, MAVA was based on a dozen or more different, empirically determinable variances in the trait being studied, each one emanating from a different degree of genetic or familial similarity, such as identical twins, fraternal twins, ordinary siblings, half siblings, or unrelated children; in addition, for each degree of similarity separate variances could be computed for children reared in the same home and for those reared apart. Cattell expressed each of these empirically measurable variances in terms of the theoretical constructs of interest, such as genetic variance and environmental variance—for the latter of which he coined the term *threptic*[96]—both within and between families, producing a complex system of equations but one in which it was possible to solve for the various theoretical unknowns. These values could then be used for direct calculation of heritability as the ratio of genetic variance to total variance.[97]

In the next few years Cattell and his associates gathered sufficient data for two studies that applied the MAVA technique: in one case, to some of the traits assessed by the *Sixteen Personality Factor Questionnaire* and, in the other, to a number of traits from the *Objective-Analytic (O-A) Test Battery*. For each trait Cattell decided whether it was "predominantly determined" by heredity, predominantly by environment, or determined in equal parts by the two influences.[98] (The language was misleading: as noted above, it was not the trait but the individual differences in the trait to which Cattell meant to refer.) But it was not until almost a quarter century later that he continued this line of research,[99] now financially supported by Robert Graham's Foundation for Advancement of Man; Graham, a millionaire inventor, was also the founder of the Repository for Germinal Choice, a sperm bank that sought to produce brilliant offspring by encouraging donations from Nobel laureates and other "geniuses."[100] Sometimes the results were quite provocative. For example, one of the highest heritabilities was for U.I. 24, "Anxiety"[101]—a finding that could have interesting implications for clinical practice as well as understanding personality. But although the method of analysis was ingenious, apparently its complexity could result in contradictory conclusions, depending on which subset of simultaneous equations was used. In one study of three traits from his questionnaire, for example, Cattell reported very low heritabilities for factor G—"Super Ego Strength": the calculation based on total population variance produced an estimate of only .05. Yet in another study of the same three traits published shortly later and seemingly based on the same data set, he found that "quite significant genetic components contribute to the rise of every one of these trait patterns"; now the same heritability estimate was .41.[102] In any event, despite Eysenck's praise MAVA was rarely used outside of Cattell's circle, and in a comparison of different methods for estimating the relative importance of heredity and environment, two leading geneticists preferred the more traditional biometric approach.[103]

At least as important to Cattell as his "pure" research program was his eagerness to apply the results. Indeed, his effort to persuade the rest of psychology to adopt his sixteen factors as the field's fundamental vocabulary was merely the first step toward what he envisioned as a host of practical applications. Even before completing the studies that produced the final set of traits, Cattell had explained to the *New York Times* how his research could lead to a scientific appraisal of the personalities of political candidates. Voters, he suggested, could then decide how to cast their ballot on the basis of candidates' profiles—their ratings on a sequence of traits such as general mental capacity, character integration, extraversion, neuroticism, rigidity, and paranoia. Although the *Times* was understandably skeptical that politicians would ever subject themselves to such an analysis, Cattell emphasized that, had his system been applied in Germany, "Hitler would never have got past the clinical psychologist"—an ironic observation in view of Cattell's highly favorable prewar opinion of the Reich, to be discussed in the next chapter.[104] The idea of evaluating political candidates might have been a bit of a lark, but Cattell had no shortage of more serious applications in mind. In one study he demonstrated how a particular specification equation—that is, the weights to be applied to a person's score on each of the sixteen factors—could be used to select the most effective leader for a group. Another study, designed to indicate the value of the *Sixteen Personality Factor Questionnaire* in clinical diagnosis and treatment, compared the profiles of "normals," homosexuals— both "convicted and unconvicted"—and criminals to determine whether "the species 'homosexual' is anything *more* than a definition of the genus 'criminal.'" Although there was "some general resemblance" between the latter two groups, there were "also specific differences," but within the homosexuals, Cattell concluded, the "convicted and unconvicted . . . were "*essentially* the same species," both groups being considerably more "neurotic" than the normals. As a consequence he recommended that homosexuals undergoing clinical treatment be administered "repeated 16 PF measurements, perhaps at 6-month intervals," to compare the "personality factor changes on those homosexuals who recover and those who do not."[105]

More than any other practical application, Cattell was interested in using the results of his questionnaire to match people to the appropriate roles, oc-cupational and educational, for which their personalities best suited them. For decades, intelligence testers had believed that test scores should be des-tiny, determining that some people were fit for leadership and others only for menial work. Lewis Madison Terman, for example, the Stanford University psychologist primarily responsible for making *IQ* a household term,[106] urged that every child be tested as early as possible—preferably in kindergarten— and directed soon thereafter toward an education and occupation for which the child's IQ was "compatible":[107] some would be given "concrete and practi-cal" instruction in order to make them "efficient workers,"[108] whereas more talented students would receive the "proper development" of their abilities.[109] For Cattell, vocational guidance was not such a "simple procedure for which a score on an intelligence test . . . will suffice." He had something much more psychometrically sophisticated in mind for making decisions about education and employment: a "two-file system" maintained in the counseling office of school systems and the personnel department of large organizations. One file would contain the personality profile for every student or employee—the in-dividual's rating on each of the sixteen fundamental traits assessed by Cattell's questionnaire. The other file would contain the "adjustment profile" for each of numerous occupations—the ratings characteristic of persons succeeding in that occupation—and the specification equation providing the weights to be applied to the score on each personality trait; indeed, Cattell actually calculated such equations for performance in a number of roles, including, for example, psychiatric technician, salesperson, and counselor. Given this information, the decision process would then place an individual in his or her appropriate niche by matching the person's profile from the first file to the job profile from the second.[110]

Naturally interested in the characteristics essential to his own chosen profession, Cattell paid particular attention to the personality profiles of creative people—artists, writers, and scientists—finding them generally more intelligent, adventurous, sensitive, dominant, and emotionally mature than the larger population.[111] In a suggestive comparison, considering his disdain for teaching and administration, Cattell also inspected the differences between those scientists who like himself were pure researchers and those involved in the other two academic areas, concluding that the former were more intelligent and dominant than the latter. "The sort of academician that the usual university administrator finds congenial and unobtrusive," he noted pointedly, "might not be the kind that would be of most use to the university in regard to its scholarly reputation."[112] Having identified what he was certain constituted the personality pattern characteristic of the creative scientist, Cattell believed that this profile should be used not only to identify potential talent but to reward it with research endowment even before any demonstrable accomplishments. In an obviously projective observation, he thought it intolerable to wait "till a man has proved himself by his works, which permits him to begin life at forty." Nor was it any more acceptable to make funding decisions "by the design submitted, rather than by the person, a practice which makes the research world safe for all, including all rule-following mediocrity."[113] In allocating research support, the results of Cattell's personality questionnaire were to take precedence over the substance of the actual research proposal.

Cattell made similar attempts to demonstrate the practical value of the O-A battery, especially in clinical diagnosis and treatment. In a number of studies he identified specific factors from the battery that could be used to distinguish various diagnostic categories from "normals." In one investigation, for example, in comparison to a control group, hospitalized schizophrenics scored systematically higher on U.I. 17, "Timid Inhibition," and U.I. 27, "Involvement"; systematically lower on U.I. 19, "Independence," and U.I. 25, "Tensidia" (that is, more psychotic); and not significantly different on U.I. 24, "Anxiety."[114] Another study found that scores on U.I. 23, "Neurotic Debility vs. Ego Strength," distinguished diagnosed neurotics from normals.[115] And just as he believed that important educational and personnel decisions should be predicated on results from his questionnaire, Cattell predicted that therapeutic progress would eventually be evaluated according to patients' changes on the factors assessed by his objective tests. "In a decade, or two decades at most," he wrote in 1966, he was certain that a "computer technician [would be] attached to the psychiatric clinic" to analyze these changes. It was essential, in his opinion, that the "laboratory and the clinic . . . get together, for the enlightenment of the former and the efficiency and objectivity of the latter."[116] Of course, none of these ambitious expectations for practical application were fulfilled: neither placement offices nor mental health clinics make much use of Cattell's proposals.

Analyzing Ability

As he had originally outlined it in 1946, Cattell's conceptualization of personality was actually much broader than the factors assessed by his *Sixteen Personality Factor Questionnaire,* involving three different types of traits: temperament, ability, and dynamic.[117] Although he sometimes referred to the traits measured by the questionnaire as *"general* personality factors,"[118] with but one exception all of them were classified in the first of these three categories. Temperament traits are stylistic in Cattell's system; they have to do with a person's tempo and persistence, whether excitable or phlegmatic, irritable or easygoing, perseverative or easily frustrated. In contrast, ability traits, as the name suggests, concern the effectiveness of a response to a complex situation—how well it assists the person to solve a problem or achieve a desired goal. Finally, dynamic traits deal with motivations and interests, stemming from the drives or needs a person wishes to satisfy.[119] Only factor *B* of the *Sixteen Personality Factor Questionnaire,* called "Intelligence" in earlier versions and "Reasoning" in later ones, was representative of the second of these categories—ability—and none of the measurements derived from the questionnaire was related to a dynamic factor. It was not until he had achieved "tolerable clarity" on the general personality factors—"about 1960"—that Cattell turned his lab's attention to the other two types of traits.[120]

Having studied under Charles Spearman, who first developed the idea of factor analysis as a technique for demonstrating the existence of "general intelligence" *(g),*[121] and being himself interested in his mentor's specialty for its eugenic implications, Cattell had proposed a "culture-free" intelligence test even before beginning his factor analysis of personality. Subscribing to Spearman's theory—that *g* was the underlying unidimensional ability common to all cognitive tests—he sought to create a test "highly saturated" with *g* yet uncontaminated by "scholastic attainment and life experience" that would allow for a comparison of different racial and national groups. To accomplish this goal Cattell constructed seven subtests, each composed of nonverbal, "perceptual" items requiring an individual to educe the relationship between figural or abstract, geometric material. In the "Relation Matrices" subtest, for example, eight geometric patterns were presented in a three-by-three matrix like a tic-tac-toe array, with the ninth element at the bottom right left blank. The examinee's task was then to decide which of six possibilities should be inserted in the blank slot to complete the systematic changes in the stimuli from left to right and top to bottom in the array.[122] (The items on this subtest were essentially identical in form to those on the Raven's Progressive Matrices intelligence test, a widely used research instrument considered one of the best measures of *g*.) Although Cattell intended the test "primarily for studying intelligence differences in social and cultural divisions of civilized countries," he saw no reason it could not be "used also with primitive peoples."[123]

Even before he published this test, however, Cattell's thinking about *g* had begun to change. Indeed, he later acknowledged that his new direction was initially "disturbing . . . personally" due to his "association with, and . . . great regard for, Spearman and his work."[124] Overcoming these qualms, in 1943 Cattell first proposed the conceptual distinction that is now an essential element in any scientific discussion of the meaning of "intelligence."[125] In place of a unitary *g*, he suggested that mental capacity was composed of two factors. "Fluid intelligence" was a "general ability to discriminate and perceive relations"; uninfluenced by education or culture, this was the type of intelligence best measured by the abstract, perceptual items in Cattell's culture-free test. In contrast, "crystallized intelligence" was involved in those tasks in which performance was mediated by learning and experience, although the earlier learning itself might have been achieved "through the operation of fluid ability." Cattell believed that scores on the standard tests of intelligence reflected a combination of fluid and crystallized abilities in unknown proportions, but that the former was predominant in childhood whereas, "owing to the recession of fluid ability" over age, performance as an adult was determined more by the latter.[126]

Because, as Cattell put it, his lab "took off on a long expedition into personality structure factoring," the evidence for this distinction did not begin to appear until twenty years later, in studies by Cattell and by John Horn, who wrote his dissertation under Cattell on the structure of mental abilities and became his mentor's collaborator and close friend.[127] In each case a factor analysis of scores on a number of tests of many different kinds—including Thurstone's "Primary Mental Abilities"; subtests from Cattell's *Culture Fair Intelligence Scales*, which were published by IPAT beginning in 1949; and some of the factors from Cattell's personality questionnaire—identified fluid and crystallized intelligence as the two largest dimensions.[128] As expected, the fluid factor was defined primarily by tests of spatial visualization, induction, and the culture-fair scales, the crystallized factor by tests of verbal ability, reasoning, numerical facility, and mechanical knowledge.[129] Cattell's analysis also found that the two abilities were not independent: the correlation of almost .50 between them indicated that people high or low in one tended to have a similar level on the other.[130] This dichotomous model quickly became one of the canonical approaches to understanding intelligence, offering a way to reconcile the conflict between the thought of Spearman, Burt, and other proponents of a unidimensional "general intelligence" and Thurstone's multidimensional theory of "primary mental abilities."

Even more than for other personality characteristics, Cattell was interested in the heritability of the two forms of intelligence. One attempt at applying his MAVA technique found that heritability was "roughly" .60 for fluid intelligence "though decidedly lower" for crystallized intelligence at .45.[131] In a revealing reminder of the problems inherent in heritability estimation, another attempt using the same set of data produced a similar result of .57 for fluid intelligence, although instead of being decidedly lower, the value for crystallized intelligence was now .61.[132] These results were of additional interest for being somewhat lower than almost all previous estimates of the heritability of intelligence unidimensionally defined, which tended to be closer to .80.[133]

But the most surprising outcome of these studies was the value of a statistic not available from any of the other models for estimating heritability: the correlation between genotype and environment—what Cattell called the "genothreptic" correlation. Though unaware of the exact value, other discussions of heritability typically assumed that this correlation was positive. As the well-known Berkeley educational psychologist Arthur Jensen explained, "Children with better than average genetic endowment for intelligence have a greater than chance likelihood of having parents of better than average intelligence who are capable of providing environmental advantages that foster intellectual development." In addition, a "genotype for superior ability may cause the environment to foster the ability," as when parents notice that their child has musical talent and consequently provide lessons and encouragement to practice. Or "a bright child may . . . create a more stimulating environment for himself" by engaging in particularly enriching activities.[134] For all these reasons, it was generally expected that genotypes more favorable for a specific characteristic would be systematically associated with more favorable environments—in other words, a positive gene-environment correlation— and the more provocative question had been whether this covariation should be counted on the nature or the nurture side of the ledger. In contrast, Cattell claimed to find large negative genothreptic correlations for both fluid and crystallized intelligence, a result he named the *"law of coercion to the bio-social mean,"* according to which cultural influences, especially in the schools, acted to coerce initial deviations, either above or below average, back toward the mean. Thus, in Cattell's interpretation, "the lock-step of unselective education presses the backward to advance more rapidly but leaves the bright to mark time," the overall effect of which was the mass production of mediocrity.[135] Rather than representing the discovery of a genuine effect, however, this negative correlation was more likely an artifact of the MAVA technique, especially since it occurred not only for the two types of intelligence but for every one of the traits in the *Sixteen Personality Factor Questionnaire*.[136] A pressure to conform so powerful that it tended to suppress any deviation from a cultural norm, no matter the trait or the direction, would suggest the robotic atmosphere of an Orwellian society more than the American obsession with individualism.

Eventually, Cattell went on to develop a much more ambitious theoretical model for the structure of intelligence, in which all cognitive abilities were subdivided into one of three types. Named "triadic theory," this system was an abstraction based on Cattell's classification of the nature and function of various abilities rather than a set of categories he had established empirically through factor analysis. In this tripartite approach, "capacities" included fluid intelligence and other abilities that Cattell regarded as an "expression of limiting properties of the brain," such as speed, memory, and fluency. "Provincial powers" were derived from what he called "local neural organization" rather than "general brain action" and referred mainly to sensory and motor abilities. Finally, "agencies" were those specific, culturally mediated abilities through which the capacities and powers expressed themselves—verbal, numerical, spatial, mechanical, and, of course, crystallized intelligence.

Although triadic theory has not exercised much influence on the field—and, unfortunately, bore a name easily confused with the much more well-known "triarchic theory" proposed by Yale psychologist Robert Sternberg[137]—the distinction between fluid and crystallized intelligence is recognized as a landmark contribution, cited not only in every book on intelligence but also in numerous introductory psychology texts. This particular accomplishment is all the more impressive in view of the fact that Cattell's work on intelligence was largely a diversion from the major focus of his research. Indeed, one of the leading experts in the factor analysis of intelligence called Cattell's interest in the subject a "sideline" but nevertheless declared that "his influence on research in this field can hardly be overestimated" and "has inspired the work of numerous other investigators."[138] The separation of fluid and crystallized intelligence has been one of Cattell's most enduring substantive contributions to psychology.

Motivation and the Dynamic Calculus

The third category in Cattell's systematic analysis of personality was dynamic traits, those related to motivation, and, just as he had for temperament traits, he believed that the crucial first step in studying the phenomenon was establishment of a taxonomy—in this case a set of basic motivational patterns. Concerned, however, that labels such as "drive" and "instinct" brought with them historical baggage that he wished to avoid, Cattell searched for some new word "in order not to get involved in all the old vendettas."[139] Eventually he settled on *erg*, which appealed to him for both its brevity and its easy conversion into an adjectival form—*ergic* (with a soft *g* as in *urge*);[140] like the identical term used in physics as a unit of work or energy based on the metric system, the word is derived from the Greek *ergon*, meaning "work" or "deed." In Cattell's psychological application, an "erg" denoted an innate propensity or disposition to react to some objects and situations more than others, to experience a specific emotion as a consequence, and to seek one type of satisfaction rather than others. Although, as always, he intended to determine the number and nature of ergs through factor analysis, before embarking on the research he anticipated that typical ergs would take the form of such innate tendencies as sexual attraction, parental protectiveness, and gregariousness.[141]

Yet again, the problem was where to begin: what sort of data should be gathered as the starting point for an analysis from which such basic motivational entities would emerge as the underlying factors? Cattell decided to focus on attitude as the unit of observation, the indication of the presence of an erg. But his approach to attitude measurement was considerably different from what he called the "ballot box" model, largely "derived from the preoccupation of applied psychology with polling" and interested only in the extent to which a person was in favor of or opposed to something.[142] Instead, Cattell conceived of an attitude as the degree to which a person was "for or against *a course of action* in relation to an object"—how much someone in a specific set of circumstances wants to take a specific act affecting a specific object.[143] From this perspective, having a favorable opinion of, for example, high-tech companies is meaningless for understanding basic motivations, such as the desire for self-assertion or security; the more instructive question would be how much someone wanted to invest his or her retirement account in NASDAQ firms during 2001.

Although attitudes were thus the starting point in Cattell's conception of the "dynamic life" of an individual, they led not necessarily directly to the most basic level of motivation but rather to an intermediate goal more general than the specific object of the attitude but not as fundamental as an erg. This culturally acquired intermediate level, which Cattell called a "sentiment," was a point of integration for a collection of attitudes—that is, a person, object, or social institution "about which *many* attitudes simultaneously exist."[144] (Actually, he coined the word *engrams* for all "acquired dynamic patterns," which included "complexes" as well as "sentiments," but conducted research almost exclusively on the latter.)[145] Attitudes were then linked to, first, sentiments and ultimately to ergs in a connective chain he termed a *subsidization sequence.*[146] In a typical example of the "dynamic structure" produced by such connections, a person's attitude toward his or her bank account might be a sentiment that, on the one hand, is affected by attitudes toward taxation, investments, and business associates and, on the other hand, is rooted in such basic motivations as the desire to protect family, satisfy hunger, and reduce the fear of insecurity. Such a structure thus produced a "chain of subsidiated attitudes" that began with specific issues or objects and ended "when no farther goal can be discovered," that is, when the chain reached "a biological goal sufficient to itself"—an erg. The relation of these concepts to each other could be best summarized, Cattell explained, "by saying that attitude, sentiment, and erg correspond to twig, bough and trunk in describing the 'subsidiation' of a tree."[147] Unlike a tree structure, however, attitudes could also be connected to a number of different sentiments, which could in turn be related to a number of ergs. In theory, the complex interlocking of all these constructs for a particular individual could be summarized in a diagram that Cattell called a *dynamic lattice.*[148]

Cattell's plan for the empirical identification of both sentiments and ergs was to conduct a factor analysis on all the intercorrelations between measurements on a large set of attitude variables. As always, he employed different methods of attitude measurement—some "subjective," others "objective"—in order to ensure that the results would not be dependent on the manner in which the data were collected. In a typical study, for example, three different approaches were used. In the subjective "preference" method, subjects were presented with all possible pairs of a set of attitude statements and were asked to choose which of each pair was his (all subjects were male) own preferred course of action; an item pair consisted of statements such as "I like to take an active part in athletics and to get exercise" and "I want America to get more protection against the atom bomb." The score for a particular attitude was the number of times it was preferred in all the pairwise comparisons. In contrast, the objective "information" method asked the subject factual questions as a measurement of attitude on the assumption that the answers "would ... be known by anyone who might be strongly and habitually interested in the given course of action." Finally, as a physiological indication of attitude, psychogalvanic responses—changes in electrical resistance of the skin due to alterations in perspiration—were measured while the subject was exposed to a series of statements on different attitudes, some pro and some con.[149] Although use of such an array of devices was certainly sound procedure, the scores derived from the different methods tended to have low correlations with each other, raising serious questions about their validity.[150]

However, once again the more immediately pressing methodological question was how to determine what specific attitudes should be selected from among the almost infinite number of possibilities for input into the factor analysis. In studying general personality traits, Cattell had begun with a list of all the trait terms in the English language before narrowing it down to a more manageable number, but no such comprehensive set of attitudes existed, nor was there any way to compile one. To make this determination he first composed "at least" two attitude statements to represent each of a list of twelve "presupposed" ergs derived from the work of other scientists, in particular the social psychologist William McDougall, who in 1908 had emphasized "instincts" as "innate or inherited tendencies which are the essential springs or motive powers of all thought and action"; whereas Charles Spearman and Cyril Burt, the major contributors to the development of factor analysis, were Cattell's methodological mentors, McDougall was the primary substantive influence on his thinking. To these statements he added another set, this time consisting of at least two statements for each of eleven "presumed sentiments ... chosen to cover the more massive attachments of the average young adult"— parents, home, career, self, and others. As in his study of personality traits found in T-data, this procedure again introduced an element of circularity into the research: an investigation designed to identify the basic set of motivations and sentiments that gave rise to attitudes began in part with a set of attitude statements specifically representative of the results Cattell expected to find. Indeed, "the more important ... ergs and sentiments" were represented by more than two statements. Finally, a few statements were added as "markers" of "radicalism-conservatism and war-pacifism," which in Cattell's judgment were important factors otherwise neglected in the set of stimuli.[151]

Unsurprisingly, the nine factors that emerged from this analysis were interpreted as eight of the anticipated ergs and the "self-sentiment."[152] Although this was but the first of a number of studies similarly designed to identify motivational roots, they tended to follow the same pattern: a set of "markers" chosen to reflect specific underlying factors largely lived up to expectations when subjected to factor analysis.[153] In fact, Cattell was somewhat exercised when the appropriate results were not obtained, declaring that one study had "regressed" because of its "failure to yield the fainter ergic factors" that he had anticipated.[154] Eventually, factors were identified corresponding to most of the ergs and sentiments that he had posited in 1950, and in 1975 Cattell summarized this line of research that had begun "twenty years ago" as demonstrating that "we do indeed have drive patterns . . . highly similar to those . . . speculated on by McDougall" in 1908.[155] Although Cattell's model of dynamic structure—the complex interplay between attitudes, sentiments, and ergs—was of unquestionable theoretical significance, much of the research seemed to be a determined effort to arrive at a foregone conclusion.

However, the study of dynamic factors did produce two other interesting results. First, it was in this substantive context that Cattell developed a type of factor analysis he named "P-technique, the factorization of the single person." The usual factor study begins with data collected from a number of persons on a number of variables—in psychology, typically scores on a test or trait—and then calculates the correlation matrix between variables as the input to the actual factor analysis. In this approach, which Cattell called "R-technique," each correlation in the matrix denotes the degree of relationship between the scores or ratings for the entire group of subjects—for example, the extent to which the people who express a desire to have the United States gain more protection against the terror of atomic weapons also want to see a reduction in the danger of death by accidents and disease. An analysis of such correlations produces common factors—in this case, ergs—based on the degree to which particular variables are associated with each factor for that group of subjects and, presuming a representative sample, for the population in general. But as Gordon Allport—the Harvard personality theorist and a severe critic of the factor approach—pointed out, that pattern of factor loadings is not necessarily characteristic of a specific individual: "The factors represent only *average* tendencies. . . . All one can say for certain is that a factor is an empirically derived component of the *average* personality, and . . . the average personality is a complete abstraction. . . . [S]eldom do the factors derived in this way resemble the dispositions and traits identified by clinical methods when the *individual* is studied intensively."[156] To address this shortcoming—and, according to some observers, in part to "appease Allport"—Cattell proposed P-technique, which collects data on the same set of variables that would be used in an R-technique study, but instead of a group of subjects it substitutes the same person on a number of occasions—ideally gathering data "from day to day for perhaps 100 days."[157] An entry in the resulting correlation matrix

denotes the extent to which a pair of variables systematically covaries over time
for this one individual, and Cattell expected a factoring of such correlations
similarly to "reveal . . . the unique trait structure in a single individual."[158]

Although it was theoretically possible to apply P-technique to the identification of general personality traits,[159] Cattell thought it particularly well
suited in practice for the study of ergs and sentiments. However, because
of the excessive demands on a subject, who would have to devote hours to
the procedure each day for more than three months, the approach did not
generate a great deal of research. In one of the few studies using P-technique,
the subject was tested in two sessions a day for forty days, a somewhat ab-
breviated version of the ideal (which Cattell improved in subsequent descrip-
tions of the research, claiming that it had been conducted over a "hundred
days").[160] A factor analysis of the three objective tests of twenty attitudes
that were administered each day produced the expected set of ergs along
with the self-sentiment, even though the reliability coefficient—that is, the
correlation indicating the consistency of measurement—for one of these
three tests was only .17.[161] But the more interesting result occurred from an
inspection of the change in the strength of particular ergs over the various
sessions. For example, the "protective" erg displayed a sharp increase after
the subject's father suffered a serious accident,[162] "as if the whole level of pity-
ing and cherishing behavior was stimulated to a new level," and changes in
other basic drives could be traced to specific events in the subject's life. In
view of this capacity by P-technique to monitor the rise and fall of specific
motivations, in 1951 Cattell predicted that it would soon furnish the basis for
a "quantitative psychoanalysis,"[163] accomplishing "with exactness what the
clinician is attempting to do by rough, common-sense methods such as free
association and observation of change of symptoms."[164] It was "just around the
corner," he wrote, eight years later, that it would be possible for a technician
in a psychological clinic with appropriate computer facilities to take the data
gathered over a series of treatment sessions and quickly "return . . . with an
objective and quantitative statement of the degrees, and areas, of ergic conflict, including the roots of motivation of the main disabling symptoms!" As
always, he was also certain that "the failure of the average clinician" to adopt
such methods could only be "due to an aversion to skilled calculation and the
hard work of acquiring new techniques." Annoyed that the method was still
not being used in clinical work in 1980, some thirty years after it had been
first proposed, Cattell suggested the need for "a diagnosis of the diagnosers,"
a reluctance to adopt his methods apparently itself being a phenomenon for
scientific examination as some sort of psychological abnormality.[165]

The other noteworthy result produced by Cattell's research on dynamic traits came from his interest not in the *direction* of motivation—its source in some specific erg—but in its strength. Curious, as always, whether the latter was truly a functional unity, he scoured the literature and compiled a comprehensive list of the many ways in which the strength of an attitude had been measured: verbal statements; physiological reactions, such as cardiovascular output and muscle tension; psychoanalytic measures of various defense mechanisms, such as projection and rationalization; measures of learning and memory phenomena; and many others—more than fifty altogether.[166] When all these devices were used to assess the strength of the same attitudes, a factor analysis of the results produced seven factors, which Cattell called "motivational components." Although the interpretation of these components was not as clear-cut as he suggested, the first three of these components did appear to be similar to psychoanalytic concepts, and Cattell named them the "Id Component in Interests" (though conscious, in this case), the "Realized Ego," and the "Ideal Self or Superego."[167] Spearman's methods had in fact led to Freud's conclusions.

The Personality of Groups

Finally, at the same time that Cattell was investigating the tripartite composition of the individual personality, he was also attempting to establish a new branch of psychology devoted to studying "the 'personality' of groups," a topic for which he suggested the name *syntality*.[168] This concept too was rooted in the thinking of William McDougall, who in a 1920 book had proposed the existence of a "group mind," which reflected the essential, shared qualities of the collection of interacting minds composing the group and facilitated the creation of art, music, and other cultural products.[169] Cattell conceived of syntality as having a parallel structure to personality, both constructs being composed of temperamental, ability, and dynamic traits, though in one case the individual's, in the other the group's. And just as he had believed that individual behavior could be predicted from a specification equation if a person's rating on each of the fundamental personality factors was known, he proposed that a similar procedure could be applied to groups once the basic syntality factors had been identified through his favorite method.[170]

As usual, the starting point presented a problem, especially since there was no set of syntality traits that could be compiled from the language, as had been done with individual characteristics. As a consequence Cattell set about the identification of these factors in two very different contexts at opposite ends of the size spectrum: small groups and entire nations. In the former case it was possible to collect data from subjects in the laboratory, and Cattell

studied six- and ten-person groups, as they engaged in numerous assigned
tasks, such as choosing a leader, deciding how to apportion free time among a
number of activities, decoding cryptograms, and providing collective answers
to questions of judgment.[171] Although a number of factors emerged from
the resulting analysis, the tasks that defined them tended to be quite varied,
requiring some imaginative feats of interpretation on Cattell's part to come
up with appropriate names—for example, "Friendly Urbanity, 'Savoir faire'
vs. Lack of Group Self Possession," "Shrewdness, Doggedness vs. Autism,
Dynamic Lability," and "Intelligent Role Interaction vs. Low Morale."[172] In
any event, the research on small groups did not last very long.

Of more enduring interest to Cattell was the search for the major psychological dimensions of national cultures, ratings on which would allow the
creation of a syntality profile for nations—or, as he sometimes called them,
"tribes"[173]—in much the same way as ratings on the sixteen personality factors produced a personality profile for individuals. In this case the studies
typically began with between fifty and eighty variables—cultural, medical,
economic, and ethnic—for each of almost seventy nations. Along with such
obvious characteristics as gross national product, per capita income, size of
population, birth and death rates, and the proportion of various racial and
religious groups, Cattell included the ratio of divorces to marriages, farm
area per agricultural worker, ratio of female to male university students,
rate of deaths from cirrhosis of the liver, number of national holidays, and
many other indexes of all sorts.[174] Once again, some creative interpretation
was necessary to derive underlying "unities" from the hundreds of resulting
correlations. In contrast to the factors identified in the studies of personality,
however, many of the factors that emerged from an analysis of these national
characteristics appeared to be as much evaluative as descriptive. The largest
factor in this analysis, "Enlightened Affluence vs. Narrow Poverty," for example, was defined by such variables as a high percentage of Protestantism, high
per capita income, the prohibition of prostitution, and legalized sterilization
of the "eugenically unfit"—which Cattell suggested were all a manifestation
of a greater than average "mental capacity" in a nation's population;[175] the
next largest was interpreted as "Vigorous Order vs. Unadapted Rigidity."[176]
These names and their accompanying explanations made both factors seem
like indexes for determining the relative desirability of a society.

This impression was strengthened by his subsequent, more detailed investigation of one dimension in particular: "Poor Cultural Integration and
Morale vs. Good Internal Morality," ratings that, he concluded, played an
important role in a nation's "success." In Cattell's analysis, unsuccessful countries such as Brazil, Burma, the Dominican Republic, Mexico, and Portugal

scored exceptionally low on this factor, an indication of their national "low morale, immorality and denial of responsibility." In another indication of the evaluative nature of these profiles, Cattell proposed the application of P-technique to identify dimensions of syntality, in which the analysis is done not on the variables for a large number of countries but for a single nation measured "every year for 100 years." In his view, the resulting factors could then be used "to give a more precise and a less subjective meaning to the term 'social progress.'"[177] These methods for making scientific judgments of a nation's success and progress would have more ominous implications in view of Cattell's social philosophy to be discussed in the next chapter.

* * *

With the exception of the distinction between fluid and crystallized intelligence, which has exercised considerable influence in the study of intellectual abilities, few of Cattell's specific, substantive conclusions have stood the test of time. Although he is universally acknowledged as the first person to apply factor analysis fruitfully to the study of personality and every contemporary discussion of trait theory begins with the obligatory recognition of his pioneering accomplishments, almost no current researchers agree with the results he obtained.[178] Indeed, the fact that numerous attempts have been unable to replicate Cattell's conclusions has served as a reminder of the subjectivity of his style of factor analysis and raised questions about the value of an approach, the results of which are so user dependent. In addition, Cattell's penchant for framing his thinking in often incomprehensible neologisms has tended to isolate his work from the rest of the field. Noting that such terms as *syntality, threptic,* and *dynamic lattice* remained "mysteries" to most other psychologists, even one of the scientists who had nominated Cattell for APF's Gold Medal Award a dozen years before he was finally named the recipient acknowledged that "perusal of journals and texts shows his to be a closed system with little impact on workers using other conceptual frameworks."[179]

Nevertheless, Cattell is deservingly regarded as one of the most productive research psychologists in the history of the discipline. A true generalist in a field known for the extent of its fragmentation, he was one of the very few social scientists to put forth a comprehensive theory of human behavior, relating abilities, attitudes, motivations (drives), and personality traits to each other, thus bringing together in a dynamic system the classic tripartite categorization of mental activity into cognition, affection, and conation.[180] Perhaps unique among psychologists, he also made contributions to theory, research, measurement, test development, and methodology; it is difficult to think of anyone else with this breadth of accomplishment. Indeed, aside from the use of P-technique, the overview of his work in this chapter has made little mention of Cattell's methodological insights. The "scree" test, for example, is a straightforward method for determining how many factors to extract in a factor analysis.[181] In some cases, such as the various techniques for factor rotation,[182] his contributions were of practical value at the time they were made but have since been rendered obsolete by the widespread availability of improved computer programs. His ingenious thinking about different approaches to analyzing data, summarized in the "data box," however, has still not been fully appreciated, perhaps because, though imaginative in concept, the methods have been applied infrequently in practice.[183]

In any event, the controversy over Cattell's recognition by the American Psychological Foundation was not predicated on concerns over his scientific achievements per se but rather stemmed from his promulgation of a system of "religious" beliefs whose moral principles were not based on what he called the traditional "superstitious" foundation of morality but were rooted in science and whose moral decisions were to be based on the data provided by the sort of scientific examination of individuals and groups to which Cattell had devoted his professional career. As he once explained, his decision early in life to move from the physical sciences to psychology was informed not only by a desire to understand "the laws governing personality" but also by a belief that "social science . . . could solve sociopolitical problems in better ways than by current rules of thumb"—through the practical application of scientifically based moral precepts.[184]

This linkage between Cattell's scientific work and his "religious" system endured throughout his career. To the latter realm Cattell brought the same absolute certainty of his own rightness that characterized his conclusions in the former and the same utter contempt for opposing viewpoints as the result of scientific ignorance or personal incompetence. However, his study of personality helped to modernize the field. In contrast, as a detailed consideration of his proposed religion will indicate, Cattell's scientifically based moral system represented a return to a tribalist thinking intolerable in the modern world.

IN THE NAME OF EVOLUTION
THE BEGINNING OF
CATTELL'S MORAL SYSTEM

A classically educated scientist for whom there was no gap between the "two cultures," Cattell was always intellectually curious and would never disparage knowledge for its own sake, but his scientific efforts were equally motivated by more practical, humanitarian concerns. Having observed in his youth both the heartrending sacrifices of the Great War and the wretchedness of life in the London slums, he was determined that his own professional accomplishments leave not only science but also society better than he found it.[1] Indeed, it was the possibility of achieving the latter goal as well as the former that had informed Cattell's decision as a graduate student to abandon a promising career in chemistry in favor of an uncertain future in a field still struggling for respect at the time. Psychology, however, offered him the appeal of a discipline whose most prominent scientists on both sides of the Atlantic consciously sought to place the results of their research in service to the principles of eugenics.[2]

Despite the tragedies of the previous decade, many scientists in the 1920s found reason to be optimistic about the future. At the dawn of the twentieth century, Gregor Mendel's laws of heredity had been rediscovered after lying in obscurity for almost four decades, and the study of genetics became an exciting new field, carrying with it the hope that the manipulation of nature would help to uplift the human condition, much as social scientists sought to do through the manipulation of nurture forty years later in Lyndon Johnson's War on Poverty. But as bioethicist and medical historian Sherwin Nuland observed, "Major steps in scientific progress are sometimes followed closely by outbursts of foolishness."[3] This was certainly the case with the beginning of genetics. Eugenics—that deformed child of the Enlightenment—promised to link scientific and social progress through oversight of the reproductive process, not only improving the quality of human beings but in the long run enabling rational control over the very path of evolution. As Ellsworth Huntington, a well-known geographer and professor of economics at Yale, explained in *Tomorrow's Children,* his aptly named book on the goals of eugenics, the possibility of evolutionary control was the latest of the "five most momentous human discoveries," the first four being tools, speech, fire, and writing. But the fifth, in his view, promised to be "the greatest of all," not just transforming the environment, as the other four had done, but allowing society "consciously and purposefully to select the types of human beings that will survive." "Today," Huntington declared, "we are beginning to thrill with the feeling that we stand on the brink of an evolutionary epoch whose limits no man can possibly foretell."[4] The knowledge was available to redeem humanity's hope of paradise, the eugenicists believed, if only it were put into practice.

This was a truly heady prospect—the possibility that the newer sciences of genetics, psychology, and sociology could solve human quality problems just as physics and engineering had solved architectural ones, replacing religion, emotion, and partisan politics with reason as the basis for social policy—and, especially at the outset, eugenics had an obvious appeal for intellectuals and the educated classes; indeed, most major universities in the United States offered a course on the topic. In addition, the emphasis on collective social benefit and the improvement of future generations was an attraction for progressives and liberal social reformers, such as Emma Goldman, George Bernard Shaw, Margaret Sanger, and Scott Nearing, who were all early supporters of eugenics. But, many eugenicists also warned, there was an ominous alternative to this starry-eyed vision of the future. Unless the present haphazard pattern of reproduction was changed in accord with the teachings of science, it would not be the meek who would inherit the earth; it would be all the dullards and mental defectives who were outbreeding their superiors. Indeed, there was widespread concern among eugenically oriented scientists that medical and social advances were themselves a part of the problem, reducing the infant and child death rate, nullifying the natural elimination of the unfit, and allowing the least capable to reproduce their kind, thus further saddling the society with what one activist called ever more "weaklings, paupers, hoboes and imbeciles."[5] It was this alarmist view that eventually came to dominate the movement, leading many of the progressives to become disenchanted.

Coming of intellectual age at the height of eugenics' popularity, Cattell recognized the concept as the ideal opportunity to combine his twin passions for scientific discovery and human elevation. He quickly became an adherent to the cause, sharing the movement's hopes for improvement and, more significant, its fears of inevitable degeneration that would take place without scientific control of reproduction in the society. As he viewed the generous British health care system in the 1930s, for example, Cattell was concerned that its guaranteed care for expectant mothers and young children would only "hasten national deterioration" unless provided in accord with the dictates of a Ministry of Eugenics, which should itself be only a temporary agency exercising a "preventive function," and eventually "develop[ing] into a more positively enterprising Ministry of Evolution."[6] Even more ambitious, he also envisioned the long-range possibilities implied by his proposal for the latter office and throughout his career sought to develop and promote a scientifically based religious system, the principles of which he believed should inform human direction of the evolutionary process.

National versus Universal Ethics

In addition to his own natural enthusiasm for eugenics, all three of Cattell's mentors and scientific role models were ardent advocates for the movement. Charles Spearman, Cyril Burt, and William McDougall—indisputably the most distinguished members of his newly chosen profession and important influences on his thinking—all joined the Eugenics Education Society shortly after its formation in England in 1907, not only personally committed to its goals but certain that their discipline was uniquely suited to the important task of determining who possessed the qualities that should be passed on to future generations. Spearman held the University of London's chair in eugenics endowed by Sir Francis Galton, the revered founder of the movement, and Burt succeeded Spearman in the position. Having recently developed what quickly became their field's most famous instrument, both these psychologists regarded the intelligence test as the ultimate measure of human worth and, ecstatic over the awesome implications of this discovery, were eager to promote its eugenical application. Spearman, under whom Cattell had earned his doctorate, maintained that

an accurate measurement of every one's intelligence would seem to herald the feasibility of selecting better endowed persons for admission into citizenship—and even for the right of having offspring. And whilst in this manner a suitable selection secures a continual rise in the intellectual status of the people taken in mass, the same power of measuring intelligence should also make possible a proper treatment of each individual; to each can be given an appropriate education, and thereafter a fitting place in the state—just that which he or she demonstrably deserves. Class hatred, nourished upon preferences that are believed to be unmerited, would seem at last within reach of eradication; perfect justice is about to combine with maximum efficiency.[7]

Eugenic progress would thus be secured not only by judicious selection of those allowed to procreate but also by an educational system that ensured a proper match between an individual's instruction and the position for which he or she was destined, thus not wasting resources either by burdening the dullards with any more knowledge than was necessary for their assigned role or by encumbering the future elites with concerns below their prescribed station in the society.

Spearman's vision necessarily assumed a view of intellectual abilities as not only genetically determined but also immutable. If individuals could improve their abilities through the process of education or acquire new ones, then the notion of a "fitting place" for each person would be rendered meaningless. A belief in a biological determinism far more rigid than mere genetic influence was thus a necessary postulate for establishment of the eugenic state, and Cyril Burt, to whom Cattell turned for guidance after Spearman departed for the United States, did not hesitate to assure the public that both premise and conclusion, as well as the logical connection between them, were incontestable.

The first British educational psychologist ever and later the first member of his profession to be knighted, Burt maintained throughout his lengthy career—from his first publication in 1909 until his last in 1972—that intelligence was "innate general cognitive ability," a view he defended in the face of criticism by producing stronger and stronger evidence for its high heritability, data that were later judged worthless and probably fraudulent.[8] Actually, the bitter debate over whether he was a "fraud or framed," as the title of one book about his work phrased it,[9] was somewhat paradoxical since, according to Burt, intelligence was *by definition* entirely genetic. But having concluded from the outset that intelligence was completely "inborn and not acquired,"[10] he went on, like Spearman, to offer a vision of education as a mechanism for directing individuals toward their genetically appropriate place. It was "the duty of the state, through its school service," Burt wrote, "first to find out to what order of intelligence each child belongs, then to give him the education most appropriate to his powers, and finally . . . to place him in the particular type of occupation for which nature has marked him out." In this plan only one-tenth of 1 percent of the population would receive a university education, which would then lead to a career in the professions or to a "higher adminis- trative" position.[11] Although the British educational system never determined occupational futures quite as rigidly as Burt had hoped, its highly selective nature, especially the separation at an early age of the few (genetically) capable students from the less fit masses, was informed largely by his ideas. A series of official reports by government committees in the 1920s and '30s—for which he served as a technical consultant, in at least one case serving on the drafting subcommittee, where he "rendered invaluable help in the preparation of the report"—reaffirmed his contentions that intelligence was "innate" and that, as a consequence, superior children, destined for the university, had to be identified before the age of twelve and placed not just in separate classes but in separate schools.[12] Indeed, it was only in response to the postwar movement for a more egalitarian educational policy that Burt produced his strongest— and most suspect—data in support of genetic influence on intelligence, which were offered as the result of scientific exploration but, in fact, intended as a political tactic.[13]

Although Cattell was less concerned than Spearman and Burt about re- organizing the educational system along eugenic lines, he shared with his mentors the belief in the power of heredity as an article of faith necessary for justification of the eugenic agenda, more than as a scientifically demonstrable result. In 1938, discussing the deleterious social effects that would be caused by the disproportionate reproduction of the less intelligent, Cattell declared it an accepted fact that "mental capacity is largely inborn," a conclusion that at best might be considered premature at the time and at worst was scientifically meaningless.[14] At about the same time, he published a study, the results of which did indeed provide support for a genetic influence on intelligence so strong that the data can hardly be regarded as credible. After "corrections" of various kinds, for example, Cattell calculated a correlation of .94 between the intelligence test scores of the two oldest children in a sample of 80 families and a correlation of .93 between the test scores of a father and his oldest child in 101 families;[15] no other study of these kinship correlations has obtained such huge values, which exceed the reliability coefficients for many intel- ligence tests—that is, the correlation between scores for the same person on the same test twice. As Yale professor of psychology Seymour Sarason, who had been a graduate student at Clark during Cattell's brief stint there in the late 1930s, recalled half a century later, "it was self-evident" to the Englishman "that heredity explained much of human behavior," and Sarason and the other students entertained themselves with the fantasy that Cattell and John B. Watson, the founder of behaviorism, "found themselves alone on a desert island," wondering "how soon it would be before they agreed not to talk with each other as a way of avoiding mutual destruction."[16]

Whereas Cattell's two factor analytic mentors were both concerned with the eugenic implications of the differences between individuals, it was William McDougall who exerted the greatest influence on his ideas about the differences between racial groups. Indeed, the scientifically based religious system eventually developed by Cattell was in many ways a more highly elaborated version of the eugenic conclusions about groups previously advanced by his prominent senior countryman. Born in 1871, McDougall had been a precocious student, entering the University of Manchester at what he later called "the absurdly early age of fifteen" to concentrate in biology and geology. Ill-content with his four years at this provincial institution and yearning to attend a school where the "academic and social prestige were immense," he set his sights on Cambridge, "the home of first-rate minds"; here was where "great men had dwelt and worked," and McDougall was determined that he "must do the same." Winning a competitive scholarship to the university, he continued his interest in science, specializing in physiology and anatomy, after which he obtained a medical degree, not with the intention to practice but in preparation for a "life devoted to the study of the nervous system." After discovering William James's *Principles of Psychology*, however, McDougall decided that neurological research was not the only route to revealing "the secrets of human nature," which, he now decided, could also be approached "by way of psychology, philosophy, and the various human sciences."[17] The year after completing his medical studies McDougall joined an anthropological expedition to New Guinea and Borneo, an experience that convinced him of the significance of biology as a major determinant of behavior.[18] When he finally changed his professional identification to psychology, this exceptionally broad scientific background proved particularly advantageous. A contributor to many different areas of the discipline, McDougall became a cofounder of the British Psychological Society and was arguably the most important psychologist in his country—and perhaps in the world—during the first two decades of the twentieth century, before coming to the United States in 1920 to accept Harvard's "very flattering" offer of the William James Chair in psychology.

Unfortunately, however, he was not well received there, his theories, according to one historian, "regarded by most American psychologists as remnants of exploded but still dangerous superstitions" and his combative personal style alienating to his new colleagues.[19] Seven years later he left to become chair of the department at Duke, where, another historian noted, the "antipathy . . . continued unabated" until his death in 1938.[20]

Understandably given his training, McDougall began his career in psychology by making significant contributions to psychophysics and brain physiology, including an important textbook on the subject, which, according to one of his students, exercised great influence on many young scientists "otherwise suspicious of psychology."[21] However, he quickly expanded his interests, publishing *An Introduction to Social Psychology*, an enormously influential work that proposed an ambitious and systematic approach to explaining human behavior as the result of the interaction of one or more specific inborn dispositions or instincts with the social environment.[22] Although one contemporary scholar has described the work as widely considered "the first textbook in social psychology," in fact, despite the adjective in the title, the book was concerned almost exclusively with individual behavior. It was McDougall's "sequel," *The Group Mind*, that actually focused on social behavior, positing the existence of a collective mental life that resulted in a national character or temperament, itself formed to a large extent though not exclusively from racial composition.[23] For this collective mind to emerge, it was thus necessary for nations to attain a certain level of racial homogeneity.

In subsequent books McDougall focused on the practical application of his scientific ideas to the most important social policy issues of the 1920s, the titles of these works indicating the wide range of areas whose deliberations he thought should be informed by the latest conclusions of science: *Ethics and Some Modern World Problems*, which he introduced as the "ethical supplement" to *The Group Mind; Is America Safe for Democracy?* which, in an "impartial and scientific . . . manner," brought the "principles of physical heredity" to "bear . . . upon the great problems of national welfare and national decay"; *The Indestructible Union: Rudiments of Political Science for the American Citizen*, which offered scientifically based measures to avert such decay; and *World Chaos: The Responsibility of Science*, which warned of the danger to the West posed by nonwhites and emphasized the importance of guidance from the social sciences in responding to this threat.[24] Actually, the concern at the core of each of these books turned out to be race—or more precisely "race mixture." Given the simplistic beliefs that dominated the new field of genetics at the time, many scientists were concerned at the possibility that human hybridization could have deleterious effects, but for McDougall it was nothing short of an obsession, a prism through which to interpret the past and predict the future.

All personality traits, according to McDougall, were racial in origin and had been "formed and fixed during long ages of the pre-historic period." As a result of this process, he explained, Nordics, the peoples emanating from northwestern Europe, were, much more than other races, instinctively curious and self-assertive—the latter trait the root from which "spring all manifestations of will-power, all volition, resolution, hard choice, initiative, enterprise, determination." This combination of characteristics accounted for their taciturn, individualistic nature and their prominence as scientists and explorers; Nordics were strong, silent types who made great discoveries and dominated less assertive races throughout the world. It was no accident, he observed in 1920, that "Britain . . . administers the affairs of one-fifth of the people of the world" and "a mere handful of British men" long ruled over the hundreds of millions in India, a group "relatively defective in character and will-power." In contrast to the Nordics, McDougall found that the Mediterranean peoples from southern Europe were characterized chiefly by the "herd instinct," a gregarious impulse that formed the basis of their more sociable nature, which found "satisfaction in merely being together *en masse*" and resulted in the tendency to congregate in cities as their "natural habitat"; unlike the reserved and contemplative northerners, the Mediterraneans were "vivacious, quick, impetuous, impulsive." Although he clearly considered Nordics the elite among whites, McDougall judged blacks vastly inferior to all the many white subgroups but, if "well handled, with firmness, but with kindness and consideration," capable of becoming "ideal followers." In keeping with this view, he found that "the main key to the history of the Negro race" was its instinctive submissiveness, a trait of docility exactly the opposite of Nordic self-assertion, which happily allowed blacks not only to tolerate without bitterness the subordinate position to which they had been assigned in the United States but in fact to enjoy being disciplined by their acknowledged superiors. As a "typical and significant incident" illustrating this characteristic, he described the "true story" of a "Negro maid," whose mistress, after treating her "with great forbearance for a time, in spite of shortcomings," finally turned on the bungling servant and "scolded her vigorously. The maid showed no resentment, but rather showed signs of a new satisfaction, and exclaimed: 'Lor', Missus, you do make me feel so good.'"[25]

Given the racial origin of these traits, McDougall maintained that racial mixture posed an extremely serious threat to human progress, causing "degeneration" in "fine races" that "mix[ed] their blood too freely with that of other stocks." The excellence of the former, he continued, could be "preserved only by continued and rigid selection," and when they were mixed with "less fine" races, the "blended progeny" not only reverted to a "lower ancestral type" but frequently displayed "disharmonies of constitution," including "an abnormal liability to moral conflict and disorder" as well as "a lack of fertility."[26] As an instructive example of the deleterious consequences of such interbreeding, McDougall cited the "astonishing" achievements of Muslim civilization, whose learning, art, and science had once been "predominant on the earth," covering "a broad belt of the old world, from eastern Asia to Spain, with splendid mosques and libraries and universities" at a time when much of Europe beyond Muslim influence was still in chaos. But, he observed, this rich culture prepared the way for its own deterioration, welcoming as it did "all comers on equal terms" and in the process "destroying race-prejudices and national sentiments"—an inclusionary ethos that led the "Arab founders [to] freely mix . . . their blood with that of many other races, and especially with that of the Negro race . . . which never yet has shown itself capable" of rising "above a barbaric level." As a result, he pointed out, Muslim civilization's "rapid success was followed by a no less rapid decline."[27]

In yet another example of the ill effects of racial mixture, McDougall considered the contrast between the peoples of northern and southern Europe. When the "Christian Englishman" spread British influence throughout the world, in McDougall's account, "typical of the more northern peoples," he "rightly . . . converted [the heathen] to his Christian creed, but, unlike the Moslem . . . never accepted his converts as his equals, or regarded them as members of one great community equal before God, and he consistently disdained to mix his blood with theirs in marriage." However, because the peoples of the South were "more completely Christianized," they were less vigilant in protecting their racial purity, and "consequently," McDougall observed, "the course of their history has run more nearly after the pattern of the Moslem world."[28]

The similar fate of southern Europe and the Muslim world constituted an object lesson, in McDougall's opinion, one that he insisted the United States could ill afford to ignore in its own deliberations on domestic policy. The most pressing issue of the time was the alarming increase of "new" immigrants: in the last quarter of the nineteenth century the major origin of newcomers to the United States had shifted from the northern European countries—predominantly the British Isles, Scandinavia, and Germany—to the eastern and southern parts of the continent. In scenes right out of *Godfather II*, steamers were docking at American ports almost daily, their steerages crowded with Italians, Slavs, Poles, Russians, Hungarians, Jews, and other exotic nationalities, bringing with them strange customs and speaking languages previously little heard in the New World. At the height of this influx, Israel Zangwill, an English Jew, wrote a play about immigrants in the United States whose title, *The Melting Pot*, captured the national imagination with its promise that in the crucible of freedom and democracy all these newcomers, no matter their background, could be forged into citizens indistinguishable from those who had arrived generations earlier.[29] In McDougall's view, the notion of the melting pot was more myth than metaphor, and a horrifying one at that; the "complete Americanization" of people who had lived "for many generations in the shade of the date palm and the banana tree" he thought plainly impossible. The new immigrants were not going to be transformed into Americans; instead, they were transforming America—so that it was already beginning to resemble their crowded home countries, "with their laborious peasants, their wan-faced patient industrial masses, their necessity for thrift, their conflict of classes."[30]

If the flood of new immigrants in his adopted country was not halted, McDougall predicted disaster for a number of reasons—social as well as biological—each of which later became a more detailed theme in Cattell's ideology. First and most significant was the danger of biological decline posed by the likelihood of widespread intermarriage between the descendants of "older American stock" and the recent arrivals—from "stocks" that, according to McDougall, had "remained through all the centuries of European civilization at or near the bottom of the social scale." It was "quite possible," he worried, that such matings would "produce a race of submen." In addition, the newcomers threatened to strike "discordant notes in the national harmony," their alien practices detracting from the cultural homogeneity at the root of the national character, itself largely a derivative of racially based traits.[31] To a large degree this particular concern on McDougall's part stemmed from the predominance of Catholics among the latest immigrants, a religious preference that again he attributed to their racial composition; it was no "mere coincidence," he believed, that the "curious, inquiring, unsociable, reflective, introverted Nordic[s]," the original European settlers, would be averse to Catholicism, a religion "of authority, of convention, of formal ritual," appealing primarily to the more subservient Mediterranean and Alpine races.[32] But the presence of the latter in such large numbers in the United States greatly increased the probability of serious conflict resulting from what McDougall called the "pretensions of the Roman Church" to the restoration of political power. Indeed, he noted, it was their members' "hostil[ity] to the organized power of the Roman Church" more than the assertion of white supremacy that was chiefly responsible for the recent resurgence of the Ku Klux Klan, a group he described as composed of "solid, seriously minded, pious, and patriotic Americans."[33] Finally and most disturbing of all to McDougall was his contention that the massive flow of immigrants tended not merely to increase the population but rather to supplant the traditional groups. He believed that the U.S. population would have enjoyed the exact same increase absent the "millions of newcomers of alien stock," room for whose presence was made possible only "by restriction of the reproduction" of the older Americans.[34] "Breed[ing] freely and naturally," the former he saw as a threat "to destroy the old stock and to put in its place a new one of different ancestry."[35]

Although the immigrants were of particular concern to McDougall because of their increasing numbers, the more grave evolutionary threat in his view actually came from the "Negroes." The former may not have been quite the equal of the superior Nordics who had founded the colonies, but only the latter, according to McDougall, were completely "incapable of absorption into the nation," constituting "a foreign body . . . which is a perpetual disturber and menace to the national life."[36] Anthropology had revealed, he wrote, that the Negro, "in the most intimate structure and composition of his tissues, of his blood and bone and brain . . . was distinct and different." In view of such a vast biological gap, the presence of blacks in the United States carried with it the risk that "the most promising civilization that the world has known" would "be deteriorated by a large admixture of Negro blood," leading to "the rapid decline of the American Nation to corruption and despotism, chaos and barbarism." Faced with this "danger . . . to the very life of the nation," he saw only one sensible solution: "thoroughgoing segregation." This scientifically prescribed course of action was not to be confused with what McDougall called the "policy of the ghetto," in which blacks were confined to their own local communities, geographically and socially separate from the whites in each town or city. Instead, he had in mind an "ample territory" to which all blacks in the United States would be transported, either in the South or perhaps in Africa or New Guinea.[37] If systematic policies were not instituted both to stop the influx of undesirable immigrants and to remove blacks from the country, McDougall foresaw a bleak future for the descendants of the original pioneers. After a century of "mingled existence," he thought that the population would be so highly blended that the "remnant of the peoples that have built up our civilization would have been absorbed . . . like a few drops of milk in a basin of coffee, leaving . . . hardly any trace of their racial qualities."[38]

Serious as these issues were for the future of the nation, however, in McDougall's analysis they were merely manifestations, albeit the most significant ones, of a more profound underlying societal need: a system of "scientific ethics" that could provide the rational basis for social policy. In language almost

identical to that later offered by Cattell in describing his own such system, Mc-
Dougall explained that ethical conduct was not "fixed . . . by some unnatural
or supernatural principle" but rather discovered from scientific investigation
of "how we may best co-operate in the cosmic process," helping to guide it to
"yet higher levels" of evolution. It was the misguided assumption that proper
behavior toward others could be derived from abstract principles, religious or
otherwise, that had resulted in what he called "Universal Ethics"—the "false
ideal" of human brotherhood espoused by almost all religious teachers and
moral philosophers, which had led to the similarly flawed belief in the equal
valuation of all human life. Indeed, he noted, although it was common to
pay lip service to such sentiments, most people knew enough to ignore them
when they would lead to "disaster and degradation." According to both "the
principles of universal ethics" and "federal law, determined by these principles," for example, blacks were entitled to "social and political equality," but,
McDougall pointed out approvingly, "the good sense of the southern white
man forbids him to obey these precepts."[39]

McDougall's scientifically based system of "National Ethics" sought to
replace this universalist approach with the realization that the proliferation of
Western white people was of paramount importance to evolutionary progress
and that, as a consequence, moral judgments were properly derived from the
degree to which an action contributed to this goal. Thus, the moral principles
informing relations between members of Western races were not to be extended to individuals from other groups. Having already achieved numerous
advances in science and medicine even when McDougall was formulating his
ideas almost a century ago, for example, the industrialized nations of the West
could contribute substantially at the time to the alleviation of suffering in less
developed areas by improving public health services, treating disease, and
reducing famine through assistance to indigenous agriculture.[40] Although
the resulting reduced death rate would be considered a humanitarian outcome by universalist ethics, a scientifically derived morality opposed all such
measures, which would only make the West complicit in its own decline.
Already, McDougall observed, "the hordes of backward peoples (aided and
abetted by . . . Western science and by the Western arts of medicine) continue to multiply ever more rapidly," while the groups that had created "our
culture and our civilization are dwindling away."[41] The result, he feared—and
it would not be long in coming if assistance to underdeveloped countries,
especially in Africa, continued "uncorrected"—would be a "swamping" of
whites throughout the world by "the swarming multitudes of other races" less
capable of sustaining civilization, the reproduction of these peoples "lowest
in the scale of culture" eventually leading to the "practical extinction" of the

white race everywhere except Europe, where its descendants would be "but a dwindling remnant."[42] Instead of this unappealing future, nationalist ethics, which would withhold Western scientific advances from other groups, could produce the outcome more consistent with the objective McDougall pronounced necessary for evolutionary progress: ensuring "that the more highly civilized races should increase faster than the more backward, so as to enable the former to prevail not merely by force, but by members."[43]

In addition to its harmfully egalitarian treatment of backward races, what McDougall called the "unchecked extension of the universal ethics" was also wreaking havoc, in his view, within the ranks of the advanced races, creating the unfortunate belief in parenthood as "the right of every man without respect to his personal qualifications." Just as it was dangerous to biological progress for a superior race to provide assistance to an inferior one, it was similarly problematic for a society to "prevent the natural consequences of unrestricted reproduction in its lower strata" through measures such as charity or free medical care that tended to reduce the death rate, especially among infants. In either case the end result of such good intentions, especially given the inclination of the "upper strata" to restrict severely their own reproduction, was an increase in the "less assimilable part of the population." The only sensible policy, according to McDougall—that is, the only one consistent with a scientifically derived national ethics—was the "social control of reproduction," if necessary through legislation that would impose restrictions on the less capable.[44]

Indeed, to cope with the presence of so many of the latter, national ethics required a major reorganization of democratic political systems, replacing the "indiscriminate" approach of "one adult, one vote" with the more scientifically sound principle of "one qualified citizen, one vote"; it was essential to realize, McDougall declared, that the franchise "must be denied to those who are obviously unfit to exercise it." Although he believed that such a restriction should apply to "all democracies," it was necessary "most of all" in the United States, "made up as it is of so many heterogeneous elements." To implement the principle, McDougall recommended that the population be divided into three classes: A, the class of full citizens; B, the class of candidates for admission to A; and C, the class of citizens deprived of the franchise due to mental defectiveness or lack of education. In the United States he estimated that class C would include between a quarter and a third of the adult population, whereas in countries such as Mexico or India the same plan would place some 80 or 90 percent in the disenfranchised category. Children of the members of class A would be born into class B and, absent any indication that they were unfit, would graduate automatically into A upon reaching adulthood; children of parents either one of whom was a member of class C would begin in that class but, after passing a qualifying test, could be promoted to B, where they would have to spend twenty years in "probationary status, with due discharge of its recognized obligations," before being admissible to class A. To discourage the squandering of superior blood in an ill-advised mixture, a citizen in class A who married a member of C would "ipso facto lose his status" and be demoted to the disenfranchised class of the spouse. This scheme of classification, wrote McDougall, would ensure that political power remained "in the hands of a reasonably select body of citizens" at the same time that it also protected the "class of full citizens . . . against the lowering of its average quality by the im-mixture of blood of inferior quality." Besides, he noted, the plan was in many ways merely the "explicit recognition and legal regulation" of the condition to which "the bulk of the coloured people of the United States" were already relegated, though at present "in an unjust and disorderly fashion."[45]

Little more than a decade after making his case for an ethical system predi-cated on science, McDougall died. In an obituary a former student described his mentor as "acutely conscious of the important role that psychology ought to play in human affairs, and at the same time regretfully aware that it was at present unfitted to play this role." Cattell certainly shared these sentiments. Indeed, shortly before McDougall's death he had edited a collection of essays—including one by McDougall himself—titled *Human Affairs* and dedicated to the notion that "every problem of social life" could be solved by scientists. The volume was intended to pave the way for an identically named journal, designed by Cattell to foster "a body of opinion among the general public in favour of referring political, social, and cultural problems to the sciences."[46] Although the journal never materialized, he remained determined not only to apply his discipline to the solution of the society's practical problems but, more ambitious, to place morality and social policy on firm scientific ground along lines almost identical to those advocated by McDougall.

Science and Race: Making Evolutionary Progress

This desire on Cattell's part to construct a scientific rationale for morality actually began to take shape when he was still a precocious teenager study-ing chemistry. As an eighteen-year-old undergraduate he crafted the outline of a long, rambling work on the use of science to facilitate social progress that took the better part of a decade to complete.[47] Eventually published in 1933—four years after Cattell had received his doctorate and already au-thored a number of articles in professional journals—*Psychology and Social*

Progress, modestly subtitled *Mankind and Destiny from the Standpoint of a Scientist,* was the first statement of a philosophy, the essential principles of which would not change over the next six decades, even as he fine-tuned some of the details. Although the eugenics movement's influence had now declined from its peak in the previous decade, Cattell still envisioned a future society organized according to the conclusions of a handful of "pioneers," who alone understood how to apply "the detached and empirical manner of science" to the study of human behavior. "We stand . . . at the beginning of a second enlightenment," he wrote, in which the use of such methods and *only* their use held out the promise "of controlling human happiness."[48]

The Goal of Life

The first and most important step down this scientific path leading to a happier world was the realization, according to Cattell, that the fundamental goal of human existence—indeed, the goal of all living things—was "to strive upwards": to "evolve 'higher' organisms, more and more complex forms of life." From this biological fact, it then followed that the "primary ideal of social life," the objective that should inform social organization and policy, "can only be that of forward Evolution." Indeed, he declared, "conscious adoption" of this objective as the basis of morality constituted "the only way to ensure human progress and to produce a system of moral laws compatible with the real nature of ourselves and the universe." The morality of any action was thus to be determined empirically, according to the extent to which it helped or hindered such evolutionary advancement. Of course, this premise of strictly linear development—which, according to Cattell, had been "discovered by an examination of nature"—was a misunderstanding of the evolutionary dynamic. In what has become a trite observation among contemporary biologists, the appropriate metaphor for evolution is not a "ladder," with its implications of upward movement, but a "copiously branching bush," in which different forms of life share common ancestors. "The history of life," observed the famous paleontologist Stephen Jay Gould, for example, "is a story of massive removal followed by differentiation within a few surviving stocks, not the conventional tale of steadily increasing excellence, complexity, and diversity."[49]

Cattell's belief that evolution was strictly hierarchical, however, was characteristic of the underlying assumption that had informed both science and philosophy for the previous two millennia. The concept of the "Great Chain of Being," rooted in the Aristotelian notion that inequality was the foundation of natural order, had been the prevailing view throughout the pre-Darwinian period and even afterward for some scientists. The premise of the chain was

the existence of a hierarchy that allocated to every form of life its appropriate position from lowest to highest—from the simplest living organisms to
human beings and even beyond them through various heavenly beings to
God, the Creator. Though originally intended as a between-species construct,
eventually this ordering was applied within the ranks of humankind, as European travelers and explorers came into increasing contact with the peoples
of Africa and Asia, and in the latter half of the nineteenth century it became
the accepted role of scientists to determine the relative ranking of different
racial groups from the lowest to the highest—from the "savage" or "barbar-
ian" groups, which were invariably nonwhite, to the superior "civilized" races,
who were not only white but, more specifically, Anglo-Saxon. This was a task
that could be carried out satisfactorily regardless of whether the ordering
of races had been ordained by the Creator or had evolved thorough natural
selection over tens of thousands of generations.

   After Darwin's brilliant insights revolutionized the study of biology, the existence of a racial hierarchy took on more significant theoretical consequences in
particular for those scientists drawn to "social Darwinism," the mixture of science and politics that sought to apply Darwinian principles to human societies.
This reinterpretation of evolution was most forcefully promoted by the English
philosopher and early sociologist Herbert Spencer; it was Spencer, rather than
Darwin, who first coined the phrase "survival of the fittest,"[50] which he regarded
as not only descriptive but also normative, that is, concisely characterizing what
was the basis of the evolutionary process and what *should* be the basis of social
policy.[51] In Darwin's subtle treatment, evolution occurred through "natural
selection," a long, gradual process in which organisms changed when chance
variations advantageous to the "struggle for survival" turned out to produce
differential reproductive success. Although Darwin had clearly intended this
expression in a metaphorical sense—explaining in *Origin of Species,* for example, that "a plant on the edge of a desert is said to struggle for life against
the drought, though more properly it should be said to be dependent on the
moisture"—Spencer and other social Darwinists literalized the phrase, arguing that evolutionary progress occurred through competition both within and
between groups; the triumph of advanced individuals and races over their
inferiors was thus the route to human biological improvement. As the prominent British scientist and ardent social Darwinist Karl Pearson observed, there
was "one way, and one way only, in which a high state of civilization has been
produced, namely the struggle of race with race and the survival of the physically and mentally fitter race."[52]

   The policies derived from social Darwinism could be described charitably
as "benign neglect"; the adjective might have been disputable, but there was

no doubt about the noun. Because traditional notions of individual humanitarian assistance to the less fortunate would only facilitate their procreation, thus perpetuating their biological shortcomings, nature was to be left to take its course undeterred by eleemosynary intervention, whether through governmental program or private philanthropy. Even modern advances in public health were suspect, because they contributed to the artificial preservation of weaklings. Such harsh policies might have seemed callous, but Spencer pronounced them "full of beneficence—the same beneficence which brings to early graves the children of diseased parents, and singles out the intemperate and debilitated as the victims of an epidemic."[53]

Since true progress could be forged only in the crucible of interracial competition, social Darwinists in the United States opposed slavery, not out of the belief that blacks too were endowed with inalienable rights but because the South's peculiar institution had artificially shielded them from the struggle, allowing blacks to flourish in what one observer called a "hothouse existence."[54] From this point of view, the purpose of attaining freedom for blacks was to create the conditions for their elimination in competition with their betters, a contest in which they were not to enjoy the assistance of such benefits as education or exercise of the franchise; to share these institutions developed by Anglo-Saxons with another race represented an artificial intrusion into the latter's evolutionary development. Some social Darwinists maintained that whites had only to ensure that blacks remained separate and unequal, and then wait for nature to take its course, a viewpoint that received temporary support when an exhaustive 1896 study by a leading economist concluded—on the basis of more than fifty years of demographic and medical data on racial differences in various illnesses and mortality rates—that "the black race is not holding its own," and it was just a matter of time.[55] But when the census four years later made it clear that this prediction was in error, there was less tolerance for such a passive attitude. Noting that the black "race is not doomed . . . in the immediate future," one scientist suggested "helping along the process of extinction," although he offered nothing specific about the form such assistance might take.[56] However, it was apparent that in some cases the social Darwinist reliance on unrestrained competition alone could not be entrusted to produce the correct outcome, and instead of being an unwarranted interference in the evolutionary process, eugenic intervention was not only justified but imperative to ensure that the rightful winners emerged from the struggle.

Cattell's moral philosophy was based solidly in this tradition of obsession with evolutionary improvement at both the individual and the racial level, but what he added to the underlying framework was a previously unprecedented degree of detail about the social organization necessary to implement its principles, the role that scientists would play in making interracial comparisons and deciding on the relative fitness of specific races, and, most important, the measures that would then be instituted to eliminate those races scientifically determined to lack the characteristics essential to biological progress. In short, he provided the intellectual justification for a highly specific plan that, in the name of evolution, would slate some races for continuation and speed others along the path to extinction.

The Science of Separation

To put this program into action, naturally races had to be rigidly separated from each other, not just the so-called major races usually associated with skin color but also much smaller, strictly endogamous populations—in the British Isles alone, Cattell identified four different racial groups.[57] It was essential, he explained, that contending groups be "relatively homogeneous" and that "the members of one . . . group be of a different inborn racial type from the other"; only under these conditions could intergroup competition lead to the selective action that alone could "result . . . in the greater prevalence of a fitter type." And it was only in these racially homogeneous groups, Cattell emphasized, drawing on McDougall's distinction between nationalist and universalist ethics, that "altruistic modes of behavior," which otherwise might seem "biologically perverse," were sound, contributing, as they did, to the security and prosperity of the group; the same ethical code, carried over to "non-homogeneous groups" composed of more than a single race, however, produced an "abominable state of affairs."[58]

To illustrate the dangers of altruistic behavior in a society populated by two races, Cattell offered a cautionary example:

> Suppose, as may well be the case, that one of these races is naturally courageous, self-sacrificing and enterprising and the other less so. The group will continue to prosper owing to the activities of inventors and explorers of the first race, who, as is generally the rule, will not pass on the usual number of children to the next generation. The nation will be successful in war because the same race has actively responded to the call to arms and to self-sacrifice. Throughout these activities, this first race will on an average be giving more to the group than it can itself recoup. Eventually only the second race will inherit the group advantages acquired largely by the first racial compound. Then like a huge parasite which has devoured its host, will the nation be bereft of all the qualities that gave it power, remain a monstrous frustration of evolution, a biological abortion able in virtue of its inherited wealth, to do untold damage to neighboring races naturally more capable.[59]

At a time when the term *parasite* was being applied increasingly to a specific ethnic group in Europe, the biological simile constituted an unsubtle hint of one source of such "untold damage," but lest the reader be unable to decode the implication, in the very next sentence the example mutated from the hypothetical to the identifiable:

> The hatred and abhorrence which many peoples feel for the Jewish (and to some extent Mongolian) practice of living in other nations, instead of forming an independent, self-sustained group of their own, comes from a deep intuitive feeling that somehow it is not "playing the game." Because our unbiologically-minded civilization cannot perceive or appreciate any intellectual causes for these feelings they are readily branded as "prejudice" by would-be intellectuals.[60]

Yet another reason that racial separation was necessary, according to Cattell, was to prevent the "evolutionary confusion" caused when a less capable group, merely by virtue of its geographic proximity to racial superiors, enjoyed the unmerited advantages of the latter's intelligence and creativity. Like his mentor McDougall, Cattell too thought that technological advancement should remain racially proprietary; the modern civilization of the West and the scientific achievements on which it was based were certainly not to be "regarded as the rightful and hard-earned inheritance of all types and all peoples," and he found the extension of these improvements to non-Westerners morally questionable "even when the races are not bound up" within the same society. "European mechanical inventions," he noted with alarm, "are increasing the wealth, the numbers and the power of Indians, Chinese and Japanese. European medical discoveries are saving millions of lives and giving rise to dense populations in Java, Africa, and India, which would never have existed otherwise. The introduction of modern machinery, etc. into Russia is making possible a relatively great increase in a relatively poor-grade Slav and Mongolian population."[61] Thus, even when other these other groups "played the game" correctly, eschewing a parasitical existence among a different race and remaining in their own society, the "free spread of culture" hindered the process of evolution, unfairly conferring a benefit on one group that had actually been earned by another.

This concern with racial accomplishments did not mean that Cattell failed to recognize an overlap of ability between races, but although he acknowledged the existence of highly intelligent members in every group, he nevertheless found it no reason to look beyond racial membership and judge an individual on his or her merits. Indeed, he reserved his harshest words for those he called "race slumpers"—people who actually argued that "positions and privileges should everywhere be given to individuals without consid-

eration of racial origin." This contention, Cattell insisted, overlooked other
characteristics that were both more important to such decisions than intelligence and considerably less likely to exhibit much overlap between races.
"An intelligent Jew, for example," he wrote, "may be the same in intellectual
capacity as an intelligent Englishman or Norwegian, but his temperament, his
way of thinking, his choice of amusement, and of ideals in art and life will be
radically different, and in these things the Englishman will be more at home
with the less intelligent members of his own race than with his intellectual
equal in a race of different temperamental constitution." These sorts of differences, he continued, had nothing to do with "superiority or inferiority,"
even though, naturally, when it came to "mental ability and vitality . . . we
are compelled to judge some races to be superior, some to be inferior." But
this "simpler matter" of temperamental differences was, if anything, *more*
important. Thus,

> to treat alien individuals as if they belonged to the same race, simply because
> their intelligence is on the same high or low level, is a mistake, for constitutional
> differences of greater importance for practical life are being overlooked. An
> intelligent Italian peasant is not the equivalent of a moderately gifted China-
> man, neither could a less gifted Scot be replaced by an advanced member of
> the negro race.[62]

The existence of these "constitutional differences," which Cattell viewed
as genetically based and racial in origin, provided yet another compelling
justification for races to remain separate from each other. Again drawing on
McDougall's concept of the group mind, Cattell maintained that "likeness of
inborn nature" was a requirement for harmonious national development.[63]
Different races, even within Europe, had to remain biologically sequestered
from each other in order for each "type" to develop "its particular disposition." The "inborn disposition of the Mediterranean type" from southern
Europe, for example, was highly gregarious, highly sexual, unassertive, inclined to crimes of violence and passion, "naively interested in the world of
the senses," and "rather vain." In contrast, Nordics—the tall, blond people
of England, Scandinavia, Denmark, and northern Germany—were strong,
silent types: self-assertive, domineering, adventurous, independent, bold,
and instinctively curious, which accounted for their interest in science and
exploration. Throughout history, Cattell noted, "the fair northern type has
been the conquering and ruling race." The Alpine race, from the middle of
the continent, was fittingly intermediate in disposition between the extro-
verted Mediterraneans and the reserved Nordics—a sturdy peasant stock
with "no urge to the noble and heroic," and more likely to rely on hard work

and economy than enterprise or creativity. Although Cattell thought that Europeans might be able to overlook some of the differences occurring between these races that had a history of close contact with each other, he found it not possible to ignore the "feeling of strangeness" that instinctively arose in regard to those "intruders into Europe"—the Jews, whose alien personalities constituted an unavoidable source of offense to their hosts. Characterizing them racially as a "Hither-Asiatic" mixture—the term popularized by Hans F. K. Günther, the Nazi anthropologist who provided the theoretical foundation for racial theory in the Third Reich and was regarded as its official ideological spokesperson—Cattell described the Jews as the intellectual equal of the Nordics but otherwise quite different: emotional, cautious, strongly acquisitive, and marked by "Jewish tenacity" and a "crafty spirit of calculation."[64]

Cattell saw these differences in personality traits between races as inevitably producing conflicts. Indeed, even *within* a group he believed that there was a need for "control of inborn characters," which, in most nations at the moment, varied far beyond "the desirable range"; a fortiori, intergroup differences led to discord. "The social ideals, the tempo of life, the recreations, the ways of thinking, the virtues and sins that excite attention," declared Cattell,

> are all dependent in a considerable measure on the inborn characters. Whenever a nation has been forcibly put together from differing races, we find a social life unnecessarily disjointed, weak, and feverish. There are thousands of misunderstandings, produced by individuals working for different goals in different ways and at different speeds. Think of the English in Ireland. Examine more closely the contacts of English and Welsh in business, politics, and education. Think of the Jews anywhere.

And as further evidence for the compatibility produced by racial similarity, in a footnote he attributed the "remarkable rapprochement" among the United States, England, and Germany since the First World War largely to "the underlying racial sympathy breaking through the crust of unfavourable circumstances."[65]

Finally, in the one argument that actually lent itself to empirical investigation, Cattell claimed that "cross-breeding" produced genetic defects in the offspring. This had been a common belief among scientists a decade earlier. In 1917, when the wave of so-called new immigrants from southern and eastern Europe was at its peak, one well-known geneticist in the United States had warned of "disharmonic mixtures" resulting from intermarriage between older Americans and the recent arrivals: a mating, for example, between a member of a tall race like the Scottish with a member of a short race like the southern Italian could produce a child who inherited the former's large stature but the latter's small internal organs and thus was afflicted with a frame for which the viscera were "inadequate." By 1933, however, when *Psychology and Social Progress* was published, support for such untenable ideas had dwindled. Nevertheless, Cattell continued to offer scientific-sounding gobbledygook as an explanation for the existence of genetic disharmonies:

> In a pure race, adapted to its conditions by long ages of selection, the inheritance of impulses in each individual is bound to be well balanced. The innate forces which are the innate material of character-building must have reached a certain mutual compatibility and potential power of good integration. If two such races inter-breed, the resulting re-shuffling of impulses and psychic forces throws together in each individual a number of items which may or may not be compatible and capable of being organized into a stable unit.[66]

Cattell had no shortage of examples for such alleged incompatibilities, some physiological, others psychological. The glands of children from parents of dissimilar race were "inharmoniously adapted to each," he claimed, which caused "the exaggerated growth of the hybrid and his disproportionately large extremities." But more harmful to social stability were the defects in personality that resulted from interracial unions, according to Cattell, who cited evidence supposedly demonstrating that "the social feuds and the unstable governments of the so-called 'Celtic' (mainly Alpine-Mediterranean) and Eastern European peoples are due to this mixed blood." However, the worst mismatch of this sort was the child of a black and a white parent. Such a "mixed breed," wrote Cattell, was "inferior to either race and frequently positively vicious"; the reason, he explained, was that "an infusion of white blood increases the intelligence of the negro, while at the same time lowering his moral qualities." Indeed, he suggested that one reason for the "alarming criminality" in the United States was the "'warring heredities' and unstable temperaments of half breeds." At about the same time that Cattell was finishing *Psychology and Social Progress,* in *Light in August* Faulkner was describing Joe Christmas's confused mulatto nature: "The black blood drove him first to the Negro cabin. And then the white blood drove him out of there, as it was the black blood which snatched up the pistol and the white blood which would not let him fire it."[67] Cattell would not have found this passage the least bit metaphorical.

For all these reasons Cattell found it imperative that "groups . . . be composed entirely of their own types"; in order for evolution to be progressive, nations and races had to correspond with each other, the former essentially being defined by the latter. But as he looked around Europe in the early 1930s,

Cattell was horrified at the extent of racial chaos. Too many nations were composed of either "racial mixtures" or "bundles of differing racial areas coupled together." These conditions, in which "the good and bad are linked up to sink or swim together," made it impossible, he complained, for competition between such heterogeneous nations to serve its proper function of "furthering human evolution in inborn characters," and until some order was imposed on these haphazard racial patterns, national competition would continue to be "of very uncertain value to human progress." In the meantime, he encouraged the "deliberate reconstruction, or even minor pruning, of present national groups" as a measure that could "eventually save . . . countries sufficiently enlightened on racial matters to do such deliberate surgery well."[68] One European country in particular would soon take on this scientifically urgent task.

Putting Scientists in Charge

It was only after racial order had been firmly established that science and, more significant, scientists could play their appropriate role in "controlling human happiness," not merely providing the theoretical justification for racial separation but engaging in the more practical task of defining and measuring specific personality traits and abilities in order to study differences both within and between groups. In the former context the purpose of such investigation would be to monitor a society's direction and judge the effectiveness of various policies—that is, to assess the degree to which individuals were developing the traits consistent with their society's goals and to evaluate whether these goals were in fact beneficial. In the latter context it would be to make the empirical comparisons necessary to determine which racial groups were in the lead and which were lagging behind in the group competition leading to evolutionary progress—to distinguish the "successes" from the "failures." It was this use for psychological measurement that had motivated Cattell to leave the chemistry lab and devote his career to the study of traits. As he noted in the foreword to *Psychology and Social Progress,* he had been "led . . . from the study of physical science . . . to psychology, where appear to lie at last the ultimate possibilities of evaluating ideals and aptly controlling social progress."[69]

To attain this sublime state, of course, it was neither "happiness" nor "progress" that would be controlled, but rather people: "The first step for the nation" that aspired to such perfection, Cattell declared, was "to control the number and quality of its citizens." Until now, he noted, the primary goal of eugenic projects had been quite modest, aimed "merely at removing the outermost edge of grossly defective and abnormal individuals." But this concentration exclusively on the lower end of the human spectrum had still left society burdened with "the excessively large families of the poor." These "families should not exist," Cattell declared, "but, since they do," he added charitably, they should receive a "minimum education and food and clothing if necessary. Society has rejected the alternative of allowing the children of the poor to die." Ensuring their survival, however, did not mean tolerating their proliferation, nor that of anyone else whose offspring might be of doubtful value. To rationalize the reproductive process, in Cattell's scheme every member of a society would be subjected to a "psychological and medical assessment," on the basis of which the examinee would be assigned "a precise factor of fertility," an appropriate number of children. Thus, he explained, if an "average" woman with a fertility factor of "one" married a man "of unusual gifts" with a fertility factor of "two," she "would normally bear three children." With proper education on the significance of such eugenic measures, an informed citizenry could be expected to adhere to the recommended number of children, but "of course," he observed, "there will be criminals in this as in every sphere." For those miscreants "who repeatedly bring weakly, diseased and mentally backward children into the world in the face of recommendations to the contrary," the state would have to take action, and among the sanctions that might be imposed on "individuals who make no effort to conform," Cattell suggested sterilization, payment of a fine, or even, in a curious use of the singular, incarceration of "the parent."[70]

The implementation of this sort of eugenic program not only was expected to increase the general intelligence of the population but in doing so, Cattell predicted, would also reduce the degree of variability, making the difference in intellectual ability between one person and another relatively slight; only in such an intellectually homogeneous society, he claimed, could democracy actually be feasible. To Cattell, Jefferson's famous observation on human equality was not an ethical principle—a "truth" that was "self-evident"—but a biological assertion, the inaccuracy of which made it necessary "to restrict the electorate in accordance with psychological tests of mental capacity" to "about two-thirds of its present extent." However, this presently unfulfilled premise of democratic theory could become a reality through "eugenic planning": the creation of a society "where each man was aware of an approximate equality to his fellows," he maintained, would make "true democracy possible for the first time." Cattell did not conceive it impossible that a society would make a conscious decision to pursue "a wide scatter of ability," but in such a case, he proclaimed, the nation had to be "prepare[d] to give up democracy and return to a . . . system of castes, aristocracies, and serfdom."[71]

Nor was democracy the only manifestation of sociopolitical equality scientifically suspect; the modern belief in equal opportunity, too, was untenable, according to Cattell, unless accompanied by eugenic measures. "The man of energy and ability," he explained, was once tied down to a position with little hope of advancement, a predicament that made him more likely "to express his energies in a home and a relatively large family." But now that such a capable person could "rise . . . socially," he "neglects to produce a family." Uncorrected by eugenic action, this inverse correlation between social mobility and family size threatened to reduce "national effectiveness."[72]

Although intelligence was the main focus of Cattell's analysis, it was hardly the only trait that lent itself to eugenic interest; any "inborn constitutional" quality—the only kind that was of "lasting importance in world affairs"— could be subject to selective breeding. For any such characteristic, social scientists would gauge the "optimum range of inborn differences" to ensure that variation in personality traits did not become excessive, thereby threatening the group's homogeneity; a "greater uniformity of type" was essential to creation of the group mind that would produce the "greater sympathy and agreement" necessary for the group to pursue its goals successfully. In addition, scientists would provide the "objective assessments" enabling a determination of the extent to which specific "temperamental factors" were best suited for these goals. That is, on the basis of "psychological and sociological knowledge," the evolutionary process would be directed toward the selection of some traits as those helpful to the society and away from others. It was entirely appropriate—indeed, imperative, according to Cattell—that scientists be granted such extraordinary influence: as psychology developed into a "true science of mental abilities and psycho-spiritual factors," he argued, its conclusions, though of unquestionable "certainty and reliability," would be "comprehensible only to highly-trained minds" who alone understood how to translate these results into their logical policy consequences.[73]

In Cattell's opinion, it was "of the first importance" that these experts, carefully selected "for ability and good judgment," be given an official role in the government, and he had very specific proposals for the form their participation should take. As a preliminary step, the scientists themselves needed to be organized to obtain "representation by a special party in parliament." Eventually, however, he suggested that the nation's legislative chambers should be enlarged by the addition of a house of scientists, composed chiefly of sociologists, economists, psychologists, biologists, medical "men," and anthropologists, who would be elected in each case by their respective professional associations. If possible, Cattell preferred that this scientific body be constructed from the House of Lords, on the grounds that such a composition would preserve certain "profoundly important principles" represented by the lords: "restriction of the electorate and the maintenance of some degree of hereditary differentiation."[74]

But this intrasocietal role played by scientific authority would be merely the beginning of a global system extending far beyond national borders, in which crucial decisions, about both individuals and races, would be made on the basis of psychological measurements of ability and personality. Cattell proposed a "co-operative world-wide movement to ensure eugenic advance by controlled direction of evolution in competitive groups." Only a "government of scientists," he insisted, could apply psychological testing properly to oversee "eugenic progress in innate powers" on an international level, thus bringing "to mankind that true control of its destiny for which it has so long striven."[75]

In Cattell's conception of this system, international oversight did not completely preclude some degree of local autonomy. Each group could make its own determination of what sort of physical or personal characteristics it wished to develop—"introvert temperaments or more extravert ones . . . more steady, reliable, persevering dispositions or more erratic but original and entertaining ones"—provided, of course, that there was scientific oversight to evaluate the consequences and decide whether a particular evolutionary direction was a "success or failure." But whether the goal was anatomical or psychological, such a decision had to be based on the rigorous measurements allowing groups to be compared to each other: "Thus one group, aiming physically at greater skeletal development, may find itself becoming slightly more susceptible to tuberculosis, or showing a slightly lower average of energy output than another group. Or aiming psychologically at a lesser instinct of self-assertion and greater gregariousness, may find itself producing fewer men of initiative and originality." Because many of these systematic differences between groups would arise out of what Cattell called the "original inborn characters" of their respective populations, he thought it would be inappropriate to make a value judgment about them in advance; each group would regard the personal traits it chose to develop as "intrinsically satisfying"—perhaps in the way that some people preferred representational art and others abstract—and thus these differences would "not [be] considered in a relative way as superior or inferior." But, he immediately added, "there will in time emerge differences which are perceived not to be merely differences but superiorities and inferiorities," and eventually everyone "will . . . recognize the fact." Groups would then be able to adjust their eugenic and cultural directions accordingly, making it less likely that they would "go . . . astray and fall out of the evolutionary race."

Yet sometimes, Cattell bluntly observed, an adjustment was no longer feasible and interference was called for: "There are bound to be leading groups and groups falling behind. There are bound to be cases where it is time to call a halt to a certain line of evolution. In uncivilized ages that surgical operation of lopping off the backward branches of the tree of mankind was done violently and without an anesthetic."[76] In the modern age, however, it was now possible to replace such barbaric processes with more scientifically enlightened paths to the same end:

> In ... clearly established cases, where it is obvious that the race concerned cannot hope to catch up in innate capacity (and therefore in cultural capacity) to other groups, the leading nations may attempt to reduce the numbers of the backward people by birth-control regulation, segregation, or human sterilization. Repeopling, by more intelligent and alert peoples, of parts of the earth possessed by backward people is merely following the highest moral considerations when it is done with humane feeling for the happiness of the generation of backward peoples then existing. Clearly the reverse process— i.e., the giving up of territory by an advanced people to a people with a lower standard of living and denser population—is highly undesirable.[77]

This was Francis Bacon's utopian "New Atlantis" with a vengeance, a world in which the scientific community exercised a degree of control over crucial decisions—about individuals and races—that would make the members of the Politburo blush.[78]

Indeed, in the name of evolutionary progress Cattell conceived of experimental designs that could be imposed on the world, manipulating racial groups on a grand scale in order to generate the data necessary for scientists to render their eugenic verdicts. If, for example,

> it is required to discover ... whether the inborn nature of white or yellow peoples is best fitted for progress in the scientific understanding of nature, it would be necessary to divide up world resources between Mongolian and European groups only. We should then start with all other conditions (economic and cultural) approximately equal and observe the course of scientific advance in each group. If now one wished to try out as well a cultural difference, say the social effect of following Christianity on the one hand and Buddhism on the other, it would be necessary to have four groups—a white Buddhist group, a white Christian group, a Mongolian Buddhist group and a Mongolian Christian group.[79]

Although Cattell went on to emphasize that smaller racial groups were better suited for such experiments, this preference on his part had nothing to do with the concept of the study but merely a desire to avoid the "passive herd opposition" he believed more likely to occur in larger units. But whatever the size of the racial units under examination, he constantly emphasized, the "most truly immoral act" was "to ruin the experiment by indiscriminately mixing the contents of the test tubes."[80]

Thus, the ultimate irony: the psychologist who disparaged simplistic methods for the study of responses in the laboratory—maintaining, with some justification, that comparing the results of subjects who had been partitioned into groups was inadequate to understand the multidimensional complexity of human behavior—was nevertheless eager to impose such experimental designs on the infinitely more complex behavior of human beings in the real world in order to make determinations that would shape the future of humankind, determining which racial groups would endure and which would be eliminated. Once "the people of the world" had all been divided "into eugenic evolutionary groups according to racial type," each of which would deliberately experiment with itself" in the interest of self-improvement, both cultural and biological, Cattell foresaw a "central laboratory" that would "collate the biological and sociological comparisons of diverging groups . . . and . . . clear away the debris of group experiments that have definitely failed." As he later added, the "expansion or contraction" of a racial group, corresponding to its respective "success or failure," would be "regulated by scientific diagnosis in the hands of international commissions."[81] Scientists would separate the usable evolutionary wheat from the disposable chaff.

A New Religion

Written between the ages of eighteen and twenty-six, *Psychology and Social Progress* might have been the result of a youthful infatuation with a utopian ideology; there is no paucity of examples of attraction to such visions—from hippie communes to hard-core Marxism—on the part of people who later looked back on this episode in their lives with embarrassment and chagrin. But in Cattell's case this was no temporary flirtation. A few years later, now in his thirties, in rapid succession he published two more books—one conceptual, the other empirical—extending the ideas in the earlier work.

Deriving moral laws as he did from the degree to which a particular course of action did or did not contribute toward evolutionary progress, Cattell insisted that morality was "thus a branch of natural science." As a consequence he was not so much dissatisfied as dismayed by traditional religious beliefs, all of which, no matter the denomination, tended to think in terms of universal principles. Instead of properly confining altruistic behavior to other members of one's own group, "all great religions," he observed, encouraged the false extension of love and cooperation far beyond the limits of biological usefulness to "all members of any group." As "the finest example" of such universal ethics, Christianity in particular disturbed Cattell, leading him, in *Psychology and Social Progress*, to call for "the halting of the Christian religion at national boundaries." Until there was widespread acceptance of the principles of evolutionary ethics, he predicted, there would continue to be a conflict between "our intuitive sense of right and wrong" and that specifically taught by traditional religions.[82] This hint at the necessity of an entirely different religious orientation was expanded in detail in *Psychology and the Religious Quest.*[83]

From the time that the English gentleman scientist Francis Galton first proposed the concept of eugenics in 1865[84]—inspired by the appearance half a dozen years earlier of his half cousin's famous book, *On the Origin of Species*[85]— through the 1930s, there was considerable interest in the relationship between eugenics and religion. Disappointed in the conventional approach to faith, not so much because he opposed its moral principles but because he found it vague, mystical, and of little practical value,[86] Galton himself proposed that eugenics be considered a "religion." He did not intend this term in some metaphorical sense: if, as he believed, evolution was the purpose of the universe, then evolutionary development was clearly the work of the deity, however one chose to understand that entity, and it became literally a "religious duty" for humans to facilitate the aim of the "divine Worker."[87] Although few others actually sought to substitute a eugenical creed in place of more traditional beliefs,[88] in the first third of the twentieth century, as Christine Rosen has described in *Preaching Eugenics,* there were numerous attempts on both sides to bridge the gap between the biological and the religious approaches to human elevation. Numerous members of the clergy incorporated eugenical concerns into their advice to the flock, requiring, for example, that couples present a "certificate of health" from a physician before exchanging vows in a church. Among other efforts at reciprocation on their part, eugenicists organized a Committee on Cooperation with Clergymen and sponsored a eugenics sermon contest with substantial cash prizes, prompting some two hundred sermons on the topic. Albert E. Wiggam, one of the movement's most enthusiastic popularizers, proclaimed that only the application of eugenics could lead to "the complete Christianization of mankind," adding that if Jesus had been present, "he would have been president of the First Eugenics Congress."[89]

More Galtonian than Galton, Cattell had no interest in any reconciliation between the scientifically validated principles of eugenics and a belief system he considered to be "a continuation of the frailties and eccentricities of unenlightened savages," of interest primarily for archaeological reasons as a "quaint illusion" now thoroughly discredited. Religion, in his opinion, appealed primarily "to the inferior, the sick, the maladjusted, the fearful, the poor, and those scorned and rejected by love, power, life and society," providing these immature unfortunates with "a pitiful accumulation of escapes and self-deceptions" as balm for their wounds and shortcomings. Yet at the same time, Cattell acknowledged the value of religious belief for society: even though demonstrably false, it played an indispensable role in maintaining order and morality, fostered a sense of purpose and community, and afforded the "deeper satisfactions" of life. Thus, despite the denunciations, he expressed "some sympathy with those practical people of good works . . . stubbornly preserving their loyalty to religious principles in spite of the fact that reason makes this position untenable." Of course, he added, "no scientist worthy of the name" could possibly adhere to an illusion, no matter how much it provided consolation to the tormented or significance to human existence.[90]

Mindful of revealed religion's obvious benefits, especially its power to give meaning to life, and concerned that its loss of credibility would result in an ethical vacuum leading to the worst excesses of individualism, Cattell sought a rational alternative, one that would allow humanity to "reach something as valuable as all that was lost with religion" yet without having to rely on myth and superstition. Although his own discipline was still in its infancy, he was nevertheless certain that in psychology lay "the foundations for a new and nobler structure of scientifically founded religion." Drawing on McDougall's concept of the group mind, he posited the existence of a "super-individual mind, built up from, yet greater than, the sum of the individual minds." For Cattell, this "super-individual consciousness" was a power greater than the self, essentially the equivalent of the traditional notion of God: the individual "depends on it, and it exercises a benevolent intervention in his life. He is, spiritually, and in some sense physically, created by the group mind. In serving it he is doing precisely what is defined as the worship and service of God. . . . It is the assurance of immortality, which is to be obtained only by giving one's life to it. It gives to the individual faith to carry out those tasks valuable to the community."[91]

The awareness that one did not exist in isolation but as a part of others who consciously identified with this superindividual entity, sharing its collective memory, native temperament, and idiosyncrasies, allowed an individual in some degree to transcend his or her own death and endure in the continuation of the group mind. As always for Cattell, this consciousness attained its "fullest and most perfect expression" when the group was composed of "biologically similar individuals"—in other words, races.[92]

Cattell was acutely aware that what he regarded as the rationalist destruction of traditional religion eliminated as well its role as the basis for "divinely derived moral law," and just as he maintained that the group mind constituted a more appropriate God substitute, providing life with a meaning that enjoyed the imprimatur of science, he sought to demonstrate that it was also superior as the foundation for morality. As he had determined in *Psychology and Social Progress,* moral laws had to be crafted in order to facilitate evolutionary progress, and evolutionary progress was encoded in the growth of the group mind, which itself was the expression of the level of evolution of the individuals who composed it; therefore, morality was whatever contributed to the "emergence of the group mind—or, if you will, of God." But the difficulty with this conclusion, Cattell acknowledged, was "the astounding discovery" that the specific moral laws deducible from such a goal were "apparently the exact opposite of those which religion and humanity have bred into our bones." After all, he observed, evolution was ensured only if humans cooperated with "nature in its vigilant and ruthless elimination of the less fit"; to further such a process would seem to justify "the absence of any law but rivalry and selfishness between individuals." The solution to this apparent dilemma for Cattell—the way to reconcile the need to strive for higher levels of evolution with the intuitive humanitarian impulse toward others—was the realization that "the type of human being we wish to evolve is one who is capable of achieving his fullest expression only in groups." Thus, the evolution of "inborn" traits such as "sympathy, unselfishness, self-sacrifice, and the capacity for enthusiastic cooperation" would be of great benefit because when levels of intelligence were equal, the racial groups more well endowed in these qualities would be more likely to survive and flourish.[93]

At first glance, this approach seemed to return Cattell to his mentor's distinction between national and universal ethics: because evolutionary progress occurred as superior groups prevailed over the less fit, either "through intertribal warfare or international rivalry," groups should be "internally closely knit by love, but externally governed only by the necessity of proving their biological worth." Thus, a rationally based religion should encourage altruistic behavior toward members of one's own group but not toward members of other groups (races). But Cattell also appreciated the natural inclination, especially among "the more intellectual leaders," to want to make altruism and charitable attitudes "ends in themselves," extending such kindnesses beyond the boundary of one's own group. Although he initially considered this universalist tendency a "mistake," which would destroy "the very conditions of competition in which love had its function of granting superior solidarity," eventually he arrived at a more nuanced view, concluding that the extension of goodwill toward other races was not inappropriate *if* it was informed by the right attitude—that groups "regard . . . each other as co-operators in the joint plan of evolving nobler types." In other words, the real meaning of human "brotherhood" was the joint dedication of different races to life's true religious purpose—pursuit of the ultimate objective of evolutionary advancement—and also to the interracial rivalry necessary to attain it. Intergroup competition in this view would not be incompatible with each side's devotion to the divine process that ensured a salutary outcome for humanity no matter which group emerged momentarily victorious. Although Cattell thought it far more desirable that this rivalry be conducted "within a circle of fundamental mutual love," violent conflict, in his opinion, was the unavoidable alternative and, indeed, preferable to the misguided universalist belief that cultures and races could be mixed without doing harm to the process of upward evolution. Thus, although he found war to be a reflection of the failure to grasp life's purpose "at a higher level," it had nevertheless "been a highroad to nobility at a lower level" and was certainly better than no competition at all.[94] Long before John F. Kennedy's famous observation about revolution, in essence Cattell had offered his own version—that those who made peaceful evolution impossible would make violent evolution inevitable.

Unsurprisingly, then, Cattell's analysis of morality brought him to the same conclusion he had reached five years earlier in *Psychology and Social Progress*, but now adorned by the underpinnings of a religious framework complete with a scientifically derived definition of God. And to do God's will was quite simple: each person was required merely to "play . . . the game" by "following his own race and culture to greater glory and more supreme service or to stagnation and perdition." Like traditional religion, there was to be an eternal reward beyond one's own physical existence, not in the promise of the soul's presence in heaven but rather in the evolutionary progress of future generations, an outcome that, for some people, meant the elimination of their descendants. A religious system based on science required "the replacement of indubitably backward peoples by a more evolved stock," and, as he had done earlier, again Cattell recommended that, if possible, this process should occur with "kindness and consideration": not through the brutality of war but "by gradual restriction of births, and by life in adapted reserves and asylums, must the races which have served their turn be brought to euthanasia."[95]

But unlike the earlier book, in which the identity of those contemporary "backward" races destined for elimination went unmentioned, Cattell was now ready to name names. The year before publishing the description of his religious system, he had singled out "Australian Blacks" as unable to create a level of civilization that could be considered "sufficient or tolerable." Slightly higher in his judgment was "the Negro," who

> has established a stable culture both in Africa and America, but . . . has contributed practically nothing to social progress and culture (except in rhythm . . .). All the social and religious notions which have been sedulously grafted upon the negro have been forcefully adapted by him, made more simple and crude

and emotional. I cite this example to show that, even when the race is a constitutionally good-natured and lovable one, lower mental capacity means reaction, crudity and a social deadweight of conservatism.[96]

In *Psychology and the Religious Quest,* Cattell expanded on this evolutionary shortcoming, explaining that the "lower mental capacity of the negro" was a consequence of a "smaller skull capacity . . . as racially characteristic as the greater projection of his heel at the other end of the skeleton," leaving no doubt that "despite endearing qualities of humor and religiosity," the "negro" was an example of a racial experiment that had to be "scrap[ped]."[97]

Another failed racial group similarly fit for euthanasia was the "Abyssinias [*sic*]."[98] In October 1935, in a conflict that helped pave the way toward World War II, Italy had invaded what was then called Abyssinia, one of the few African states not subject to European domination at the time; although the League of Nations condemned the act, voting to impose sanctions, they were not widely supported, and seven months later Italy annexed the object of its aggression, proclaiming King Victor Emmanuel III as emperor of Ethiopia.[99] To Cattell, this was not an instance of imperialism but a sign of progress. "By evolutionary morals," he declared, "the substitution of Italian culture for Abyssinian is good." Although "the way it has been done is bad," Cattell pointed out, relying on the "old-fashioned" resort to violence, he saw no reason to criticize the invasion, as long as "Italy has no hypocritical objection to being displaced in turn by similar methods."[100]

Nor was Italy the only country whose policies lived up to the moral standards of Cattell's religious system. In *Psychology and Social Progress,* written just before the ascendance of fascism, he had predicted that the nation to adopt eugenic measures would hold "an enormous advantage over its neighbors" in the competitive struggle. In the discussion of racial temperament, he had also warned against the forms of art "intrinsically satisfying only to the Hither-Asiatic and Oriental races of Poland [that is, Jews]." Looking around the world in the late 1930s, Cattell saw that a number of countries were indeed following the path he had prescribed. Especially in Germany, he observed, "the community boldly acts upon the wisdom of the biologist and the medical man and . . . eugenic laws are instantly put into operation." The Reich, in his opinion, deserved "the credit of being the first to adopt [involuntary] sterilization together with a positive emphasis on racial improvement."[101] At the time Germany had passed the Nuremberg laws, encoding separation between Aryans and alien races into official state policy, and thereby forcing the Jews to "play the game" correctly by stripping them of citizenship and depriving them of basic rights. The Reich had also recently confiscated thousands of pieces of *entartete Kunst*, degenerate art inimical to the Aryan racial soul.[102] Although he was concerned that the Axis powers[103] had mistakenly elevated the state above the group mind, nevertheless Cattell believed that all three countries were on the right moral track, inspired by "elements of purpose which our democracies have lost," and he urged the less enlightened nations to take heed:

> At the moment . . . the Atlantic democracies are bewildered, envious, and hostile at the rise of Germany, Italy, and Japan, countries in which individuals have disciplined their indulgences as to a religious purpose. These nationals fear the gods even though they are partly false gods, in comparison with the vast numbers in our democracies lacking any super-personal aim. Their rise should be welcomed by the religious man as reassuring evidence that in spite of modern wealth and ease, we shall not be allowed to sink into stagnation or adopt foolish practices in fatal detachment from the stream of evolution.[104]

To Cattell, developments in the totalitarian nations were hopeful signs for the emergence of true religious values.

The Crisis Confirmed

Although his evidence was entirely impressionistic, in *Psychology and Social Progress* Cattell had complained bitterly over the generally low intellectual level of so much of the population in his native England. With effort, he wrote, the "university-educated man" might be able to tolerate all those "bank holiday proletarians moving like locusts across our countryside," but could "find no satisfying companionship with a man whose reading extends to a credulous devouring of newspapers . . . and whose ideas on all subjects are grossly immature."[105] His point at the time was that such widespread mediocrity could be changed only by the implementation of appropriate eugenic measures. Appointed three years later to the first Leonard Darwin Research Studentship—essentially a research fellowship—by the British Eugenics Society, Cattell was afforded the time and the resources to gather data on intelligence in order to demonstrate not only that the problem of dullness was severe but that it was projected to become much worse as well.[106]

The resulting study, *The Fight for Our National Intelligence*, was more rant than research—a few tables of data intended to justify hysterical predictions of genetic and social catastrophe that Cattell felt compelled to repeat every few pages. The data came from administration of a "specially designed nonverbal intelligence test" to all the ten-year-old children in Leicester, a "typical industrial city" and in an "unspoilt rural area" in Devonshire, consisting of a number of scattered villages; altogether some thirty-seven hundred children were tested, of whom three-quarters came from the urban sample. Cattell also collected information on the parental occupation of each child and the number of children in the family. Computing the average number of children per family at each IQ level, he found that the "grim evidence runs with relentless consistency": less intelligent children came from systematically larger families, an effect that was true for both samples but especially strong in the rural area. "For a dysgenic trend we were prepared," he noted, but "not on this scale and not of so uniform a nature" that "there is no redeeming feature to the situation"; the population was being "recruited increasingly from the sub-men." At the present relationship between level of intelligence and degree of reproduction, Cattell calculated, the average IQ of the population would be expected to decline about one point per decade, meaning that in "three hundred years half the population would be mentally defective." This rate of change, he added, "must be one of the most galloping plunges to bankruptcy that has ever occurred," presaging first, as the title of the study's introductory chapter suggested, "the twilight of Western civilization" and eventually "the lingering death of civilization . . . across the world."[107]

The culprits—or, more properly, the caricatures—in this precipitous decline were to be found at both ends of the intelligence spectrum. Near the upper extreme were the insecure arrivistes Cattell called members of the "National Suicide Club": pretentious social climbers so obsessed with superficial appearances that they could not "afford" to educate more than their one fairly intelligent but "egocentric and over-anxious" child. These people he described as "carriers of a fatal and contagious moral disease." Close to the opposite end—not so much the "actual certifiable defective" at the lowest rung of the intellectual ladder but the "'dull' group just above deficiency"—was the kind of person whose "life . . . has never had any life." Through their "unchecked fecundity," which typically resulted in a "half-witted litter," such parents were "going to . . . bring civilization down about their ears . . . [b]lindly, unconsciously gnaw[ing] . . . away at its foundations, impoverishing themselves and other people, converting their misery into an acid corroding the foundations of society." These "subcultural" families Cattell named "Civilization Wreckers, Unlimited."[108]

Although Cattell viewed these two groups as equally culpable threats to national survival, both his rhetoric and his recommendations were directed primarily at the dullards. To be sure, he proposed a number of measures that would encourage greater proliferation of the more intelligent, including scholarships for their children and other ways to "make the able child an economic asset" (whereas "the dull child must be made to some extent a fine upon his parents"). And he also condemned the "weltanschauung of false values" characteristic of so many upwardly mobile parents who produced neurotic "only children," warning that "the thoughtful citizen may well avoid the 'only' daughter as he would the plague!"[109] But, as was true for most of the eugenics movement, control of the less capable was Cattell's major focus. In addition to their deleterious effect on the population's average intelligence, he resented the opportunity cost of their existence, which consumed resources that could otherwise be devoted to research. Science, he complained, was being deprived of "its true rewards" by a society that preferred "to support half a million dull individuals uselessly on a pittance rather than a thousand brilliant individuals fully in creative labors."[110]

Cattell had no shortage of ideas to reduce both the number and the influence of the intellectually subnormal. Most important, he proposed expanding the legal definition of "feeblemindedness," which at the time designated "mental defectives" as the lowest 3 to 4 percent of the population, so that it would encompass the additional 20 percent that Cattell labeled the "subcultural social defective." Although the latter group did not require the full institutional care accorded to the former, its members, he insisted, did need "'care, supervision and control' in a modern society which wishes to be as jealous of its good standards as it is kind to those who cannot reach them." Such assistance, Cattell explained, was to include regular medical examinations and the provision of "birth control facilities" along with "employment in State-run specially adapted workshops." "That the sub-cultural should not exercise a vote . . . goes without saying," he added. Presumably, those subjected to such regulation would have no objection: the less intelligent, observed Cattell, "seem to realize that their greatest happiness lies in a benevolent dictatorship." For persons judged capable of being parents, legislation would adjust their birthrate "to the magnitude of their contribution to civilization and the need which society has of them" (a policy that seemed to leave the door slightly open for reproduction by the subcultural, since Cattell acknowledged the demand for "simple repetitive and routine industrial tasks" best performed by individuals with IQs in the socially defective range). Such intrusive measures were unobjectionable in his view: "The begetting of children" was "far from being a personal matter but must admit of fine regulation by the state on behalf of the happiness of all."[111]

Based on data and featuring lurid predictions about the nation's fate, *The Fight for Our National Intelligence* received substantially more attention than Cattell's other early works on eugenics, and much of it was unfavorable. Even before the book's publication, he had announced its conclusion of civilization's imminent decline in a series of journal articles[112] and public lectures, eliciting hostile reactions from some other scientists[113] and no small amount of press coverage under such sensational headlines as "Peril of Race Deterioration," "English Children Getting More and More Stupid," and the alliterative "Ban Balmy Babies."[114] J. B. S. Haldane, the distinguished geneticist and evolutionary biologist, himself a member of the British Eugenics Society, took particular issue with Cattell's claim in *Eugenics Review* that "about 75 percent of the children of the feeble-minded are also feeble-minded, and the remainder are not far above the borderline,"[115] citing previous studies with dramatically different results and suggesting that the journal "could do an immense service to eugenics by setting a higher standard of accuracy." Cattell replied rather lamely that the concept of mental deficiency was only "a rough sociological and administrative notion" and "by its nature incapable of being used precisely," apparently unperturbed that his assertion about children had done exactly that.[116] When the book appeared, many of the reviews were also critical.[117] Behind the scenes, prominent members of the Eugenics Society expressed concerns about the recipient of their own fellowship. "Our friend Cattell has been letting himself go in a rather stupid way," wrote one official in the society to another after Cattell had given a lecture titled "Is National Intelligence Declining?" at a professional conference. And the society's former chair and still its honorary president, Major Leonard Darwin, who had written an introduction to Cattell's book and in whose name the society's research fellowship had been established, called him "an irritating writer . . . verbose and rather tactless."[118]

However, Cattell was always impervious to criticism. Foreshadowing the attitude that would inform his factor analytic studies, he viewed others' disagreement with his ideas as an indication of their personal intellectual shortcomings and their inadequate education. Those who did not concur that the intelligent sector of society was being steadily replaced by "innately dull and limited types," or were not sufficiently exercised over this prospect, failed to grasp the statistical analysis and suffered from "an utter ignorance of biological principles and an arrogant intellectual timidity which are the consummation of the traditional education to which our ruling classes were subjected in the last generation." In *Psychology and Social Progress,* Cattell went through journalism and the academic disciplines one by one, systematically disparaging each profession as a "false beacon" and an obstacle to any real advance. People "with a lust for power" but lacking the ability for "success in some particular subject . . . drift[ed] into journalism"; historians, "by natural professional selection . . . of retrovert temperament," failed to realize the importance of racial differences as an explanation of historical phenomena; philosophers displayed "distinct peculiarities of character" that made them "automatically unfit . . . for true research" and served "as a bar to all true intellectual advance"; among philosophers, ethicists in particular were the worst of the bunch, prompting Cattell to call for "an enquiry into the[ir] psychological make-up"; and the entire public education system was "founded on dogma instead of on science," leading to the "sterilization of our best minds."[119] With the exception of a small number of like-minded individuals, Cattell had a bad word for almost everyone.

Thirteen years after *The Fight for Our National Intelligence*, Cattell had the opportunity to confirm his predictions of intellectual degeneration. Again supported by the Eugenics Society, he conducted an almost identical study, administering the same intelligence test to a similar sample of ten year olds. Not only had the expected decline of one IQ point per decade not occurred, but the data showed the exact opposite: there had been a "significant increase" of 1.28 points, an effect attributable entirely to "higher test scores among those of average and sub-average intelligence." Cattell was loath to accept a result so diametrically opposed to the tocsin he had been sounding, and so he didn't, claiming years later that the second study had shown "absolutely no change" over the period of "half a generation" since the first. Dismissing as "mere artifacts" the many studies by other researchers showing gains in test scores, he even argued that IQ had actually dropped slightly if changes in the relation between intelligence level and death rate, celibacy, and childlessness could be taken into account; he acknowledged having no data on these points but was nevertheless certain of the effect they had exerted.[120]

After emigrating to the United States, Cattell remained committed to finding a way to divert his adopted nation too from a similarly dysgenic future. When Robert Klark Graham, a wealthy California businessman who had invented plastic lenses for eyeglasses, turned out to share Cattell's obsession with the proliferation of idiots, the scientist collaborated with the entrepreneur, becoming in 1963 one of the original members of the advisory board of Graham's sperm bank. Like Cattell, Graham too was concerned with humankind's evolutionary direction, and sought to counteract the downward spiral by encouraging brilliant men to donate their seed, which could then be used for artificial insemination, each donor thus creating numerous talented children.[121] Cattell also provided expert assistance in the preparation of Graham's book, *The Future of Man*, based on the curious notion that human brain size, and thus mental development, had peaked some twenty-five thousand years ago with the Cro-Magnons, whom Graham called "the most magnificent folk the race has ever produced," and had drifted downward ever since.[122] (Cattell apparently shared this belief, claiming in 1987 that the Cro-Magnon's brain was "probably a little better than ours.")[123] However, Cattell himself never again conducted any empirical research on trends in the population's intelligence.

* * *

By the second half of the 1930s, the racial approach to eugenics, outlined in its most extreme form in Cattell's moral system and put into practice by the Third Reich, had lost most of the appeal it once enjoyed and was now largely the province of Nazi sympathizers. For all but the most virulent racists, the postwar revelation of the lengths to which the Nazis themselves had gone in the name of racial purity dealt their concept of "political biology" a lethal blow. Having found so much to commend in the Reich's policies, designed to improve the quality of their progeny and to protect both Aryan genes and the Aryan racial soul—its group mind—from contamination by other racial groups, Cattell had relatively little to say in the postwar period about the regime that had once been the object of his admiration; the few instances in which he did comment on the Reich indicated that his earlier praise for its policies remained an unrecovered memory. In 1972 he compared Hitler to roving bands of killers such as the "thugs" in India or "murderous Hippie sects," ignoring the obvious difference between individual renegades and a system officially organized by the state and justified by the latest conclusions of science—the same conclusions that Cattell himself had reached. And he characterized the Nazi movement as "a revolt . . . of the less cultured, lower-middle-class, immature youth against the established religious authority of Christianity," again neglecting to mention that he had dismissed the latter as a dangerous illusion and extolled the former for its discipline and the sense of purpose it imparted to the nation.[124]

Naturally, at the time that Cattell had praised the Reich, he could not have foreseen the pile of bodies at the bottom of the slippery slope down which National Socialism was descending. But Nazi racial theory was not objectionable to Cattell primarily for the brutality committed in its name. What he found particularly unforgivable about the Nazis was the führer's "crass and unsubstantiated claim . . . for German racial superiority, imitating in a new key the Jewish claim to being a Chosen People." (Well read in history and literature, he must have known that the claim of chosenness has nothing to do with Jewish superiority, although neo-Nazi and white supremacist groups typically attempt to make such an association; instead, it refers to the belief that Jews were chosen by God at a time when idolatry was common to receive and spread the message of monotheism.) Yet apart from the outrageousness of the comparison, it is noteworthy that Cattell was offended not so much by Hitler's claim but by the fact that it was "unsubstantiated." As he had made clear in the description of his religious system, Cattell was not at all averse to determining the relative merits of racial groups, but such judgments were properly the province of science; the führer had come to his conclusion without the data to support it. In addition, Cattell judged the Reich responsible for the subsequent inability of educated persons "to think objectively on the inheritance of individual differences in mental characteristics." For many people "it became imperative," he explained, "to assert exactly the opposite of the Nazi unscientific assertion, even though it might turn out to be equally unscientific." In Cattell's view this attitude of "ignoracism"—the refusal to recognize the existence of genetic differences between races—was the true harm done by the Holocaust. Ignoracists, he declared, were even "more opprobrious" than racists—guilty of "greater immorality."[125]

Refusing to acknowledge racial differences was certainly not an error to which Cattell would fall prey. Nor did the events of the Nazi era create any substantial change in the social ideology that he based on such differences. For more than half a century following the end of the war, Cattell continued to promote a religious system requiring the separation of racial groups as the first step in determining which ones should be allowed to carry a banner in the evolutionary race.

BEYONDISM AND THE
NECESSITY FOR "GENTHANASIA"
CATTELLIAN MORALITY
IN THE POSTWAR PERIOD

Despite Cattell's intense interest in the subject of intellectual deterioration, *The Fight for Our National Intelligence*—a project conducted for a specific purpose under the auspices of the Eugenics Society—was nevertheless a diversion from the major focus of his research: human personality. The latter interest no less than the former was intended to serve his scientifically based ideology turned religious system. In *Psychology and the Religious Quest*, Cattell had stressed the importance of identifying those "extremely slight" differences in personality, "frequently subtle and unexpected," that resulted in "one group mind [that is, racial group] being far more powerful, wise, and highly developed than another." In particular, he was interested in identifying the specific traits responsible for the fact that different racial groups of, in his opinion, approximately equal intelligence nevertheless displayed great variation in their actual accomplishments. Although, for example, the "intelligence of the average German" seemed to him essentially the same as "that of the average Spaniard," he was "at a loss to account for the far greater contribution to culture made by a nation of the former." Seeking the explanation for such differences in the personal characteristics of the individuals in each group was "a field of vitally important research"—one to which Cattell intended at the time to devote much of his professional career.[1]

His initial attempts to study an important trait, one associated with achievement aside from intelligence, focused on the variable of "perseveration," the tendency to persist at repetitive tasks. Not only was perseveration believed to be one of the most important elements of personality—or "temperament," as it was often called at the time—but, of particular interest to Cattell, there was already evidence of racial differences: one earlier study of elementary school children in Leeds had found that Jewish boys scored consistently higher on tests of perseveration than their English counterparts. Since Cattell had already concluded that Jews and Nordics were the two most intelligent racial groups, here was an opportunity to investigate a variable other than their intellectual capability that might account for the differences between them, explaining why, despite their high intelligence, the Jews' record of accomplishment lagged behind that of Nordics.[2]

However, in his first attempt to gather data on perseveration, conducted in 1934, none of the five different measures Cattell administered to a sample of college students displayed any relationship to each other—in other words, there was no reason to believe that any of these tests were valid. And unsurprisingly, there was no significant correlation between the combined measures of perseveration and measures of "general character" and "general temperament." The best that he could report was that the negative relation between perseveration and character "approach[ed] significance." Undeterred by this marginal result and having no evidence other than the earlier research that had found Jews to score higher on the variable, he nevertheless went on to construct an elaborate characterization of the systematic difference between low and high perseverators, in which the former were industrious, hardworking persons of "uncompromising individuality" who displayed "astute" judgment and a respect for others' privacy, whereas the latter were "languid, slow or desultory workers" inclined to be "more sentimental" and "suspicious, jealous, and fault-finding toward others." In a subsequent paper a year later Cattell even provided a developmental explanation for the genesis of these differences: the low perseverator, "brought up in a framework of consistent strict and objective discipline," turned out to be "less likely to suffer from emotional conflict and frustration," whereas the high perseverator, "bound by a close affection to his parents, and governed by the sometimes capricious withholding of that affection," was first "spoilt . . . and later intimidated"—a combination that left the child "to find his own salvation or to retreat into regressions." As a consequence of these differences, Cattell concluded, high perseverators tended to have "significantly fewer friends and more enemies," and were generally "more warped natures, less free and natural, and more given to mental conflict."[3] Since Jews were high scorers and hence exhibited the poor "character integration" associated with all these tendencies, he speculated on the assessment of "an English subject of high perseveration score (and therefore not of very good character integration") who "would be only a moderate perseverator in a Jewish community": perhaps in the latter context such a person might be "considered to show good character integration."[4] Someone disordered by English standards would be psychologically well grounded compared to most Jews.

Although there were no Jewish subjects in Cattell's own studies of perseveration, he did categorize each person into a specific European racial subgroup on the basis of hair color, eye color, stature, and cephalic index (the ratio of the head's breadth to its length, multiplied by one hundred to remove the decimal point). This procedure produced six groups: Nordic, Mediterranean, Alpine, and their three pairwise mixtures. Ignoring the fact that the Nordic-Alpine mixture scored the lowest on perseveration of any group in both his studies, Cattell focused on the tendency for Nordics to score lower than Mediterraneans, a result that "point[ed]" him "in the same direction" as the Leeds study because Jews were "a racially mixed people in whose composition the Mediterranean element is large."[5]

Having offered these racial differences as "the quickest way of deciding" whether perseveration was determined by a "hereditary factor," five years later almost as an afterthought Cattell conducted a study of the extent to which individual differences in the trait were heritable. At the time the standard method for estimating such genetic influence was to compare the differences on a trait for monozygotic (that is, identical) twins with that for dizygotics (nonidenticals); since the monozygotics have all their genes in common whereas dizygotics share on average only half their genes, the extent to which the intratwin differences for the latter exceed those for the former provided an indication of the effects of heredity. Strangely, however, he found the differences for the monozygotic twins to be "slightly greater," meaning that there was no genetic basis whatsoever for perseveration. But, as always, Cattell was ready with a saving explanation, allowing him to preserve the assumption of hereditary determination in the face of such hostile data: someone with an identical twin, "conscious of his individuality," felt the need "to distinguish himself emphatically from another being who resembles him too closely," and this need produced "a 'protest' reaction," in which "one or both of the twins react away from the personality" of the other.[6] This convenient interpretation made empirical investigation superfluous: data consistent or inconsistent with genetic influence nevertheless led to certainty of its effect.

Indeed, Cattell culminated this series of studies by converting low scores on perseveration into what he called "the genetic syndrome of 'Nordic-Low Rigidity.'" This hereditary trait, he explained, was responsible for the Nordic "irrepressible drive or energy which expresses itself . . . in conscientious will-character, in dominance, and in surgency [that is, cheerfulness and sociability]"; it also played a role in the tendency for Nordics to have a greater interest in mathematics and science than other groups and to pro-duce a larger number of "famous scientists, explorers, soldiers, and political radicals." And once again Jews and Mediterraneans were at the other end of the spectrum, as Cattell transformed the result of the now fourteen-year-old comparison of Jewish and English schoolboys on a neutrally defined variable called "perseveration" into a conclusion that Jews displayed "significantly higher disposition rigidity," which, despite high levels of intelligence, ac-counted for their interest in the humanities rather than the more Nordic fields of science and engineering, and their attraction to "emotional and revealed religions" rather than the more practical morality that appealed to the tough-minded Nordics. In 1946, outraged that no one else had pursued the role of disposition rigidity in "racial mental differences," even though he had published the initial work on this topic more than a decade earlier, Cattell suggested that other researchers were interested in science only for propaganda purposes.[7] Mere absence of disagreement with Cattell was insuf-ficient to establish one's scientific bona fides; others were required to pursue the topics that he considered important.

It was thus both ironic and puzzling that Cattell himself immediately dis-continued this line of research directed at identifying the specific traits that distinguished between two groups of approximately equal intelligence—the embodiment of what he had previously viewed as a central purpose of the social sciences. No doubt in his new position as director of the Laboratory of Personality Assessment and Group Behavior at the University of Illinois, Cattell was expected to engage in more basic science. Then, too, in the post-war scientific atmosphere in which an emphasis on the importance of culture and learning had replaced the notion of innate group characteristics as the prevailing explanatory framework for the diversity of human behavior, he must have realized that his own obsession with racial differences—and espe-cially those associated with the tripartite categorization of Europeans—was viewed as an anachronism by most of his professional colleagues, including, naturally, the editors of professional journals. But most probable of all is that

Cattell came to the conclusion that a more well-grounded delineation of the basic variables constituting the concept of personality was necessary before returning to the kind of judgments so important to human progress that he thought scientists should be making. Especially at a time when psychologists were conceptualizing personality as composed of a number of separate traits, it was important for any serious program of eugenic selection first to establish a comprehensive taxonomy in order to identify and then to measure the specific characteristics on which individuals might differ. In any event, in the late 1940s Cattell himself abandoned the line of research that he had just excoriated the rest of his discipline for not pursuing in favor of the factor analytic approach to defining the building blocks of personality, the endeavor resulting in the achievements for which he became justifiably well known.

This sudden cessation of studies of interracial differences was in no way a sign that Cattell had abandoned the ideology and the agenda that lay behind them. When, in the late 1940s, a number of prominent social psychologists began to apply the tools of their profession to the study of "racial prejudice," he was horrified, calling such attempts a "sad blot on the escutcheon of the social sciences." Cattell was especially disturbed to see that support for segregation was considered to be an indication of racial prejudice. "A prejudice by definition," he declared, "is an attitude which cannot be rationally defended," and Cattell saw nothing rationally indefensible about the need to keep races separated from each other.[8] It was the *study* of prejudice that constituted the real prejudice—"woefully unscientific bigotry," Cattell called such research.[9] Indeed, he insisted, "the very use of the term 'prejudice' as a scientific concept in connection with social attitudes should automatically disqualify the user as a social scientist." And as was often the case when others took positions that Cattell thought wrongheaded, he attacked personally those who wished to study prejudice, raising questions about their integrity. "Wholesale distortion is inevitable," he charged, when science was allowed into "the hands of tendentious men . . . incapable of being honest with themselves," and to prevent such misuses of his discipline he called for greater attention to the "characters as well as the intellectual capability of those who become professional social scientists."[10] In the next few years some of the most eminent names in American social science—Otto Klineberg, Jerome S. Bruner, David Krech, M. Brewster Smith, Kenneth Clark, Stuart Cook, Isidor Chein, and many others—lent their expertise to the NAACP's attempt to overturn segregated education in the cases leading to the *Brown* decision by testifying on the psychologically deleterious effects of prejudice and discrimination.[11] According to Cattell's reasoning, none of these researchers, a virtual who's who of social psychology at the time, was ethically fit to qualify as a social scientist.

The Birth of Beyondism

Whenever he complained of these misguided attempts to introduce what he considered false values into science, Cattell offered his own concept of "evolutionary ethics," first posited almost two decades earlier, as the proper relation between science and morality, one in which the latter was derived from the former by assessing the extent of a policy's contribution to evolutionary progress. In one such discussion, published in 1950, he referred to his system for the first time as the "Ethics of Beyond," with its implication of concern for the welfare of generations "beyond" the present, alluding to a book in preparation that would provide a "fuller and more systematic treatment of this science of morality."[12]

However, it would take more than two decades for this work to appear in print, by which time Cattell remained the only scientist who had been active during eugenics' ancien regime—the last link between the post–civil rights era and the days when much of the scientific establishment supported the concept of eugenics and prominent researchers were concerned about the genetic disharmonies caused by racial interbreeding. For that matter, he was one of only a handful of well-known contemporary scientists who still called himself a eugenicist—and possibly the only one in this group not viewed as a kook or an extremist. In 2001 a book intended to reestablish eugenics as a respectable, "essentially correct" concept observed that from 1970 until the end of the century, "eugenics had only four articulate supporters in the Western democracies: Robert Graham, William Shockley, Raymond Cattell, and Roger Pearson." Graham, the multimillionaire who publicly solicited contributions from brilliant donors to his Repository for Germinal Choice, was treated as a figure of ridicule by the press, who derisively renamed his project the "Nobel sperm bank."[13] Shockley, a Nobel laureate in physics for his invention (along with two colleagues) of the transistor, became interested in eugenics late in his life and was widely known for an artless campaign— dubbed by one journalist a "traveling carnival of racism"—to convince his fellow scientists and the public of blacks' intellectual inferiority; after the seventy-year-old Shockley announced that, on more than one occasion, he had made his own contribution to Graham's sperm bank, his public image changed from menacing to mocked.[14] And Pearson, a British-born anthropologist who founded and directed an institute in Washington, D.C., was a disciple of Hans F. K. Günther, the Reich's major authority on race, and had made a number of attempts to establish a Nazi international.[15] Cattell stood out as the only member of this group to enjoy mainstream credibility.

In 1972, just as he was leaving his position as head of the personality laboratory at the University of Illinois in order to direct the Institute for Research on Morality and Adjustment, an independent organization he had created in Colorado to integrate further his scientific research with his religious system, Cattell finally published *A New Morality from Science: Beyondism*, a 480-page prolix tome describing his religious thought in detail; fifteen years later *Beyondism: Religion from Science* provided some elaboration of Beyondist principles.[16] Together these two books constituted the most comprehensive statement of his sociomoral beliefs and their relation to social science. Despite the adjective in the title of the earlier volume, Beyondism showed no significant discontinuity from the "evolutionary ethics" of the 1930s. If anything, the intervening decades had made all the traditional approaches to morality more contemptible than ever to Cattell. "The notion of 'human rights'" was nothing more than "an instance of rigid, childish, subjective thinking,"[17] and other humanistic principles "such . . . as 'social justice and equality,' 'basic freedom' and 'human dignity,'" he dismissed as "whore phrases."[18] As always, conventional religion was the worst offender of all in his eyes, one of its "chief raisons détre [*sic*]" being the "succorance of failure." Religion's encouragement of compassion for all only produced an "indulgence of error" by prolonging the duration of genetic failures—both individuals and groups—which, "from the perspective of Beyondism," Cattell called "positively evil."[19] In contrast, in a religion based on evolution as the central purpose of humankind, "religious and scientific truth [would] be ultimately reducible to one truth . . . [obtained] by scientific discovery . . . therefore . . . developing morality *out* of science." Embodying this unified truth, Beyondism would define "the finest ways to spend our lives."[20]

Just as in Cattell's earlier works, the tenets of Beyondism specified not only what should be the goal of all human activity but also the method by which it was to be attained: evolutionary change, he maintained, occurred not so much through the operation of natural selection on individuals but on groups, that is, on races. Thus, "in the interest of evolution," he observed elsewhere, "if races did not exist, we . . . should have to invent them."[21] And because natural selection exerted its most important effects primarily on groups, the "central requirement of ethical life" for Cattell—the only way to ensure biological progress—was group competition, a process "in which some survive and some do not."[22] It was because none of the traditional sources of moral authority, from Jesus to Gandhi, recognized this essential principle that he rejected them all in favor of the apostle of social Darwinism, Herbert Spencer, whom Cattell described as the only "respectable philosopher recognizing the natural appearance of a 'code of amity' among citizens and a 'code of enmity' among groups."[23]

In this view, the individual person in the group was "like a cell in the human body," and the body had a soul—a racial temperament or group mind. A person's primary loyalties were to the other cells that composed this body and to the "organic unity" of body and soul—the racial group to which the individual belonged.[24] As a consequence it was appropriate—indeed, an obligation, informed by loyalty to the group—to display cooperation, unselfishness, and willingness to sacrifice for other members of one's own group; to treat members of other groups with such consideration, however, was not only unnecessary but "dangerously wrong" and to be "unquestionably . . . regarded as a 'heresy' from a Beyondist standpoint." Yet this concern exclusively for the welfare of one's own racial group did not preclude a sense of "brotherhood" with the rest of humanity, though not one informed by the erroneous belief that all people are the same. Instead, Beyondism's version of "brotherhood" was predicated not merely on the recognition of racial differences but on the necessity of their preservation—on the requirement that "all men cooperate to sustain and produce such differences, and give their lives to testing their validities."[25] Indeed, Cattell maintained, those who were reluctant to recognize and investigate racial differences—"ignoracists," he called them—were the real threat to progress, far more dangerous than "racists," the "misguided person[s]" who assumed without proof that their own group was superior to others.[26]

Thus, as Cattell had argued decades earlier, a devotion to "the common glory of evolutionary endeavor" was the true expression of "love" for all humankind, one that appreciated the role of group competition as "an indispensable tool for progress," even if it had to occur through war.[27] But whether the rivalry was peaceful or violent, the Beyondist welcomed it with the attitude best expressed by Henry Newbolt in a poem Cattell quoted in many of his discussions of religion:

> To set the cause above renown
> To love the game beyond the prize.
> To honour while you strike him down
> The foe that comes with fearless eyes.[28]

Thus, in addition to group loyalty, everyone had an "ethical obligation to the Evolutionary Principle in the universe itself." It was the devotion to this principle of evolutionary progress through group competition that Cattell recognized as the Beyondist equivalent of "God."[29]

"The Musical Beat from the Jungle"

Although, as his earlier writing had done, this religious framework again provided a justification for strict racial separation, much of the accompanying discussion was phrased more euphemistically; it was unlikely that Cattell's views had changed, but in a more politically correct era, apparently he felt compelled to make a modest accommodation to the changed zeitgeist. In 1932, for example, he had pointed to the "'warring heredities' and unstable temperaments of half breeds" as one reason for the alarming extent of criminality in the United States.[30] More than half a century later, in only slightly less inflammatory language, he referred to the "hideously wrong inscription on the idol in New York Harbor" and went on to describe the behavioral consequences of interbreeding with immigrants from different racial backgrounds.

> In the U.S.A., praises are traditionally sung to the Melting Pot, but the first requirement in successful plant hybridization is a rejection of perhaps 90% of the hybrids as unsuccessful. As in the case of the foundry, the scoria produced must be removed from the melting pot if the remaining produce is to be above the average of the contributors. The appearance of unfortunate combinations goes on naturally, and this, rather than the sociologists' wild western frontier, is very likely partly responsible for the higher crime and insanity rates in the U.S.A. than in the parent countries.[31]

Despite the veneer of science suggested by the reference to plant biology and the metallurgical metaphor, there was no doubt about the meaning: at the dawn of the genomics era, when the richness of Tiger Woods's racial mosaic was viewed as a cause for celebration rather than concern, a prominent scientist still maintained that racial interbreeding caused criminal behavior and insanity in the offspring—a belief for which there was not an iota of evidence.

The fear of harmful consequences from *some* interbreeding did not mean that Cattell remained opposed to all racial mixture. With what he called proper "genetic management," it was possible to make "effective progress ... by the path of hybridization" but only under certain highly controlled conditions. First, there had to be a "shrewd choice of the second race" to ensure that it had the appropriate properties; then "an unfettered exercise of the right of self-determination in terms of knowing when firmly to put the lid on, and let the melting pot boil, i.e., to begin the second phase ... in which the best is to be 'brewed' from the mixture"; and, finally, the "institution of an effective within-group eugenic selection program to screen out the many defective combinations."[32] The lack of any explanatory detail, such as the definition of a "defective combination" or the process by which it would be "screen[ed] out," made this proposal sound all the more ominous—the mad scientist remaking humanity according to his own design, combined with the power of the state. Adding to this image, at the same time Cattell also argued that it was imperative for humans to "diverge into several distinct non-interbreeding species." Although he acknowledged that such divergence appeared improbable in an increasingly interconnected world, he thought it could occur either through the establishment of space colonies living in isolation for some centuries or from "'genetic engineering,'" in which some groups chose to follow "Beyondist ideals" under the supervision of "federal world government." In fact, Cattell claimed that "*relative* sterility—the forerunner of interspecies infertility" already existed between "distant racial types," although he offered no specific example.[33]

But even if races whose mixture would be genetically unproductive were kept from interbreeding, the presence of different races in the same nation or society still produced the threat of racial "parasitism" that Cattell had warned of in the 1930s, a time when his chief concern of this sort was the disruptive "Jewish . . . practice of living in other nations" in Europe.[34] When Beyondism first appeared four decades later, however, he had been a longtime resident of the United States, which was becoming more and more multicultural. Although Cattell now mentioned no group by name, his description of parasitism left little doubt exactly what race he had in mind as the new source of the problem. As a hypothetical example, he suggested,

> Let us take a case where one type has genes more favorable to high intelligence and the other to resistance to malaria. A society composed of the first type might succeed as a society by virtue of its gifts of intelligence (and malaria deaths need not reduce the total population, granted an appropriate birth rate). On mixing the two, however (in a malarial environment) the differential in immunity endowment to malaria would result in the intelligent maintainers of the culture being completely replaced by lower intelligences.[35]

Lest anyone missed the implication—unaware that the gene for sickle cell anemia, carried by many people of African origin, also conveys immunity to malaria[36]—Cattell immediately followed this example with another one just as pointed: "Or again, in a welfare society," he wrote, "any tendency of a group to a birth rate less controlled by social standards—and this normally happens with the less intelligent and the less temperamentally foresighted—will result in that genetic sub-group inheriting the society." Supported by its "cultural momentum," such a society might continue for a while, he predicted, "but eventually just like a great ceiling beam, which is eaten from within by death watch beetles and no longer what it appears to be, it crashes and has to be replaced." To avert such catastrophes, there had to be "a regular cost-accounting for parasitisms, cultural and genetic."[37] The insinuation of the effect of blacks on U.S. society could not have been clearer. Less well defined, though certainly sinister sounding, was the unspecified action—the "cost-accounting"—that Cattell thought should be taken in response to this effect.

The important point for Cattell was always to ensure that the consequences of culture—the costs and benefits—were not separated from their genetic origins. Underlying this view was the assumption that culture was a manifestation of, and therefore essentially indistinguishable from, race; in fact, he often referred to the units of evolutionary selection as "racio-cultural" groups.[38] As a consequence of this linkage, a culture could not be imposed, willy-nilly, onto a race genetically unsuited for it. Naturally, Cattell viewed intellectual ability as the most important consideration in an appropriate pairing, since the culture developed by a superior group could not be adopted successfully by a race of lesser talents. As a specific example of this problem in 1937, he had bluntly observed that all the cultural advances that "have been sedulously grafted upon the negro have been forcefully adapted by him, made more simple and crude and emotional," demonstrating that "lower mental capacity means reaction, crudity and . . . social deadweight."[39] Half a century later, he expressed an almost identical sentiment but with much less candor and without reference to any particular group. For natural selection to be most effective, "it would be desirable," Cattell now wrote, to avoid an "'unlucky' tie-up of, say a good culture with a poor race." In such a mismatched attempt to apply "a complex and exacting culture to a race to whom it is not particularly suitable in virtue of their average mental capacity," he elaborated, "we may expect the memory storage to be inadequate to the program and certain subroutines to be missing, so that only a fragmentary imitation of the original program is possible," necessarily resulting in a "partial deformation" in the "borrowed culture."[40]

Although intellectual ability was the *primary* consideration, it was not the *only* factor in determining the culture genetically appropriate for a particular race. Again, throughout Cattell's professional life this principle had remained unchanged in substance though moderated somewhat in expression. In 1933 he had railed against the "race-slumpers," who failed to appreciate that culture and race were inseparable—not just intellectual capacity but also "temperament, . . . way of thinking, . . . and ideals in art and life"—and, as a consequence, mistakenly believed that it was possible to treat "alien individuals as

if they belonged to the same race" simply because they were of equal intelligence.[41] In 1972 Cattell offered a slightly more subtle version, warning of the
dangers of "culture borrowing" and in particular that "the musical beat of the
jungle, or even the mood of the literature of Dostoyevsky, [could] introduce
incompatible elements in . . . Anglo-Saxon culture." And fifteen years later
Cattell still complained about the "'racial and cultural slumping' [advocated
by] self-styled progressive social movements" but neglected to explain what
he meant by the term. At the same time he warned that a "borrowed" cultural
element could "prove indigestible, functionally inconsistent and disruptive
of the existing pattern in the borrower."[42] Of course, this assumption at the
core of Beyondism that culture was a derivative of race would make non-
Anglo-Saxons in the United States the eternal other, destined to remain aliens
no matter how many generations they had been citizens or how deep their
commitment to what are commonly considered American values.

Scientific Improvement within Groups

In the process of interracial competition demanded by Beyondism, each
group was obliged to apply eugenic measures vigorously within its own ranks;
the failure to do so would place it at a severe competitive disadvantage. In
addition to the careful management of any interbreeding with other racial
groups, this concern for quality within ranks meant the avoidance of any mis-
placed humanitarian assistance, which would only "weaken [a group] in the
long run . . . by aid[ing] the survival of the weak at the expense of the strong."
Although he cited no studies, Cattell claimed that "psycho-social research"
had demonstrated that the "poor" were not "downtrodden" but occupied a
social level commensurate with their "inherent properties," much as "an oil
level separates out from a shaken mixture of oil and water."[43] If their poverty
was merely an appropriate social reflection of their genetic worth, then the
poor did not need financial assistance as much as they needed birth control to
avoid burdening the group with yet another generation of incompetents.

As another method for within-group improvement, Cattell wished to
exploit advances in science and genetic technology, both those that had
already occurred and those he anticipated in the future. His evolutionary
ethics of 1933 had described a plan in which each racial group would determine for itself which traits to develop—anatomical or psychological—most
likely through selective breeding. Four decades later, again sounding like the
caricature of a mad scientist, he expected that it would soon be possible to
pursue the same end through "a scientifically controlled increase in mutation
rate." Acknowledging, however, that for every favorable mutation there could

be a thousand that were unfavorable, he found a scientific solution for this problem also: medical technology had advanced to the point where it was able to recognize "genetic failures of certain kinds in utero," which meant that "the majority of the undesirable mutations could be caught shortly after conception, and aborted." This "monitoring of gestations" would be concerned with eliminating not simply "physical defect and physiological abnormality but also neurological deviation incompatible with a healthy social life."[44]

The selection of spouses was yet another decision that Cattell believed could benefit from scientific expertise. He worried that physical attraction had become "a backward eddy in the stream of natural selection," resulting, as it now did, in a sexual preference for "broad shouldered and heavily jawed men, and women with extensive fore and aft projections"—traits that were hardly conducive to evolutionary progress in the modern stage of human development. Indeed, noting that "a desirable birth rate . . . scarcely demands a sexual activity of perhaps 50 years," Cattell called for the eventual development of an "antiaphrodisiac," which would allow couples to form a stable long-term bond by focusing not on sexual pleasure but on "congenial temperaments and common purposes." Though conceding that there was some good in allowing the present generation to determine its descendants "through marriage choice," nevertheless, he speculated, this sort of eugenic selection by the average person might be "less beneficial than the directions that social scientists work out," undistracted by irrelevant corporeal considerations.[45]

The most important area in need of immediate scientific assistance within a group, however, was how to contend with the large number of the less intelligent that Cattell insisted were swamping every society. His earlier predictions of a one-point decline in IQ per decade in England had been disconfirmed. In addition, beginning in 1984 a series of studies had provided a wealth of evidence for what is now one of the most firmly established results in psychology: the "Flynn effect," named after the New Zealand political scientist James R. Flynn, who first demonstrated that, in every country for which data were available, there had been "massive gains" in IQ scores over time, the different increases averaging about fifteen points, or one standard deviation, per generation.[46] Nevertheless, in characteristically alarmist language Cattell continued to see intellectual deterioration occurring on an unprecedented scale throughout the twentieth century—"the worst backslide in human quality in ten thousand years," not merely halting the process of natural selection but shifting it "into reverse gear," thereby multiplying the ranks of the incompetent and nonproductive.[47]

One of the major consequences of this proliferation of the unfit was yet another form of parasitism, in which Cattell saw the talents of managers and inventors being exploited by the "less gifted" proletariat, whose use of the franchise to encroach on the prerogatives of their genetic superiors constituted what he called "robbery . . . by the ballot box." This was "an injustice and an unethical procedure," he declared, exerting a deleterious effect on "the survival potential of the society as a whole." Democracy, in his view, may have been a "tool of freedom" in some earlier, more primitive era, but it was now in need of "radical improvement" to correct its "maladaptations to a more complex scientific society" and make the voting process consistent with "a Beyondist set of evolutionary values." Cattell offered a number of suggestions for accomplishing this goal. One recommendation was to reduce the electorate to some 60 to 75 percent of its present size[48] by establishing educational and intellectual criteria—"historical knowledge adequate to the issue" and an IQ greater than 90,[49] the latter requirement disenfranchising the majority of the black population in the United States, whose average IQ score is estimated to be in the high 80s in most studies. Another proposal was to restrict the ballot only to taxpayers, a measure that Cattell estimated would eliminate some 10 percent of the population from eligibility.[50]

A final possibility for reconciling democracy with evolutionary progress was some sort of "explicit weighting of the votes of individuals according to their intelligence, sanity, and education." This approach would address the inequality between voters that Cattell illustrated with two "personal acquaintances." The first was a famous "classics professor . . . with a deep grasp of the political and social wisdom of the ages"; the second was "an ordinary person who did some gardening" for Cattell. Despite the obvious differences in their intelligence, the present practice of democracy, he observed, would allow the latter's opinion "to completely cancel" the former's "long-sighted contribution to the community," and a society that granted "equal voting powers to individuals so disparate" could not survive, Cattell claimed. In all likelihood, the classics professor he had in mind in this example was Revilo P. Oliver, a friend and colleague at the University of Illinois, whom Cattell thanked in the preface to his 1987 book for "improvements and clarifications" in his thinking about Beyondism. One of the most prolific and erudite American adherents to Nazi ideology, Oliver was a virulent Jew hater who hoped that if the Aryan race eventually "recovers its lost vigor and ascendancy, a future religion may recognize Adolf Hitler as a semi-divine figure."[51] In Cattell's example the Beyondist improvement of democracy would grant systematically greater influence to a Nazi intellectual than to a less intelligent "ordinary person" who earned a living with his hands.

Thus, although the principles of Beyondism had not changed substantially from Cattell's evolutionary ethics in the 1930s, the proposals were much more specific. Between monitoring gestations, informing marriage choices, and eliminating the flaws in democracy, Beyondist science would play a significant role in determining who was born, who mated with whom, and who was appropriately equipped to exercise the franchise.

Successes and Failures

Because the central principle of Beyondism was intergroup competition as the mechanism for evolutionary progress, the purpose of within-group eugenic improvements of all kinds was not merely to enhance a racio-cultural group's quality of life but to increase its probability of being judged "successful" by what Cattell envisioned as a "central clearing house," created under the aegis of a "world federal government," to oversee the process of racial comparison.[52] A system of coordinated research institutes, composed of "the finest brains science can produce," would assist individual societies by collecting the kind of data that could reveal which specific policies "contribute maximally to evolution at each point in the history of a society and under each condition of the social and physical environment," thus enabling a group to translate findings into ethical principles and make "readjustments in faulty directions of progress."[53] Through such careful, scientific assessment it would also be possible "to measure the signs of health or sickness of a society so that a graduated 'probable survival index' can be assigned." A low value on this index would not only eliminate "the need to wait on complete collapse" but, by providing the opportunity to study "a misconceived racio-cultural experiment as it demonstrates its failure," could lead to greater understanding of the laws and principles of evolutionary advancement.[54] Although such a "World Research Institute" would begin by analyzing the data from already existing groups, Cattell believed that it should eventually "move from passively recording and analyzing to advising and creatively designing." In other words, as he had recommended in the 1930s, scientists would "manipulate" societies, matching different racial groups to various cultures in a "factorial experiment" to find the most suitable "culturo-genetic combinations."[55] Cattell thought that UNESCO might be the starting point for such an organization, but only if it first abandoned its misguided "'social work' values," exemplified by "free food distribution and other acts that need revision by Beyondist principles."[56]

Once such a research enterprise had made a proper accounting, however, Cattell saw no reason to postpone the inevitable. As morality was brought "increasingly . . . into the area of science," he wrote,

so does tolerance in the moral field become increasingly pointless and undesirable. . . . In goodness, as in truth, if the right answer is known with greater
certainty, there is good reason to apply it with greater rigor. There is no virtue in
tolerating known evil. And failure to apply moral laws with a degree of authority
proportional to their certainty is as debilitating to the social organism as would
be failure of the body to obey the psysiological [sic] laws of its functioning.[57]

Since evolution took place through natural selection among competing
groups, there was no doubt how such moral certainty was to be translated
into action: "Failing groups should either be allowed to go to the wall, or be
radically re-constituted, possibly by outside intervention. By contrast, successful groups, by simple expansion or budding, should increase their power,
influence and size of population."[58]

Nor was a failing group to enjoy any assistance in its struggle either with
another group or with nature. Any "external 'charitable' support from other
groups, or even their failure to expand as the defective group retracts," was
considered by Beyondist religious principles to be "immoral acts militating
against evolution"; such responses only reinforced the strength of the faulty
culture, or, "if the defect is genetic, they postpone the reduction of genetic
defect." According to this scientifically derived moral code, instead of stag-
ing concerts to feed starving peoples in African countries—the sort of act
Cattell considered a "pernicious and evil interruption of group evolution"[59]—
dominant racial groups in the United States and Western Europe should be
preparing to confiscate their land and preside over their extinction.

Similarly forbidden by Beyondism was "culture borrowing," in which one
group was assisted by inventions or advances developed by another, a practice
that again only separated rewards from their genetic origins, thus confusing
the process of natural selection between groups. Indeed, despite all his praise
for scientists Cattell complained that they failed to appreciate the need for
"national restriction of discoveries."[60] In this view, a society whose scientists
had developed a cure for a deadly disease was to keep it to itself, lest it save
the lives of persons in a different, competing group, one not entitled to benefit
from an advance that its own members had been unable to discover.

Beyondism thus required the steady elimination of failing races, an essential process if the earth was "not to be choked with . . . more primitive
forerunners." The decision that a group was due for extinction was not to
be taken lightly, Cattell acknowledged, but the more advanced races could
not be realistically expected to continue to allow substantial space to be
set aside for "museum 'storage.'" The "maintenance of the status quo," he
declared, could not tolerate "making ninety-nine hundredths of the earth

a living museum." But there was no reason, Cattell emphasized, that in an enlightened era this goal could not be attained through "newer and more humane methods," avoiding the brutality with which extinction had been carried out in the past. Instead of the term *genocide,* which he wanted to reserve only for "a literal killing off" of all the members of a group, Cattell proposed the neologism *genthanasia,* for the more sensitive process of "phasing out" a "moribund culture . . . by educational and birth control measures, without a single member dying before his time."[61]

Beyondism was obviously not a religion that could be practiced by an individual in isolation; to be meaningful it needed not just a congregation but an entire society. However, much to Cattell's frustration, none of the traditional sources of cultural influence showed any inclination toward the kind of scientific values that were necessary for Beyondism to be accepted on a widespread basis. Literature and the arts he judged at present no better than "revealed religion," similarly based on intuition rather than investigation and capable only of empty posturing; authors such as Tolstoy, Dickens, Shaw, Orwell, and others lacked "any marshalling of scientific evidence" and, as a consequence, produced only what Cattell called "obviously emotionally biased, nonsensical fabrication." (Interestingly, among contemporary authors, only a few science fiction writers, one nonfiction science writer—Paul De Kruif—and the creators of *Star Trek* met with Cattell's approval.) For the arts to have any real significance, they too had to be informed by the "human evolutionary purpose," revealing to the public all the "consolations, insights and emotional convictions appropriate to founding moral values on the broad developments of biological and social science"—that is, they had to promote Beyondism. The press, including both print and television journalism, was another institution unaware of scientifically based moral values, and Cattell saw ample justification for a "national censoring authority" that, in the name of "democratic 'quality' controls," would impose some restraints on what could be published or reported.[62]

Unable to "offer the reliably-checked inferences . . . [of] a scientifically-based Beyondism," all these cultural influences in the United States had become more burden than benefit, in Cattell's opinion, out of touch with the spiritual needs of their time and hence contributing nothing to the survival of their racio-cultural group. There was no separate truth of the heart; only science could provide the foundation for a set of moral values in harmony with the process of evolution. But not just any branch: it was biology and the social sciences—the disciplines that studied human beings and their behavior—that could inform a religion consistent with the true purpose of life. And most important among the social sciences was psychology, whose potential for rescuing morality from its illegitimate involvement with the humanities had lured Cattell away from the chemistry lab half a century earlier. In particular, his special field of expertise, the application of complex statistical techniques for defining and measuring the most important characteristics of individuals and groups, could provide the methodology necessary to assess evolutionary progress and to determine which outcomes were "successes" and which "failures." This is not to say that Cattell was not interested in basic science but rather that his interest, especially in mathematically sophisticated techniques of measurement, was, to a large extent, informed by the role he foresaw advances in this field playing in implementation of the Beyondist agenda. The decomposition of personality into its constituent elements, the development of methods for their assessment, the estimation of the degree to which each of these elements was heritable, the specification of the most important variables for characterizing and evaluating societies— these goals of Cattell's research program were all essential preliminary steps in the journey toward the final destination: the scientific measurement and evaluation of the characteristics of individuals and groups necessary to Beyondism's unforgiving judgments. Mathematics, Cattell observed, had been considered the "queen of the sciences, and as in other complex sciences it is going to have as great a role to play in connection with the new science of morality. But if Beyondism is aptly so called, then this new science, with its rugged experimental problems, its supreme importance for human life, and its central integration of all sciences, may well be called the king of the sciences."[63] Cattell's own scientific efforts were intended throughout his career to contribute to this royal endeavor.

Cattell and the Far Right

Although Cattell occasionally alluded to the concept of Beyondism in his journal articles, it was typically in a cursory, tangential observation, an afterthought to the main point of the publication;[64] it is doubtful that a mainstream social science journal would have had much interest in accepting a submission devoted entirely to the necessity of intergroup competition as a moral postulate, much less a proposal to use psychological data to determine the winners and losers. In the late 1970s, however, a few years after his retirement from the University of Illinois, he began an association with an obscure anthropological journal, as both a board member and a frequent contributor, that was eager to provide an outlet for Cattell's social ideology. Known primarily for its history of support for racial segregation and white supremacy, the *Mankind Quarterly* had been founded in 1960 in Scotland with financial backing from Wickliffe Preston Draper, an American multimillionaire with Nazi sympathies, who had previously funded a campaign by a Klansman to repatriate all blacks in the United States back to Africa.[65] Fifteen years after the fall of the Nazi regime, the journal had brought together racist intellectuals from both sides of the Atlantic, reflecting its twin emphases on restoration of the ideology of *Rassenhygiene*, which had informed racial policy in the Reich, and opposition to the growing movement to grant blacks their long-denied constitutional equality. Indeed, whether European or American, all the participants in the journal's establishment viewed the southern struggle to preserve its way of life as part of a larger movement for white supremacy, seeking to keep blacks segregated and powerless not just in the southern United States but also in South Africa and what was then called Rhodesia, now Zimbabwe. The purpose of the journal, acknowledged its first editor in chief candidly, "was to provide our small group with the opportunity of being published," especially because "our views" were no longer being tolerated in other outlets.[66]

The *Quarterly*'s staff was a clear indication of the journal's point of view. Editor in chief Robert Gayre had been a disciple of Hans F. K. Günther, the leading Nazi anthropologist, and boasted of his own prewar acquaintance with the great German "expert."[67] One associate editor was a British geneticist who had contributed to the Nazi literature on racial hygiene and had been cited in the 1930s as the scientific authority for "biology's warning against intermarriage between Jews and those of Germanic . . . race."[68] The other associate editor, an American psychologist, was one of the expert witnesses in the legal attempt to reverse the *Brown* decision on the basis of scientific testimony—supplied almost entirely by members of the journal's advisory board—that blacks were intellectually inferior; in private correspondence he suggested that "our best bet" to prevent integrated education was to "make the white schools so unpleasant for them that the Negroes withdraw."[69] He also authored articles calling blacks the descendants of "savages in an African jungle,"[70] unfit for association with whites, and warning that the real goal of the civil rights movement was to weaken white society through "widespread amalgamation."[71]

Under such leadership the *Quarterly* churned out a steady stream of justifications for racism. One article explained that racism was an "instinctive feeling . . . rooted in man's nature" and serving "a biological function." Thus, the presence of "different races . . . in the same community . . . automatically provoked" hostility because "each group is endangering the genetic integrity of the other"; in the South, for example, "whites tend to go berserk against

... negroes ... suspected of physical relations with Caucasoid women." The only solution, the author concluded, was to prevent the establishment of any multiracial community in the future and to resolve "existing communities ... into separate societies on a racial basis." Another article proposed restricting the participation of blacks in the polity because it was "obvious that the Negro in the United States is ... inferior" and "even if ... of adequate intelligence ... may be temperamentally unsuited for citizenship." And in the journal's book review section, every demeaningly essentialist portrayal of non–western Europeans received accolades. One book warmly praised in the *Quarterly* argued that "Easterners"—a term encompassing Asians, Indians, Turks, Arabs, and Jews—might be capable of copying what western Europeans had originated, but "under the skin" these groups were all "alien to constitutional government, the study of biology, the motorcar, or the Universal Declaration of Human Rights" and as a consequence had "contributed nothing to our modern world, not even a single idea." The "Western Jew" was characterized in this work as "a germ plasm which for its sustenance feeds on a basically alien soma." To absorb such inassimilable outsiders into "our institutions" was a "logical impossibility," according to the English author, who called for Britain to be "cleared of its multi-racial jungles, and be reconstituted as a homogeneous society." The journal's reviewer recommended that the book be read by everyone "in authority" wherever there were attempts to "mix" different races in the same community.[72]

In 1978 financial difficulties forced Gayre to relinquish editorship of the *Quarterly* after losing his suit against a critic who had called him a "racist"— which, under the British legal system, required him to pay more than fifty thousand dollars in court costs—and control of the journal was acquired by Roger Pearson, director of the Institute for the Study of Man, based in Washington, D.C.[73] The transfer of proprietorship produced little change in the publication's ideology. A Güntherist like his predecessor, the British-born Pearson regarded the Nazi anthropologist whose conclusions had informed Nazi racial policy as "one of the world's greatest names in the field of raciology" and attempted to publish new editions of Günther's work from the Nazi era at his own expense.[74] After an unsuccessful postwar attempt to form an international organization for former Third Reich officials as well as new adherents to Nazi thought, Pearson emigrated to the United States, where he engaged in a number of publishing ventures under various pseudonyms. As "Edward Langford," he coedited *Western Destiny*, dedicated to the view that the racial foundation of Western civilization was under systematic attack by Jewish "Culture Distorters," anxious to "destroy race ... consciousness" among white youth by peddling cultural debasement and moral degenera-cy.[75] Then, as "Stephen Langton," he edited and published the *New Patriot,* a periodical espousing an interpretation of the Second World War, in which *Germans* had been the victims of a genocidal attempt by Jews who had de-manded their complete "extermination."[76]

Pearson's scientific writing had much in common with Cattell's. In an observation similar to Cattell's concern with parasitism, early in his career Pearson had written that if a group with "a superior set of genes mingles with . . . an inferior tribe, then it commits racial suicide, and destroys the work of thousands of years of biological isolation and natural selection."[77] As editor of the *Quarterly,* he wrote and published what was essentially the same article five times between 1978 and 1995—once under his own name, the other four times under a pseudonym—arguing that society no longer ap-preciated the "evolutionary purpose of 'race prejudice.'"[78] Often in identical language, each of these articles declared that racial prejudice was a biological necessity essential to evolutionary development, leading "healthy-minded people . . . to maintain . . . reproductive distance" from other races in order to "maintain the integrity of the gene pool." Declaring that the tendency to "distrust and repel" members of other races was "one of the main pillars on which civilization was built," Pearson feared that this natural reaction was "weakening under the pressure of human ideologies which are antithetical to biological realities," resulting in "distorted human beings," who exhib-ited such "perversions" as "interracial sexual experimentation," much like animals inappropriately attempting to "mate with animals of other breeds." Contemporary appreciation of these biological imperatives had so deterio-rated, Pearson noted with outrage, that acts of racial prejudice had come to be considered, erroneously, as "immoral" or—worse yet—"hate crimes."[79]

An Outlet for Beyondism

Soon after Pearson took the helm, the *Mankind Quarterly* announced its re-organized Editorial Advisory Board, which now included Cattell. Before his involvement with the journal, the board was composed primarily of obscure academics, and its few well-recognized members were known primarily for their opposition to civil rights or support for National Socialism. The addi-tion of Cattell's name to the masthead was thus something of a coup for the *Quarterly,* his own prominence conferring a modicum of academic respect-ability on a publication that had served largely as a platform for the opinions of unabashed white supremacists and neo-Nazis. In return, as it were, Cattell now had an outlet for a stream of articles unlikely to be acceptable in mainstream professional journals despite his prestige. For example, in an article titled "Virtue in 'Racism'?" he offered an analysis similar to Pearson's, arguing that racism was an innate "evolutionary force—a tendency to like the like and distrust the different" that in most cases had to be respected as "a virtuous gift"; the mere fact that society "has had to battle racism" was for Cattell "sufficient evidence that an innate drive exists." And rather than regarding such a natural inclination as a "perversion," the appropriate response to racism, in his opinion, was "to shape society to adjust to it," no doubt by keeping groups separate from each other. Among academic publications late in the twentieth century, only the *Mankind Quarterly* was likely to welcome such an interpretation. In another article in the *Quarterly*, Cattell analyzed the relationship between blood types and personality traits, the former variable possibly suggesting a link to race, which some scientists have attempted to define in part according to the frequency of different blood groups. This analysis was quite similar to one he had previously published in the *American Journal of Human Genetics* sixteen years earlier only to have it ridiculed by two experts in the next issue. In extraordinary language for a scientific journal, Alexander Wiener, codiscoverer of the Rh factor, had called Cattell's study a "waste" of journal space, finding some "consolation" in the fact that "the article is probably harmless, because few readers will take it seriously." In addition, a specialist in the statistical technique used in the study had called the analysis "incorrect" and concluded that "the 'results'... should be ignored."[80] In the *Quarterly*, however, Cattell found a much friendlier venue for an almost identical study, secure in the knowledge that Pearson would not allow the work of the chief proponent of evolutionary morality to be savaged.

In a particularly bizarre incident, a paper titled "Some Changes in Social Life in a Community with a Falling Intelligence Quotient"—originally published by Cattell in 1938, based on the study of children's intelligence in England that he had conducted as a British Eugenics Society research fellow—was reprinted in the *Quarterly* in 1991 with no mention of its actual provenance. A footnote explained that the article was "condensed" from a paper that had appeared in a 1983 collection edited by Cattell and published by Pearson's Institute for the Study of Man; a version of the 1938 paper had appeared in that volume also.[81] In fact, the article in the *Quarterly* was identical to the original 1938 publication with the exception of some minor changes, no doubt made by Pearson, eliminating the reference section as well as any other indication that the social and cultural decline described by the paper and "the present study" on which it was putatively based was actually more than half a century old or that other "recent research" cited in the paper had been published six decades earlier, in 1932.[82]

But for Cattell the most important function of his association with the *Quarterly* was the opportunity to spread the gospel of Beyondism to an audience that was likely to be sympathetic. Indeed, his first publication in the journal, appearing in the issue just before he was formally named to its board, presented a summary of his thinking about Beyondism, once again insisting that science had to be the source of religious values. To a readership hardly in need of being persuaded that some racial groups were superior to others, he explained the need for a "mechanism for expansion of successful cultures and retraction of moribund societies," defending colonialism and imperialism as ways of promoting natural selection by ensuring greater resources to those races that "make a better adjustment to the natural world." As always it was to be left to scientists to determine what constituted a better adjustment and who had made it. But once science had arrived at its evaluation, both individuals and races found wanting would have to accept that they "have been anvil and not hammer" in the shaping of the future, a metaphor Cattell repeated verbatim from *Psychology and Social Progress* in 1933. As an inevitable step in the evolutionary process, races as well as individuals were "born to die," he told the readers of a journal that had led the scientific opposition to civil rights, and to make room for their more capable successors, "genocide, like individual death, is the only way of clearing space."[83]

It was also in the *Quarterly* where Cattell returned to the Beyondist implications of his work on "syntality"—the equivalent in a group of personality in the individual and in many ways the reconceptualization of his mentor McDougall's concept of the group mind. More important, syntality represented the beginning of an attempt to define and measure the specific variables that would allow a scientific determination of the degree of "adjustment," the criterion on which a group's prospects for survival and expansion was to depend. In his original discussion of syntality in 1948, Cattell had emphasized the need to eliminate "harmful" group behaviors in order to prevent "failure." For example, he noted, "a group which tolerates parasitic subgroups fails," as did "a group which errs in establishing correct orders of loyalty." Almost two decades later in a mainstream journal he offered the first hints at a syntal dimension significantly related to a group's success or failure: a factor interpreted as a "*morality* contribution to morale" with loadings from such variables as the society's syphilis death rate, alcoholic death rate, homicide rate, and proportion of illegitimate births (a high weighting on each of these variables obviously indicating low morality). Applying this result to data then available, Cattell concluded that Brazil, Burma, the Dominican Republic, Mexico, and Portugal were the nations that most fit the "syndrome of low morale, immorality, and denial of responsibility," whereas Denmark,

Iceland, Israel, and Sweden were at the other end of the spectrum. Though Cattell refrained from pointing it out at the time, in a world organized along Beyondist principles, presumably the latter societies would be entitled to expand at the expense of the former.[84]

Lacking the grant support for this work that he enjoyed for most of his research, Cattell had to postpone further studies on syntality until well after retirement from Illinois, when he was "rescued" with financial assistance from the Foundation for the Advancement of Man, established by Robert Graham, whose sperm bank he had helped to launch.[85] Upon resuming his study of syntality, Cattell arrived at a more specific conclusion in the *Quarterly*, finding that there were four main dimensions—level of technological development, affluence, morality-morale, and cultural creativity—all of which were to a large degree manifestations of the underlying racial level of intelligence. Given this relationship between intelligence and the first of these dimensions—development—in particular, "the practical politician," wrote Cattell, "will have to face the fact that, despite full cultural communication, some countries are likely to remain undeveloped."[86] Again as Beyondism had made clear, very specific treatment was to be accorded to backward groups with little hope of catching up to the more advanced races.

More than a decade later, this line of research, and in many ways Cattell's larger scientific agenda, culminated in a book, published by Pearson's Institute for the Study of Man as a Mankind Quarterly Monograph and bluntly titled *How Good Is Your Country? What You Should Know*, his most detailed and ambitious treatment of the relation between personality, syntality, and group selection. In the preface Cattell thanked "Dr. William Andrews," one of Pearson's many pseudonyms, for his assistance in preparing the manuscript for the printer; having already worked with Pearson and the *Quarterly* for some time, it is unlikely that Cattell was unaware of this ruse, the psychologist's willingness to cooperate with the editor's deception an indication that the two had more than a formal relationship.[87] As always in Cattell's discussions of Beyondism, *How Good Is Your Country?* emphasized the need to control compassion, especially in international affairs, and to prevent the alleviation of famine by "superficial 'do-gooders' who have no conception that failures will and should be tolerated." Just as he had described an individual's personality through a profile on sixteen basic factors, Cattell proposed to characterize nations by their "syntality profile" on nineteen similarly basic dimensions, the most important of which was now judged to be "cultural pressure"—a combination of creativity and progress that he called "the primary hope of mankind." Although the answer to the question in the title was to be determined by "an international research center," in which "doctors of social science" would conduct "the equivalent of a 'medical examination'" on entire nations, Cattell did not hesitate to speculate on the prospects of some countries right away. Grouping nations by the similarity of their profiles, for example, he concluded that the "New World Mediterranean" group in particular—composed of a number of South American, Central American, and Caribbean countries, along with the Philippines— showed "poor promise," rating low on factors of development, affluence, orderliness, and democratic maturity; this unpromising profile he attributed largely to the mixture of native and European populations that were "difficult to mend [*sic*] into a definite pattern." Another problem area was what Cattell called the "Balkan block," though "southeast European" might be a better designation for a group composed of Bulgaria, Romania, Hungary, and Czechoslovakia, the last two of which are not usually considered Balkan. These nations, whose "unstable governments" he had attributed in 1933 to the racially "mixed blood" of eastern Europeans, now rated low on factors of affluence, cultural pressure, and population control, which Cattell found to be indications of their "resistance . . . to civilization as we know it." Though he acknowledged that this study was merely "exploratory" and that its results needed "further verification," Cattell looked forward to "the day . . . that the State Department and the Foreign Office appl[ied] these findings—in lieu of guesswork" to international and national affairs.[88]

In examining the relationship between syntality and the probability of eventual success or failure, it was important to consider, Cattell noted, that the syntality profile for a group was in large part a function of the personality of its members; as McDougall had similarly argued, the group mind was a function of the (racial) characteristics of its constituent individuals. In administrations of the *Sixteen Personality Factor Questionnaire*, for example, the English scored systematically higher than other nationalities on introversion, Mexicans lower on intelligence and dominance, and Brazilians higher on "protension" (the tendency to blame others), and Cattell had no doubt that a nation's syntality was directly related to such characteristics of individuals. As a consequence, he thought it possible to trace "an objective path," in which personality traits could be used to predict syntality traits, which in turn could be used to predict the likelihood of a group's survival.[89] The entire project of defining and measuring the human personality thus found its ultimate raison d'être as the source of data to be used in the scientific determination of nations' futures.

Such a scenario was predicated necessarily on the willingness of a population to provide a wealth of personal information to researchers, whose conclusions might not be particularly salutary for the people being studied.

Cattell believed that the importance of such a context required "a new attitude to privacy," a form of freedom that he thought catered primarily to the needs of "the criminally and shadily-occupied." Researchers, he insisted, should have "complete access to data on financial, social, sexual and educational lives of citizens" as information that a person "owes his country," and the reluctance to comply with such demands he pronounced due to "surliness." After all, Cattell pointed out, "a truly private piece of behavior"—one with no implications for society—"does not exist."[90] Again, the needs of Beyondism were to take precedence over constitutional guarantees.

"Intellectual Comrades"

Nor was Roger Pearson the only extremist to whom Cattell had ties. The factor analyst's return in the 1970s to writing on his ethical system also brought with it a return to the marked affinity for the work of racists and anti-Semites that Cattell had displayed earlier in his career. His 1933 discussion of racial characteristics, especially among Europeans and Jews, relied heavily on the writing of Nazi ideologue Hans F. K. Günther—the same tracts that had been used to provide scientific justification for the regime's racial policies— and as authorities for his conclusion of Nordic racial superiority, Cattell also cited both Günther and Joseph-Arthur de Gobineau, the nineteenth- century French aristocrat whose ideas were revived and popularized in Nazi Germany as another intellectual rationalization for the Reich's emphasis on racial purity.[91] Insisting that differences in racial value determined the fate of civilizations, Gobineau had maintained that whites in general were superior to other races, but that the white subgroup of "Aryans" in particular—his term for Nordics—constituted the silver and gold threads in the human tapestry; this elite racial group, in Gobineau's analysis, had constituted the aristocracy throughout European countries, creating civilizations through their domi- nation of weaker peoples, which then declined when Aryans intermarried with their inferiors.[92] Although a eugenically based Nordicism was popular among some American intellectuals in the 1920s and it was not uncommon to see Gobineau and Günther cited as authorities in their writing, only Cattell adopted the latter's racial analysis of Jews, regularly referring to them, in the Nazi anthropologist's terminology, as the "Hither-Asiatic race."[93]

For his treatment of racial differences in religion, Cattell had turned to Mathilde Ludendorff as his source of expertise, citing what he called "her eloquent and powerful appeal for a return to the spirit of the Nordic God belief" in her 1928 book, *Deutscher Gottglaube*. One of the few women neu- rologists at the time and the wife of General Erich Ludendorff, an early Nazi figurehead who had taken part in Hitler's failed putsch of 1923, the metaphysically inclined Mathilde attempted to inject into the Nazi movement a pagan religious philosophy that, difficult though it may be to believe, was critical of Hitler for not being sufficiently anti-Semitic; according to *Beyond Eagle and Swastika,* political scientist Kurt P. Tauber's authoritative overview of German nationalism, both Ludendorffs were "fully convinced that Hitler had become merely the terror instrument of the Jews, the Freemasons, and the Jesuits," and, though finding much to praise in the führer's anti-Jewish boycotts, pogroms, and Nuremberg laws, they complained that "all these measures were far too slow in coming and not sufficiently rigorous in their application."[94] In the lengthy passage from *Deutscher Gottglaube* quoted in the original German with obvious approval by Cattell as an illustration of the religious differences between Jews and Nordics, Ludendorff described how the Semitic peoples humiliate themselves by groveling in the dust before their God as an indication of their so-called piety, in contrast to the Germans, who sense God within themselves, a realization that gives them pride, courage, confidence, and the determination never to dishonor this inner deity.[95]

Whereas Cattell's citation of such extremists as Günther and Gobineau was unfortunate but perhaps unsurprising in the context of the time, the lengthy anti-Semitic quotation from a fringe source that had never been translated into English suggested his intellectual engagement with an obscure literature even further from the scholarly mainstream than more traditional Nazi writers. To the extent that Mathilde Ludendorff was known at the time that Cattell adduced her work in support of his own, it was as a crank attempting to promote an even more irrational, radical variant of Nazi ideology, and *Deutscher Gottglaube* was in no way a contribution to the scholarly literature on religion but rather an artless polemic aimed at convincing the Nazi movement to adopt Ludendorff's neo-pagan religious beliefs as a central element of its ideology.

Half a century later in his development of Beyondism, Cattell again found ideological compatibility with the small handful of writers and academics still promoting segregationist and even National Socialist beliefs on race. Indeed, instead of merely citing their work as support for his own assertions, he now acknowledged the similarities between their thinking and his own, expressing gratitude for their "contributions that proved happily integrable into the Beyondist viewpoint."[96] Among others, this group of persons whose ideas had been integrated into Cattell's ethical system included two of the most prominent leaders of the attempt to stop the civil rights movement on the grounds that blacks were genetically inferior to whites in intelligence and thus not entitled to political equality. In the 1960s University of Georgia psychology professor R. Travis Osborne had been a star witness, testifying on racial differences in aptitude and achievement test scores in two legal cases brought by segregationists seeking to reverse the *Brown* decision; he later became a director of the Foundation for Human Understanding (FHU), an organization created and funded by activists for segregation, whose chief activity was the mass distribution, gratis, of literature on blacks' intellectual inferiority.[97] Carleton Putnam, though an attorney and businessman who had studied history and politics, led the scientific resistance to civil rights, claiming to speak on behalf of "a muzzled group of scientists." In a series of open letters, books, and pamphlets, all published and widely disseminated with funding from Wickliffe Draper, who had also supported Pearson's *Mankind Quarterly* and Osborne's FHU, Putnam argued that the courts and politicians had been hoodwinked into supporting political equality for blacks by a cabal of Jewish scientists intent on weakening white civilization by persuading the society that all races were equal in ability.[98] In one of the two books cited by Cattell as "integrable into the Beyondist viewpoint," Putnam declared that blacks in the pre-*Brown* era were victimized not by political oppression but by biology: "It is what he is that makes the average Negro a second class citizen, not segregation." In the other book Putnam opposed not only integration of the school system but also extension of the franchise to blacks, expressing his horror at the prospect of "inject[ing] into the bloodstream of the body politic, without any control whatever, a virus of Negro votes which . . . is absolutely certain to undermine our 'constitution.'"[99]

Other writers on Cattell's list of compatible thinkers espoused ideas even more directly rooted in Nazi ideology. Alain de Benoist, for example, was the editor of *Nouvelle Ecole,* a French version of the *Mankind Quarterly,* some half the latter's editorial staff, including Pearson, and a number of members of its advisory board serving on the former's Comité de Patronage; under the pseudonym Fabrice Laroche, Benoist had earlier been a contributing editor of *Western Destiny,* the neo-Nazi periodical coedited by Pearson under the name "Edward Langford" and officially devoted to protecting the white race from its sworn enemy, the Jewish "Culture Distorter." *Nouvelle Ecole* was the official publication of Groupement de Recherche et d'Etudes pour la Civilisation Européenne (Research and Study Group for European Civilization), whose French acronym, GRECE, formed a tributary pun on the homeland of Nordic culture. An organization dedicated to protecting Nordic purity from the usual threats, GRECE placed particular emphasis on pre-Christian societies in which Aryan aristocrats ruled over the inferior races.[100] According to Stanford professor of religion Thomas Sheehan, "The rosters of GRECE and *Nouvelle Ecole* read like a high-school reunion of old reactionaries and fascists." Invited to participate in a gathering of neo-Nazis from around the world organized by Pearson, the delegation from Benoist's group met with William Pierce, a former American Nazi Party functionary, who left to found yet another Nazi party, the National Alliance, and, under the name "Andrew MacDonald," authored *The Turner Diaries*, a fictional blueprint for race war that inspired Timothy McVeigh, who was convicted and executed for the bombing of a federal office building in Oklahoma City; as Pierce explained, the French organization was "working along lines very close to ours."[101]

In addition to citing their ideas as merely "integrable" with his own, Cattell expressed particular gratitude to some of these "intellectual comrades" for their specific contributions to the evolution of his thinking—the "improvements and clarifications" they had helped him to make over earlier versions of Beyondism. Specifically named among this group were three persons whose writing has been canonical in the modern Nazi movement: Roger Pearson, Revilo Oliver, and Wilmot Robertson. Through numerous articles in the *Mankind Quarterly* decrying interracial relationships as a "perversion" and a raft of similar publications emanating from his Institute for the Study of Man, Pearson had conducted a decades-long campaign for the United States to emulate the Nuremberg laws. And in private correspondence he blamed race mixing on Jews, bent on "the destruction of all potential rivals to the Jewish community in their apparent eagerness to obtain world power" and establish "rule over a vast subnormal mass of sub-humanity."[102] Oliver, Cattell's erudite colleague at the University of Illinois and a scholar of some distinction in his own field of classics, was a founder of the John Birch Society but had been forced to resign from that organization after referring to the "beatific vision" that could be realized on earth if only "all the Jews were vaporized at dawn tomorrow"; in his own account of his departure, Oliver declared that "the Society had become a Jewish auxiliary used to keep the *goyim* confused and docile." One of the chief intellectual authorities of the neo-Nazi movement, he was also an editorial adviser for the Institute for Historical Review, the center of Holocaust denial. Oliver's book *America's Decline*, one of the works listed by Cattell as "integrable into the Beyondist viewpoint," was essentially a neo-*Mein Kampf*, venerating Hitler as a future religion's deity and praising the führer's most well-known literary effort as a "cogent" and "persuasive" work, the veracity of which "the Jews immediately proved." "Without cunning and deceit," wrote Oliver, the Jews "could not survive. . . . [T]hey are the only human race that is by nature parasitic on other races," and during the 1930s, he observed, after these "inassimilable and uncivilized aliens" had "infested the nation" earlier in the century, many Americans believed that "'we need a Hitler here.'" This lack of sympathy for the plight of European

Jews endured, according to Oliver, until "they invented the hoax about 'gas chambers' and . . . 'extermination.'"[103]

It is important to emphasize that none of these publications praised by Cattell for their influence on his thought could be characterized as a far-ranging discussion, perhaps offering some valuable social insight apart from its preoccupation with the suppression of various minorities. From cover to cover, for example, each of Putnam's two books consisted of an unrelenting attack on any measure of social or political equality for blacks on the grounds of their genetic inferiority. Similarly, evident on almost every page of Oliver's book was his single-minded focus on Jews as the underlying source of all contemporary social problems.

Cattell had particularly close intellectual ties to the pseudonymous "Wilmot Robertson."[104] At almost the exact same time that Cattell's first major work on Beyondism appeared in print, Robertson, also with financial support from Draper, published *The Dispossessed Majority*, which Oliver called "the most important book published in this country since 1949—perhaps since 1917."[105] Robertson's opus explained that almost all the nation's contemporary problems stemmed from the presence of "inassimilable minorities"—not just blacks but also Asians, Hispanics, Greeks, southern Italians, Arabs, American Indians, and Jews. These groups, estimated by Robertson to compose 30 percent of the population, were not entitled to the Bill of Rights and other constitutional protections because, he maintained, "rights *earned* by one [racial] group" could not be "*donated* to another." Moreover, he wrote, the *Brown* decision overturning segregated schools had "kill[ed education] by destroying its binding force—the homogeneity of teacher and pupil."[106]

Like Pearson and Oliver, Robertson's chief criticism of Hitler was that he had been unsuccessful. In Robertson's analysis, the führer "did not think racially, at least in regard to his Japanese alliance," an error that eventually gave "Roosevelt and his high finance camorra of Jews and bought wasps" the opening they had been seeking to enter the war. As a consequence, wrote Robertson, Hitler's attempt to establish German dominance in Europe "failed, and his failure was shattering to Northern Europeans, both in Europe and America."[107] Although Robertson saw the "Staatsvolk" in the United States, "preponderantly Nordic and Nordic-Alpine in composition," as threatened by an "agglomeration of minorities," he obsessed in particular over "Jewish hegemony," and was the publisher of a slick periodical titled *Instauration*, which argued for "rational anti-Semitism" on the grounds that Jews are "arrogant, obnoxious, and hypocritical . . . aliens" who "distort our culture" and "promote race-mixing."[108] As a result of "their fear and loathing of Western civility" and their "vendetta . . . against all things non-Jewish," declared Robertson in

The Dispossessed Majority, Jews had set out "to bruise Western culture"—to undermine the intellectual disciplines and "divide and destroy the Western political and economic order"—through their leadership "of every divisive force in the modern era, from class agitation to minority racism, from the worst capitalist exploitation to the most brutal collectivism, from blind religious dogma to atheism and psychoanalysis, from total dogmatism to total permissiveness." Noting that Jews had infected most of western Europe as well as the United States with the same "social diseases," Robertson pointed out that despite its severe defeat, Germany had emerged from the Second World War as "the one large Western nation almost free of Jewish financial domination" and as a result had become "the most affluent and most stable nation in Europe." To put a stop to "the Jewish envelopment of America," he concluded, "history should not be repeated"; this time, "the operation ought to be accomplished with finesse."[109]

After Cattell published his first major work on Beyondism in 1972, he reported being contacted not only by some "well known writers in the field" but also by a few correspondents whom he characterized as "relatively unknown, but unexpectedly independent and original thinkers." Wilmot Robertson was almost certainly in the latter group. His books are not reviewed or advertised in mainstream journals; as one historian points out, "no one simply stumbles upon Robertson's publications. You are either a white supremacist or an expert on the far right." Moreover, Robertson soon began to suggest a reorganization of the society based directly on Cattell's writing. In 1974 he proposed the establishment of a "commonwealth" to be called, with no sense of irony, the "Utopian States of America," in which all "inassimilable" racial groups would be subject to "obligatory" separation and relocation, each in its own enclaves, thus removing the "horde of parasites which have fastened on to our body politic." Jews represented "the most urgent item on the separation agenda" for Robertson; unable throughout history "to establish a constructive and peaceful relationship with the non-Jewish population," they were to be "resettled" in Miami Beach, Beverly Hills, and a portion of the New York metropolitan area as a way to "sever Jews politically, economically and culturally from their host populations." Although he viewed separation of blacks as a "problem of much greater magnitude," Robertson believed such a salutary outcome could be achieved by formal division of rural areas into all-black and all-white counties combined with de jure confinement of blacks into urban ghettoes in a system of "cities within cities"; many blacks, he suggested, could also be repatriated to Africa, perhaps in exchange for the white South African population. Puerto Ricans, Cuban Americans, Asians, and various Mediterranean minorities— southern Italians, southern French, Spanish, Greeks, and others—were each to be subjected to a similar process in Robertson's scheme. This organized system of American Bantustans—in many ways what Cattell had called for in his own writings—would produce what Robertson called an "ingathering" of northern Europeans as well as the basis for a biologically correct "world order whose geographical frontiers matched its racial frontiers, once the minority elements were separated out."[110]

Unsurprisingly, given the similarity in their thinking, Robertson and Cattell quickly developed a mutual admiration for each other's work. Howard Allen Enterprises, founded by Robertson as a publishing and distribution center for extremist literature, soon added Cattell's *New Morality from Science* to its list of "books that speak for the Majority," advertising it in a brochure alongside Robertson's own writing and other works in the neo-Nazi canon, such as "Carleton Putnam's Modern Classics on the Negro Problem," which described how Jewish scientists had duped the nation into extending political equality to blacks.[111] Shortly after Cattell's second book on Beyondism appeared, the psychologist and his recent publication were featured on the cover of Robertson's magazine, *Instauration,* and a lengthy and, naturally, favorable review stretched over two issues.[112] Then, in 1992, Robertson published *The Ethnostate: An Unblinkered Prospectus for an Advanced Statecraft,* a book-length elaboration of his plan for racial balkanization of the United States, rooted in Cattellian social thought. Now convinced that the presence of so many minorities had rendered "America . . . beyond saving," Robertson viewed the creation of a "Euro-American state cut out of the dying husk of America" as the only "sensible means of assuring white survival," a goal to be sought by Nordics and Alpines in the United States "not for their own sake but because of their special place in the order of things": the race that had risen the highest on the evolutionary ladder and on whose accomplishments the entire planet was dependent for salvation, he emphasized, was "the one that has a patent on white genes."[113]

Much of *The Ethnostate* read like a compilation of ideas from Cattell's writing throughout his career. Robertson, too, believed that humanitarianism was "the greatest 'drag' on evolution," propelling whites further along "the road to self-destruction," and that the society also had to guard against "human parasitology"—some people "feeding off" the bodies and minds of others. Citing Cattell as his authority, Robertson argued that, in order to solve these and other social problems, science should "supplant religion as the primary source of morality." And what scientifically derived morality preached, once again, was the necessity for racial separation into independent regions in order to "protect the gene pools of . . . races and population groups"; there could be no such thing as "human rights without ethnic rights," he declared.

The racial homogeneity of the resulting geopolitical entities was expected to make laws prohibiting miscegenation unnecessary, but in the rare case that a mixed-race pregnancy did occur, abortion would be "mandatory."[114] In addition to the putative importance of these individual "ethnostates" for evolutionary progress, Robertson enumerated the many practical advantages that Cattell too had pointed out previously. In addition to eliminating the "grave misunderstandings" due to innate differences in personality when members of various groups were present in the same society, racial homogeneity was an essential condition for the production of high art. In particular, separation would prevent instances of what Robertson called "cultural aggression," in which one racial group adopted another's cultural form, a process he compared to "an individual exposed to a disease-carrying virus." For example, jazz, he warned, had made "unhealthy inroads" in cultures whose music differed "so radically from that of the Negro" (an observation that white jazz musicians, as well as millions of white jazz fans, would find questionable, to say the least). Most important of all, in the competition between the different ethnostates, each group was to rely solely "upon its own capabilities and resources," prohibited from "borrowing" from more complex cultures advancements that "it could not create under its own power" or otherwise benefiting from outside assistance. Finally, Robertson, again like his main scientific authority, believed that extensive psychological data should be collected on every individual—naturally IQ scores, but also tests for "defects, . . . attitude, concentration, feeling, taste, control, moral balance," and many other traits, including "most notably, the multiple personality tests developed by Raymond Cattell"; all the results were to "be guarded like state secrets."[115] The conscious embodiment of every one of Beyondism's basic principles, *The Ethnostate* was more Cattellian than Cattell.

Of course, merely the citation of Cattell's work as justification for a political proposal, no matter how crude or racist it might be, does not imply his endorsement; after all, there is no shortage of extremist schemes that purport to be derived directly from Darwinian concepts, a claim that hardly can be used to reflect badly on Darwin. There is little doubt, however, that Cattell enthusiastically approved of Robertson's plan for the practical application of Beyondist thinking. In his 1987 book Cattell announced establishment of the Trust for the Advancement of Beyondism, dedicated to spreading the gospel and funded from his own resources. Six years later a group of Cattell's friends and supporters gathered in California for the "First Annual Meeting . . . [of the] Beyondist Society." A document describing the purpose of the meeting noted the importance of evaluating the "survival value" of different racial and cultural groups or "ethnostatics [*sic*] as Robertson calls them."[116]

Although the typed document was unsigned, the words "For John" appeared at the top in Cattell's unmistakable handwriting. And, in fact, shortly after this meeting John Horn sent a memo to members of "the Beyondism working group—the self-appointed executive group," asking for their reactions to "Ray's suggestion for the first Newsletter of the Beyondism Society." The recipients of the memo, presumably the same people who had participated in the meeting, included Robert Graham, who had created the Repository for Germinal Choice—the so-called Nobel Prize sperm bank—and a number of Cattell's former students, among them Jerry Brennan, John Horn, and Richard Gorsuch.[117]

The first issue of the projected newsletter—the *Beyondist*—soon appeared, describing itself as the "Quarterly Organ of the Beyondist Foundation" and listing as its editors Cattell and Brennan, who had collaborated in some of the research on syntality.[118] Its lead article explained that the founding "group of intellectuals" had adopted a Beyondist constitution with nine principles, one of which called for the creation of independent "ethnostates" along the lines in the eponymously named book by "Robinson." Immediately following the constitution was a review of Robertson's book—this time with his name rendered correctly—calling it "a very timely supplement to the argument of the *Beyondist*" and recommending that "every seriously thoughtful citizen should read and ponder" the work. Although there were no authors indicated for any of the brief articles or reviews in the newsletter, much of the writing was unmistakably Cattell's style, sometimes using examples that had appeared in his work elsewhere. In addition, as editor, presumably he exercised control over the newsletter's contents, and Horn's memo had made clear that the first draft had come from Cattell; others had only been asked whether they thought it needed "editing." In any event, it is unthinkable that anything appearing in a publication devoted to Beyondism did not enjoy the full support of the philosophy's creator and chief exponent.[119]

Indisputably the most prominent scientist in the latter half of the twentieth century to propose a comprehensive ideology justifying outright racism, Cattell became a hero to numerous fringe hate groups in search of intellectual justification. An editor of *National Vanguard*, for example, the official periodical of the National Alliance, cited Cattell as the only other person besides the organization's deceased founder, William Pierce, whose thinking pointed toward a "faith of the future" in harmony with the facts of science.[120] Looking to Nazi Germany as a model, the National Alliance was dedicated to "regaining" control of the "Jewish media" and the government, "led by collaborators with the Jews," in order to institute "racial cleansing of the land" and create a "White living space," in which all "Semitic and other non-Aryan values and customs" have been completely eliminated.[121] According to one of its editorial statements, the group "would like to see . . . all heterosexual White men and women on one side and all Jews, homosexuals, Blacks, Asians, and mestizos on the other. Then we would be ready for the shooting to start, and we would settle matters pretty quickly." In another instance, the first edition of *Heritage and Destiny*, an anti-Semitic "white nationalist" magazine later taken over by the American Friends of the British National Party—a Virginia-based group associated with David Duke and affiliated with the British National Party, England's foremost neo-Nazi organization—paid tribute to Cattell's "masterful attempts to build a new moral system upon the findings of modern biology."[122]

In at least one case, Cattell subsequently chose to cooperate with an extremist periodical that had praised his work. *American Renaissance* was predicated on the belief, similar to the one at the core of Cattell's ideology, that race must be the essential ingredient of citizenship; as a consequence, the magazine bluntly observed, neither minorities nor third world immigrants belonged in the United States and certainly could never be "real" Americans. Any notion that two races could exist in the same society "on equal terms," insisted the publication's editor, was "but wishful thinking and leads only to disaster and oblivion."[123] *American Renaissance* published excerpts from the oral histories of former slaves, emphasizing how they had found life under the South's peculiar institution far less burdensome than coping with the demands of freedom.[124] And even after emancipation, according to the magazine, blacks were entitled only to personal liberty and the right to hold property, not any of those "phony" rights to participate in the polity and economy that had been "fabricated" for them in the 1960s.[125] Until recently, the editor pointed out, there had been widespread agreement that blacks were "a perfectly stupid race," and although they could "neither be killed nor driven away," no one expected "civilized white men" to work alongside them.[126] After attending a conference sponsored by the eponymous organization that published *American Renaissance*, even Dinesh D'Souza—the well-known conservative and author of one book that launched the war against political correctness and another that called for the repeal of the Civil Rights Act of 1964, so that employers could engage in what he called "rational discrimination"—labeled the group "racist."[127]

American Renaissance gushed over Beyondism in a review stretching over three issues, with a special section devoted to Cattell's claim that the practice of altruism was appropriately limited only to one's racial comrades and became a "perversion" when extended to members of other groups; because religion turned out to be wrong about life's creation, it was equally "wrong," both Cattell and the magazine concurred, "to tell a man to love his neighbor as himself."[128] Cattell later welcomed *American Renaissance*'s editor to his home in Hawaii to provide a personal interview, implicitly lending his approval to the publication. This "conversation with a pioneer" was obviously quite a cordial occasion, Cattell mentioning "with a smile" that he had five children as evidence that he was "both a theoretical and practical eugenist." Noting that the psychologist's thinking had "laid the groundwork" for Robertson's *Ethnostate* and other schemes for racial separatism, the interview quoted Cattell's observation that "any religion that preaches against competition must be dysgenic" and that Christianity was a particular cause of mischief because of the "moral impetus" it provided to "the belief in racial equality." Cattell was "a hero to his admirers," declared the magazine that opposed civil rights for blacks, clearly believing that its readers should be numbered among the appreciative.[129]

* * *

A critique of Cattell's ethical system based in part on his involvement with others espousing odious opinions naturally runs the risk of charging guilt by association. But the argument advanced here is far more substantive. It is not merely that he has cited a long list of Far Right authors and activists as significant influences on his own work, including arguably the three most important English-speaking Nazi theorists of the last thirty years—Pearson, Oliver, and Robertson. It is that, in addition to citing their writing as support for his own ideology, Cattell has acknowledged their ideas as "integrable"— that is, compatible—with his thought; expressed his gratitude for the influence these ideas have had on the evolution of Beyondism; graced the pages of their journals with his own contributions, thus lending his considerable prestige to publications dedicated to keeping blacks in second-class status; registered no objection when schemes of racial balkanization were predicated expressly on his writing—and indeed edited a publication that praised such a scheme for its intellectual indebtedness to his thought and called for its implementation; and provided a friendly interview to a periodical directly advocating that constitutionally protected rights be withheld from blacks. This is not guilt by association but rather guilt by collaboration: it is indisputable that Cattell and numerous segregationist or Nazi ideologues share a core set of beliefs and a common vision of an ethnically cleansed future, and that his support for such a society has lent his academic prominence, consciously and deliberately, to their intolerable goals.

THE CATTELL CONVENTION
THE CONTROVERSY
OVER THE AWARD

Every August the American Psychological Association holds its annual convention, an opportunity for thousands of psychologists, professional and academic, to gather in formal and informal groups in order to present their own research, discuss issues of concern to both researchers and practitioners, and listen to invited talks by some of the most distinguished members of their profession. Two particularly noteworthy events at every convention are the keynote address, often delivered not by a psychologist but by someone prominent in public life, and the awards ceremony, at which members of the profession who have made outstanding accomplishments are honored by their peers.

There are two different categories of awards. The APA awards are given for distinction in each of a number of areas: Scientific Contributions, Applications of Psychology, Early Career Contribution to Psychology, Contribution to Psychology in the Public Interest, Contribution to Research in Public Policy, and various others. Although these awards are certainly prestigious, each year there is a second, even more select group of honorees: recipients

of the American Psychological Foundation Gold Medal Awards, which recognize "Life Achievement" in each of four areas—Psychological Science,
Public Interest, Practice of Psychology, and Application of Psychology. The
APF is a nonprofit philanthropic organization, established in 1953 by a group
of former APA presidents who, according to the foundation's own description, understood the field's "unparalleled potential for understanding human
behavior and advancing human welfare" and sought "to promote psychology
and to help extend its benefits to the public," in part by recognizing those
psychologists whose careers "light the way for what can be done to benefit
humanity."[1] For the first three decades after its founding, the APF honored
one outstanding psychologist each year until 1985, when it began to give
multiple awards for science, application, and public interest; the practice
category was added in 1994. Gold Medal recipients must be sixty-five years
or older and must have made "enduring contributions" in the category of
the award. Almost all these persons have been household names in psychology, the men and women whose research has informed the direction of the
discipline.[2] Unlike the APA awards, the winners of which are announced
earlier in the year, the APF Gold Medal recipients are named only weeks
before the convention takes place.

The Convention

In July 1997 the *APA Monitor*, the organization's monthly magazine, announced that Raymond B. Cattell had been chosen as that year's recipient
of the Gold Medal Award for Life Achievement in Psychological Science for
his "landmark contributions to empirical knowledge and theory in psychology"; the award was to be presented in a ceremony on August 16 at the APA
convention, held that year in Chicago. According to Joseph Matarazzo, a
behavioral neuroscientist at the Oregon Health Sciences University School
of Medicine and president of the APF at the time, six other candidates had
been nominated for this specific honor, but Cattell had been the unanimous
choice of the Board of Trustees, composed largely of psychologists who had
served as president of the APA, including Matarazzo.[3] As the APF process
required, a statement on behalf of Cattell had been submitted by one person,
whom Matarazzo called the "major nominator," and buttressed by a number
of supporting letters. Though unclear whether it was the former or one of the
latter, a nominating letter appeared for a time on the Web site of the Institute
for Personality and Ability Testing (http://www.ipat.com), which had been
founded by Cattell. Written by his longtime friend and collaborator John
Horn, understandably it emphasized Cattell's "methodologically sophisticated

and theoretically comprehensive program of research into human behavior and the qualities that uniquely define individuals"; there was no mention of Beyondism or of any attempt on Cattell's part to promulgate a system of evolutionary ethics, and certainly no indication that his research program had been intended to serve such a purpose. This was the likely model for all the letters on Cattell's behalf: submitted by well-known former students with notable research careers of their own, but omitting any reference to his socioreligious views. These Cattellians long believed that their mentor had never received the recognition merited by his accomplishments, and there had been attempts on their part as far back as 1985 to nominate him for the Gold Medal Award.[4]

Nor is there any doubt that many of his disciples were well aware of Cattell's Beyondist thought. Horn, for example, was named in Cattell's 1987 book as one of the social scientists to be contacted by anyone interested in the "Trust for the Advancement of Beyondism" and then played a prominent role in the Beyondist Society's first meeting, conveying to other members of the Executive Committee "Ray's suggestion for the first Newsletter of the Beyondism Society," which pronounced Robertson's *Ethnostate* so compatible with Cattell's own thinking.[5] In the double issue of *Multivariate Behavioral Research* edited by Horn and dedicated entirely to a discussion of the impact of Cattell's work, Cecil Gibb—an Australian psychologist who had earned his doctorate under Cattell's direction and gone on to collaborate with his mentor—referred to *Psychology and Social Progress,* published in 1933, as the origin of the research program that Cattell had pursued for the next fifty years. And in the same issue of the journal Richard Gorsuch, too, who delivered the eulogy at Cattell's funeral, cited the 1933 publication as the beginning of what developed into Beyondism, though he provided little sense of the actual content of either the book or the religion.[6]

However, there is little reason to believe that the APF board was familiar with Cattell's more ideological work. Interviewed two weeks before the beginning of the convention by Barry A. Mehler, a professor of history at Ferris State University who had just published an analysis of Cattell's writing on ethics,[7] Matarazzo maintained that he knew nothing of the Gold Medal recipient's interest in eugenics, a fortiori disavowing any knowledge of something called "Beyondism."[8] Nor did the formal statement of the award that appeared in *American Psychologist,* the APA's professional journal, make any reference to the honoree's social thought, although the accompanying bibliography did include a book incorrectly referred to as *Religion from Science* (omitting *Beyondism,* the first word in the actual title). Matarazzo also insisted that none of the other six former APA presidents who served on the

APF board had ever heard of Beyondism.[9] Although, obviously, he could not be certain of the veracity of such a claim about others' knowledge, it was probably true: if anyone on the board had in fact known of Cattell's writings on ethics, it is hard to believe the issue would not have been mentioned in the discussion leading to his selection.

In the spring of 1997, a few months before the convention, the APA announced that Elie Wiesel would give the keynote address. By coincidence, in June Wiesel had been invited to the University of Guelph near Toronto to receive an honorary degree as part of the school's commencement ceremonies. During his presence at Guelph he had a brief conversation with Andrew Winston, a professor in the Psychology Department. Though originally trained as a developmental psychologist at the University of Illinois, Winston had become more interested in the history of psychology, becoming a noted scholar in that field—a fellow of the APA's Society for the History of Psychology and the executive officer of Cheiron, the International Society for the History of the Behavioral and Social Sciences; one of his specialties was the history of social scientists' collaboration with neo-Nazi groups, including those dedicated to Holocaust denial. At the university's postcommencement reception Winston informed the honorary degree recipient of his area of research, and Wiesel, interested to learn that there was a small community of scholars writing on this topic, asked the psychologist to send him some articles. However, Winston delayed doing so, and by the time he got around to putting some material together, Cattell had been named the Gold Medal recipient. Concerned about the APF's choice of honoree and knowing that Wiesel would deliver the keynote address at the APA, Winston included some information about Cattell along with a few papers of his own in the packet he sent to Wiesel.[10]

Winston and Mehler also each took steps to oppose Cattell's receipt of the award. Less than two weeks before the start of the convention, Mehler, as director of the Institute for the Study of Academic Racism, issued a lengthy press release about Cattell's background, noting that "the potential awardee has a lifetime commitment to fascist and eugenics causes and openly affiliates himself with Wilmot Robertson's work, which the Anti-Defamation League [ADL] characterizes as 'racist and anti-Semitic.'" Among other outlets, the press release was distributed to the New York Times and CNN, to Mehler's contacts at organizations such as the ADL and the American Jewish Committee, and to a number of individuals, Wiesel among them.[11] At about the same time, Winston wrote to Matarazzo, the president of the APF, with a copy to Raymond Fowler, the APA's chief executive officer, enclosing two of Cattell's articles from the Mankind Quarterly as evidence for his "life-long commitment to eugenics and racism" and declaring that "the APF award to

Cattell will be a moral stain on our discipline and our organization." Despite questioning the wisdom of the APF's decision, the letter was worded decorously, observing that the details of Cattell's views "must have been unknown to you, and will be distressing to you."[12] Although Matarazzo did not reply, Fowler responded in equally courteous fashion, thanking Winston for sending the material and calling it "thoughtful" for him to have done so. According to Fowler, the information provided by Winston had given the APF board pause. "I am confident that they did not know about Dr. Cattell's social and political views when they named him as awardee," he wrote, adding, "The award will not be presented at the convention in Chicago. The Board will meet during the convention to determine its disposition of the matter."[13]

Because I had written about Cattell in a book published three years earlier, Winston also contacted me to ask if I would communicate my own reservations to the APF. I faxed the relevant ten-page section of the book to Rhea Farberman, the APA's public affairs director, to be passed on to the APF board, along with a cover letter observing that Cattell's insistence on racial segregation was inseparable from his scientific thought and that, for two-thirds of a century, he had been arguing for the importance of segregation so that "unsuccessful" races could be "phased out"; I added that, during the civil rights movement when other social scientists began to study racial prejudice, he had continued to maintain that "apartheid—not in South Africa but in the United States—was a scientific necessity."[14]

Mehler, Winston, and I also made arrangements to meet at the keynote address for the first time; all our previous communications with each other had taken place by phone or e-mail. In fact, before the Cattell nomination, none of the three of us had planned to attend the convention; Mehler was not a psychologist much less an APA member, and neither Winston nor I was a participant in any of the paper sessions or symposia that year.

Arriving on Friday, August 16, less than an hour before the address was scheduled to begin, I met Mehler, who informed me that he had been able to arrange for the two of us—Winston had not yet arrived—to speak briefly with Wiesel. In the ten minutes or so available, I showed Wiesel a few pages photocopied from Cattell's work. Particularly concerned at Cattell's prewar opinions that seemed to provide an intellectual foundation for Nazi policy, Wiesel asked to keep a passage from the 1933 book, in which Cattell had first offered a scientifically based rationale for the "hatred and abhorrence which many peoples feel for the Jewish . . . practice of living in other nations," and then castigated the "would-be intellectuals" who "readily branded [these reactions] as 'prejudice'" out of an inability to appreciate their biological causes.[15]

The largest attendance at any single event at the APA convention is almost always the keynote address, and 1997 was no exception given the international stature of the speaker. Occupant of a named chair at Boston University and the recipient of numerous prestigious awards including the Nobel Peace Prize, Wiesel was the author of more than forty books, fiction and nonfiction, dealing primarily with the Holocaust and the moral obligation to oppose racism and genocide, a responsibility to which he had dedicated much of his own life through the establishment of the Elie Wiesel Foundation for Humanity and his defense of the rights of oppressed minorities from Nicaragua to Cambodia. Wiesel was a particularly appropriate choice for the 1997 convention, which featured a special "Miniconvention on Psychology and Racism" organized by the APA Public Interest Directorate, and an audience estimated at two thousand persons gathered to hear him.[16] Focusing on the need to honor the elderly and to advocate for their rights as a victimized population, Wiesel stressed the importance of preserving their memories for younger generations and spoke movingly of his own commitment to the preservation of the memories of persons who had suffered under the Third Reich. It was important, Wiesel emphasized, that these painful recollections be used not to seek revenge but to prevent others from suffering.[17] Near the end of his remarks Wiesel described his own agonized decision to terminate a close friendship of fifty years' duration after learning of his friend's earlier complicity with the Nazis, an anecdote that he compared to the difficult decision that the APA now had to confront. Alluding obliquely to the postponed award, Wiesel refrained from mentioning Cattell by name but congratulated the APA on its willingness to reconsider conferring honor on a supporter of odious policies. "Theories that are so close to Nazi theories," he observed, "are to be repudiated, not honored." Though brief, the reference to the award was done gracefully, focusing on the principle rather than the individual. Wiesel later wrote to me that "it was too bad the award was offered in the first place," adding that he hoped "such a disgrace doesn't happen again."[18]

However, at the time most of the audience probably had no idea what Wiesel was talking about. It was only on the previous day that the APA had issued its statement, announcing that the presentation of the Gold Medal Award to Cattell, scheduled to take place the next evening, had been "postponed due to new information presented to the APF Board which requires further study" and explaining that "in order to provide full due process," a Blue Ribbon Panel of senior research scientists would be appointed to "advise the Board on its further actions";[19] posted by the convention office in the registration area, where it appeared along with a hundred other announcements of various kinds, the statement was not widely distributed to the attendees. And only in that morning's New York Times was the story carried for the first time in a mass media publication, making it unlikely that very many people listening to Wiesel's 11:00 o'clock address were aware of the situation alluded to in his concluding comments.[20]

In a bizarre coda that only added to the audience's bewilderment, as soon as Wiesel's talk ended, Joseph Matarazzo seized the microphone to deliver an impromptu lecture on due process and the difference between accusation and truth; though well known as a former president of the APA and the current president of the APF, he was not listed in the program as a participant and had no formal role in the instant event. Omitting, like Wiesel, any mention of the object of the controversy, Matarazzo declared that the APF was taking the charges very seriously and would appoint a Blue Ribbon Committee to investigate their validity. Yet he also emphasized that the researcher in question had written many books, was a leader in a number of fields, and had been chosen by the board of the APF for his lifetime of achievement in science, and that in addition, announcement of the award had already been published in *American Psychologist*. It was hard to escape the impression that, at least in Matarazzo's opinion, due process was intended as a mechanism to produce a specific outcome. When he concluded by telling the audience, "You will all be pleased, I'm sure, when the Blue Ribbon Committee makes its report," there was little doubt that he believed the source of this pleasure would be found not so much in the fairness of the process as in its result.

This impression was strengthened further by the interaction that occurred immediately after the keynote address. Seeing Mehler, Winston, and me together in the corridor, Matarazzo waved around the just published *New York Times* story—which had reported that, according to a recent fax from Cattell, his views of eugenics had "evolved over the years" and that the creator of Beyondism "now believes in eugenics only on a voluntary basis"[21]—and bellowed, to the three of us and anyone else within earshot, that the article rendered our charges baseless. In his interview with Mehler two weeks earlier, Matarazzo had disavowed any knowledge whatsoever of Cattell's work on eugenics and had never even heard of the religious system to which Cattell had devoted entire books and numerous articles. Yet he was now prepared, on the basis of a single line in an eight hundred–word newspaper article, to dismiss the concerns of those of us who had actually read the thousands of pages on evolutionary ethics written by Cattell.

Immediately after the convention I sent a letter to Farberman, the public affairs director, providing a list of Cattell's works that the Blue Ribbon Panel might want to consider. I prefaced the list by observing that an official in the APA Press Room at Chicago had asked me whether I had any criticisms of Cattell's scientific contributions—a question that appeared to me to indicate an intent to separate Cattell's research from his advocacy of segregation and other discriminatory policies. "Although I do not agree with this position," I wrote to Farberman, nevertheless I acknowledged "that it is one with an intellectually defensible rationale," but wished to emphasize the "difference between separating Cattell's research from his repugnant ideology and pretending that the latter does not exist"; in particular, the fact that Matarazzo had thrust a newspaper at us in the corridor "proclaiming some sentence in it a refutation" of all the scholarly work on Cattell's ethical system made me "concerned that there may indeed be an attempt at such a pretense." I soon came to the conclusion, however, that these fears were unfounded. Only a few days later, the APF director e-mailed me to request a copy of my own writing on Cattell; the fax of that material that I had sent unsolicited some weeks earlier had been unclear, and she wanted a clean copy to submit to the Blue Ribbon Panel once it had been appointed.[22] This seemed to me a favorable indication, suggesting that there would be a serious process of review.

The Withdrawal

In early November the APF board did indeed announce the appointment of a five-member Blue Ribbon Panel, selected to represent expertise in a broad range of areas, scientific and ethical. Chaired by M. Brewster Smith, an eminent social psychologist and past APA president, who in 1952 had been an expert witness for the plaintiffs seeking to overturn segregated education in one of the four cases eventually consolidated as *Brown v. Board of Education,* the panel included a former president of the Society for Multivariate Experimental Psychology, which had been founded by Cattell, as well as two other prominent researchers in psychometrics and cognitive processes, one of whom had been chair of the APA's Board of Scientific Affairs.[23] The fifth member of the panel, and its only nonpsychologist, was Arthur L. Caplan, director of the Center for Bioethics at the University of Pennsylvania and the nation's leading expert on issues of medical ethics.[24] The panel's charge was to examine Cattell's writing, balancing the importance of protecting science, particularly politically unpopular science, against "psychology's opposition to the inappropriate use of science to promote destructive social policy," and to issue its report to the APF board by early February 1998.[25]

A month later, however, Cattell withdrew his name from consideration for the award, and the panel was disbanded without issuing a report. According to Fowler, the APA's chief executive officer, Cattell had been inclined to withdraw from the beginning of the controversy but had been dissuaded from doing so by his many friends and supporters who encouraged him to fight back. In a widely circulated "Open Letter to the APA" announcing his decision, Cattell sought "to correct misunderstandings and misrepresenta-tions" of his beliefs that had been propagated by "misguided" critics, whose accusations had been "based on (a) incorrect interpretation" of his writing, "(b) statements taken out of context," and "(c) statements . . . made as a young man in the 1930's . . . later amended based on subsequent observations." Be-fore proceeding to clarify his beliefs, Cattell emphasized, "To the extent that any other statements I have made, in the 1930's or at any other time, conflict with the statements I make in this letter, I would like to publicly retract those statements."[26] Or as Ron Ziegler, Richard Nixon's press secretary, famously observed after a sudden, dramatic change in the administration's position, "This is the operative statement. The others are inoperative."

Of course, until this declaration, issued fifty-three days before his death, Cattell had never given any indication that his earlier views had changed. Nowhere in his voluminous writing, for example, did he ever acknowledge that his earlier call for the genocide of blacks—by peaceful means, to be sure—had been misguided, or ever even mention his praise for the eugenic measures of the Third Reich, much less express regret for having supported the regime's policies. Indeed, his two later books on Beyondism both began by pointing out that they were his attempts, after a lengthy hiatus devoted almost exclusively to research, to return to the ethical belief system outlined in the prewar writing of his youth. As Cattell put it in the introduction to his first major statement on Beyondism, published in 1972 when he was "three score years and ten," this latest effort was "a *fuller* scale of presentation" (emphasis added) but not in any way a departure from the ideas expressed in *Psychology and Social Progress*, written four decades earlier. Quite the contrary, he emphasized at the time, "I have . . . gone much further back into the past for good thought in this area." And in 1987 Cattell referred to the 1972 book as an "expan[sion]" of *Psychology and the Religious Quest*, his 1938 attempt to create a religious system informed by science. In Cattell's brief 1974 autobi-ography, too, he wrote that his social thought had "endured" from his books in the 1930s to its latest incarnation as Beyondism.[27] All these reflections on his prewar writing emphasized their continuity with Cattell's later religious system; there was never an intimation that he wished to disavow anything in the earlier work, only to expand on it.

Nevertheless, in his "Open Letter to the APA," Cattell went on to espouse a credo totally unrecognizable from any of his previous writings—not just those published in his youth, from which Cattell now sought to distance him-self, but articles that had appeared quite recently as well. "I believe in equal opportunity for all individuals," he suddenly wrote, "and I abhor racism and

discrimination based on race." None of his earlier public pronouncements
had suggested that behind the numerous proposals to restrict the franchise
and the constant admonitions against the extension of altruistic impulses to
members of other races lurked a closet egalitarian. Indeed, only five years
earlier in the *Mankind Quarterly*, the academic journal that had spearheaded
the scientific attempt to prevent blacks from obtaining equal opportunity,
Cattell had insisted that racism was an "innate drive," an "evolutionary force"
not substantially different from the sex drive, and "like all instinctive forces,"
he pointed out, "it has its virtues and its vices." There were some situations, he
conceded, in which this tendency to dislike other races could be "a source of
trouble" but emphasized that, even in those occasional circumstances where
it might appear necessary to restrain such a natural reaction, it was still important to recognize the danger of "suppressing innate drives." Rather than
sharing his abhorrence of racism with the *Quarterly*'s readers, Cattell called
for social scientists to recognize it as the "virtuous gift" that it was and to
study "how best to shape society to adjust to it"; one method, he suggested,
was to avoid racial diversity within a society.[28]

In an even more astonishing volte-face, Cattell's open letter also declared
that there was no valid evidence for racial differences in intelligence; his previous certainty that blacks were *Untermenschen* notwithstanding, all studies
that had been offered to substantiate racial differences he dismissed now as
biased, "influenced by education, culture, and environment." This startling
pronouncement, going beyond endorsement of the mere ethical principle
of equal opportunity to an uncharacteristic reluctance to draw an empirical
conclusion, actually made Cattell considerably more environmentalist on the
subject than many less eugenically oriented social scientists who nevertheless believed that racial differences were to some degree heritable. Richard
Herrnstein and Charles Murray, for example, argued in their controversial
bestseller, *The Bell Curve*, that "both genes and the environment have something to do with racial differences" in IQ scores, though they declined to offer
an estimate of "what might the mix be."[29] In any event, it was Cattell's allies
as well as his critics whose "misunderstandings and misrepresentations"
were sorely in need of correction. There is no way that publications such
as the *Mankind Quarterly* or *American Renaissance*, devoted adherents to
white supremacy, would have gushed over Cattell's socioreligious thought
or allocated such prominence to his writing had they known of his newly
announced egalitarian sentiments.

Finally, Cattell's open letter professed that he believed only in "*voluntary*
eugenics as a means to contribute to the evolution of the human race."[30] This
previously unmentioned emphasis on volition, however, would seem antitheti-

cal to almost every policy recommendation informed by Beyondist principles. Restriction of the franchise; the "monitoring of gestations" in order to identify and eliminate through abortion "undesirable mutations," not just "physical defect and physiological abnormality but also neurological deviation incompatible with a healthy social life"; a "cost-accounting for parasitisms, cultural and genetic"; the control of "hybridization" through "genetic management"; implementation of "an effective within-group eugenic selection program to screen out the many defective combinations"; the expansion of "successful" groups at the expense of "defective" ones; the "phasing out" of moribund cultures through "birth control measures"—on the face of it, none of these vague but ominous-sounding proposals was likely to be accepted willingly by the individuals or groups intended as their target. Indeed, one of these recommendations—the control of "hybridization" through antimiscegenation laws, based in part on the same pseudoscientific claims espoused by Cattell of deleterious consequences for the offspring of interracial matings—had for many years been statutory policy in all the southern states and a number of others outside the South, until being judged unconstitutional by the Supreme Court in 1967;[31] anything but voluntary, these laws prescribed prison terms for offenders. Or when Cattell declared, for example, that "a society under any real pressure cannot survive if it gives equal voting powers" to a classics professor and a gardener, it is hard to escape the conclusion that he was calling for the latter, and others similarly considered to lack sound judgment, to be *deprived* of the ballot. Indeed, it would be disingenuous to maintain that the intent of this observation was for persons of putatively low capacity to relinquish their right as citizens only *voluntarily*. Although it is not possible to know what was in Cattell's heart and mind when he crafted the open letter expressing his abhorrence of discrimination and his commitment only to voluntary eugenic measures, it is, however, undeniable that these eleventh-hour assertions were repudiations of almost all the beliefs he had previously committed to print, not merely those from the 1930s.

The circumstances under which Cattell issued his declaration provided yet a final reason to be skeptical of its sincerity. As two of his supporters frankly noted in an article praising their deceased friend and colleague and decrying the "shameful treatment accorded him," Cattell's "public statement denouncing both racism and fascism" had been "prompted by the occasion" of the last-minute postponement of his award.[32] That is, absent the controversy over the award, there would have been no fervent condemnation of racism or ringing endorsement of equality. This sequence of events suggested that, rather than being informed by a desire to set the record straight, the statement was in part an attempt at damage control.

The Aftermath

The decision to postpone Cattell's award produced considerable outrage, not only from scientists who had been his friends and associates over the years—the so-called Cattellians—but also from a number of other researchers who resented what they perceived as the inappropriate intrusion of political considerations into what should have been a decision based solely on scientific merit. According to Cattell's daughter, the APA received more than one hundred letters in support of her father but refused to print any of them. The Society of Multivariate Experimental Psychology, which Cattell had founded, unanimously approved a recommendation that the award be "immediately finalized" with a formal ceremony, although, perhaps because many members of the society were actually familiar with their founder's ethical thought, adding that it "did not seek to determine the truth or falsity of the allegations made against Cattell but did agree that even if those allegations were true, that would not be reason to rescind the Gold Medal award." The four winners of the previous year's APA award for Early Career Contributions crafted a letter urging reconsideration of the postponement, and one of the four—Rutgers University neuroscientist Mark Gluck—attempted, unsuccessfully, to persuade his three cosigners that they should all return their own awards as a protest.[33]

However, unwilling to accept the fact that the APA/APF had made a decision on the merits of the concerns about Cattell, some of his supporters invented a completely fictitious account of the reasons for the deferral of the award, claiming that the presentation ceremony had been canceled at the last moment only because Cattell's critics had threatened to foment a disturbance. The thought that three middle-aged academics, the only people at the conference who had expressed reservations about the honoree, could or would create such a ruckus is amusing—perhaps even flattering—but it had not a shred of truth. Indeed, all our communications with the APA or APF about Cattell were professional and courteous, sometimes to the point of deference. Winston's letter expressing reservations about Cattell had been gracious, complimenting the APF's president for his history of "deep commitment to human welfare," and had elicited a cordial response from the APA's chief executive officer, expressing gratitude for Winston's "thoughtful[ness]."[34] In my own conversation with an APF official I stressed that, despite my personal opposition to the association's choice of honoree, I was not demanding that they change the decision; I wanted only to ensure that it was fully informed. Particularly ironic about the concocted charge is the fact that there *was* a disruption at the convention: Matarazzo's decision to seize the microphone and deliver a spontaneous reply to the comments at the end of Wiesel's address. One can only imagine the outrage that would have ensued had either Winston or I—both of us APA members—attempted such an impulsive act to announce our own reaction to the postponed award and the impending process.

Some of the people who spread this fiction were longtime right-wing activists with a history of paranoid claims that true science was being subjected to an "Inquisitional attack" by radical egalitarians. In the *Mankind Quarterly*, for example, Florida State University geneticist Glayde Whitney maintained that, just as Christian theology had sought to stifle Galileo, Lysenkoism—an ideology shared, according to Whitney, by Joseph Stalin and Hillary Clinton—was now attempting to suppress genetic heresy in the United States, and in the service of this cause Cattell's critics had planned a disruption of the APA event reminiscent of the riots at the 1968 National Democratic Convention also held in Chicago.[35] Though a well-known researcher and once president of the Behavior Genetics Association, Whitney, like Cattell, believed in the existence of "hybrid incompatibilities between blacks and whites," attributing the "very wide range of health problems" suffered by the African American population, especially its high infant death rate, to the presence of disharmonious white genes undetected because of the "one drop" convention, which defined all "hybrids" as black.[36] Only months after condemning Cattell's critics, Whitney contributed the foreword to David Duke's autobiography, comparing the ex-Klansman and neo-Nazi to Socrates, Galileo, and Newton, and warning that the NAACP and other "front organizations" had been created "in furtherance of the Jewish agenda"—to preserve "Jewish distinctiveness . . . by eliminating distinctiveness among the non-Jews." Two years later, as one of the featured speakers at the annual conference of the Institute for Historical Review—the center of Holocaust revisionism—he provided additional detail on the source of the conspiracy to suppress genetic truths, explaining to an audience filled with Holocaust deniers and Nazi sympathizers that Jews were using the same tactics in science as they had used to invent the Holocaust: creating a "fake" to advance their own interests, in this case subverting European-American civilization by convincing whites to accept blacks as equals.[37] For Whitney, the plan to disrupt the APA convention fitted nicely into this larger plot by Jews to discredit contemporary science in pursuit of their own agenda.

Unfortunately, the myth that a riot had been planned was also spread by a number of scientists with no political ax to grind. In a letter announcing his resignation from the APA because of the way Cattell had been treated, Case Western Reserve psychologist Douglas Detterman, for example—an APA fellow and noted expert on the study of intelligence and mental retardation—described how "fear of demonstrations . . . led to the withholding

of the award." Ralph Mason Dreger and Irwin Berg, who had been Cattell's
friends and collaborators in work on personality and clinical psychology,
also perpetuated the notion that the award had been "'postponed' at the last
minute because there were threats of rioting . . . were it to be presented." Probably the most illustrious researcher to repeat this invention was University
of Minnesota professor David Lykken—an internationally prominent researcher in personality assessment, psychopathology, behavior genetics,
and psychophysiology, and one of the very few persons ever to receive APA
awards for distinguished contributions in two different areas—who later
wrote that "a small group of zealots had . . . threatened a protest demonstration" and called the APF's consequent decision to withhold the award
"craven."[38] It is particularly disappointing that scientists who would never
pass on unreferenced and unfounded rumor as fact in their research did
not hesitate to retail this piece of nonsense in professional journals when
it fitted their preconceptions.

One other strange event occurred as a consequence of the postponed award.
In the desire to explain our opposition to Cattell to other psychologists, so
many of whom seemed unaware of the ideological motivation for his research,
I submitted a proposal for a discussion titled "Raymond B. Cattell's Social
Thought" at the 1998 APA convention in San Francisco, conducted by a panel
of speakers who would explore the relatively unknown system of ethics that
was inseparable from Cattell's science. Composed of Winston, Mehler, Jerry
Hirsch—a behavior geneticist, longtime colleague of Cattell's at the University
of Illinois, and director of a program in "institutional racism," in which he had
mentored Mehler—and myself, the panel would discuss the evolution of Cattell's ethical system from its roots in social Darwinism to its present form, the
relationship between his work and the thought of other contemporary social
theorists, and the Beyondist Foundation created to further the development
of his system. Such proposals must be submitted to a specific division of the
APA, which then sponsors the event, and I sent this one to Division 45, the
Society for the Psychological Study of Ethnic Minority Issues. In early March I
received a boilerplate note of congratulations sent to everyone whose proposal
had been accepted. Enclosed with the note were the comments from the four
anonymous reviewers to whom the proposal had been sent for evaluation, all
of whom were enthusiastic, calling it "very timely" and "much needed"; one
reviewer thought that the title should be changed to "reflect Cattell's racism,
anti-Semitism, and use of his fame to propagate hatred, Nazism, and anni-
hilation of racial groups," while another suggested that a "counter-point if
available" be included on the panel.[39] Believing that the latter suggestion was
quite sensible, especially in view of the fact that Cattell was no longer avail-

able to defend his writing, we began to consider who would be an appropriate spokesperson, and Mehler, who had been in contact with Cattell's daughter, wrote to her seeking a recommendation.

More than a month later, and only because one member of the panel, for personal reasons, had expressed a preference for the specific day on which our discussion was to take place, I called the APA to ask if scheduling information was now available. Informed first by the APA office that there was no record of the event, I finally managed to speak to an official who explained that there had been an "error": I had been sent the "approval" letter when I should have received a rejection. At least one person on the projected panel had already purchased an airline ticket, which could not be returned, causing him to lose the cost of the flight. Given the outrage directed at the APA over Cattell's treatment, the entire sequence of events seemed somewhat suspicious, as well as disappointing, depriving us of an opportunity to make a public statement of the reasons for our criticisms. In the absence of any strong evidence to the contrary otherwise, however, I decided to accept the explanation of inadvertent error.

In Denial

The disbanding of the Blue Ribbon Panel before it could examine the issues and, to a lesser extent, the rejection of the panel discussion of Cattell's work deprived the profession of an opportunity for exploration of an important set of issues: the relation between scientific contributions and ideology, and the degree, if any, to which the latter is a proper consideration in according recognition for the former. Fortunately, or so it first seemed, another outlet for such a discussion quickly arose when, six months after Cattell's death, Marvin J. McDonald, a psychology professor at Trinity Western University in British Columbia specializing in the study of religion and science, proposed that the *History and Philosophy of Psychology Bulletin*, the journal of the History and Philosophy Section of the Canadian Psychological Association, publish a special issue, "Psychology, Eugenics, and the Case of Raymond B. Cattell." McDonald, who then served as editor of this special issue, was not a partisan in the debate. As he noted to a prospective contributor, the collection of articles on Cattell was intended to be part of a "longer-term process which eventually depolarizes the issues, maintains respect for . . . Cattell & his family, and gives full consideration to the wide range of defensible positions."[40] Although the broader audience at an APA event would have been preferable to a relatively obscure academic publication, I was nevertheless thankful that the journal was going to provide an opportunity to air views on the controversy—not just the narrow issue of whether postponement of the award was justified but larger questions, such as the ethical responsibilities of social scientists, the interplay between sociopolitical or religious views and a researcher's scientific contributions, and the relationship over the past century between eugenics, psychology, evolutionary biology, and behavior genetics. Presumably, Cattell's supporters as well as his critics would be invited to participate, and there would be an opportunity for a genuine exchange.

In sensible fashion, McDonald began by forming an e-mail discussion list of the "recipients of invitations to contribute," which included, among others, Mehler, Winston, and myself as Cattell's critics; a few well-known scientists with no connection to Cattell; and a number of his closest friends and collaborators, including Richard L. Gorsuch, Ralph Mason Dreger, and John Horn.[41] Gorsuch, a professor and the director of research in the Graduate School of Psychology at Fuller Theological Seminary as well as a Disciples of Christ ordained minister, had written to Matarazzo, claiming that the quotes cited by Cattell's critics were "sentences taken out of context" and then used by "one or two extremists to intimidate us . . . and . . . to lead others to think that we listen to lousy scholarship." In what appeared to be an intentionally deceptive communication conveying the false impression that he was previously a neutral observer unaware of Cattell's work and initially inclined to believe the criticisms, Dreger—who later helped to spread the fiction that the award ceremony had been canceled due to "threats of rioting"—had written to the APA, stating that he had approached the controversy with one opinion but then changed his mind after digging into the details and realizing that the charges were unfounded. According to the *National Psychologist,* a bimonthly newspaper for practitioners in the field, Dreger explained that this "change of heart . . . resulted notwithstanding the 'glowing tributes' by colleagues he respects about a volume written by Richard Tucker on *The Science and Politics of Research.*" In his letter to the APA, the *National Psychologist* reported, Dreger went on to declare that "I am prepared to charge Tucker with obfuscation, quotation out of context, and placing quotations in contexts which distort the meaning of the original," although no example was offered.[42] Presuming that the newspaper account was accurate, I took some comfort in Dreger's inability to render accurately either my name or the title of the book—*The Science and Politics of Racial Research.* But now I looked forward to an academic exchange in which these serious accusations by Gorsuch and Dreger could not be made unadorned by evidence.

Unfortunately, however, after having delivered these uncontested statements in letters or interviews, none of Cattell's supporters were inclined to participate in a public discussion in which they would have to engage with critics of their mentor. Much to my dismay, Horn—well known for his work with Cattell on the distinction between fluid and crystallized intelligence and a core participant in the Beyondist group of intellectuals—responded to McDonald's invitation by contending, in an e-mail message sent to everyone who had been invited to contribute to the *History and Philosophy of Psychology Bulletin*'s special issue, that Mehler and I "would not be appropriate contributors" to the discussion and objecting to our involvement. Mehler, a professor of history at Ferris State University, was "more a journalist" than an academic, according to Horn, and "It should be known," he continued, "that Tucker's writings on Cattell are not objective, that he is not a scholar: he's an advocate . . . [who] has strung together quotations of out-of-context phrases and sentences to support a priori indictments that were not based on scholarly examination of the evidence." The book that led Horn to this conclusion received a number of academic awards—an observation that I make with no intention whatsoever to preclude his right to argue that the work was wrongheaded or worthless, but merely to suggest the presumptuousness of his attempt by fiat to expel from the entire domain of scholarly literature a book that had won, among other honors, the American Political Science Association's Ralph J. Bunche Award "for the best scholarly work in political science in the previous year which explores the phenomenon of ethnic and cultural pluralism" and to single out its author for exclusion from a discussion of the issues addressed in the book. But the very fact that an invitation had been extended to Mehler and myself was an indication for Horn that McDonald, too, was academically suspect, "behaving mainly as a journalist, responding to fads, pandering to popular [*sic*], making [his] way into Who's Who's [*sic*]."[43] From Horn's point of view, if there was to be an exchange over Cattell and eugenics, it had to begin by systematically removing from the list of discussants the people who had raised in print the issues that were at the core of the debate; otherwise, neither he nor the other Cattellians would be willing to participate.

Of course, it would be dishonest to pretend that I do not have a viewpoint about the controversy over Cattell. In that limited sense, it is indisputable that I am an "advocate," but it is for a position reached a posteriori—after lengthy examination of Cattell's work. Indeed, before reading his voluminous writing on science and ethics, I knew only of his contributions to the study of personality, intelligence, and quantitative methodology, and was both surprised and, at first, resistant to the conclusion to which the evidence eventually drove me. But in this sense of arriving at a position based on evidence, very few academics are *not* "advocates." Indeed, that term would certainly apply all the more so to Cattell, who concluded in 1949 that there were sixteen basic factors of personality and then insisted on the validity of this claim for the next half century despite the inability of any other scientist applying the same methods to arrive at a similar result.

McDonald tried to persuade Horn that his misgivings were unfounded in both cases. Judging from Mehler's recently published article on Cattell in *Genetica*, an "international journal of established scientific reputation" and after inspecting some of the "primary source material" on which that article was based, McDonald was confident that the historian would "provide an academically viable essay for the special issue." Similarly, after reading my book and a number of the primary sources on which I had relied, the editor of the special issue concluded, in his response to Horn, that "your characterization of Tucker's work is a caricature." However, McDonald continued, in what was clearly intended as an incentive for Cattell's defenders to remain engaged in the discussion, if subsequent analysis demonstrated that my conclusion was "shortsighted," then "publishing that analysis will make a substantive contribution" to the debate.[44] Unfortunately, these efforts proved fruitless, and none of Cattell's supporters contributed to the resulting special issue, necessarily omitting an important perspective from the discussion. My own brief article concentrated on Cattell's arguments for racial separation, making two observations: that there was no scientific evidence for the various aberrations that he claimed were a result of racial interbreeding and that his assumption that culture was indistinguishable from race was misguided.[45]

Although Cattell's supporters thus refused to participate in a public exchange, I took advantage of the e-mail discussion list assembled by McDonald to respond to their accusations that I had distorted the record. In an effort to dispel the image of Cattell's critics as politically correct fanatics planning to riot, I tried to begin courteously, replying to Horn's attempt to bar me from any published discussion by thanking him for having raised the issue of context of quotations, which I agreed was an important consideration. In response to his charge that I had "strung together quotations of out-of-context phrases and sentences," I then provided for the list members a set of lengthy excerpts from Cattell's books written between the 1930s and 1970s, all of which emphasized the need for the intelligent and successful races to eliminate less advanced peoples, preferably using nonviolent methods, to prevent the latter from blocking evolutionary progress. There were no ellipses in these passages, I pointed out—not a single word had been omitted—but if anyone still thought that they had been "strung together" to create a false impression, I offered to provide additional material. Finally, I confessed to some degree of puzzlement at being labeled an "advocate" for documenting Cattell's lifelong advocacy for an ethical system and a resulting set of social policies that, by all traditional standards, are considered morally intolerable.⁴⁶

There was very little reaction from the Cattellians. Although Dreger had told the *National Psychologist* that he was "prepared to charge Tucker with obfuscation, quotation out of context, and placing quotations in contexts which distort the meaning of the original," he made no response. Neither did Gorsuch or any other of Cattell's defenders on the list who had announced previously that the critics' characterization of his thinking had been essentially a hatchet job. Horn did reply eventually, but only to observe that, although he "did not have time to go into all the instances" in which I had allegedly distorted Cattell's thought, he would cite one example. I had quoted the passage from *Psychology and Social Progress* in which Cattell argued that there were indisputable "cases where it is time to call a halt to a certain line of evolution" and that in previous, less civilized ages this "surgical operation of lopping off the backward branches of the tree of mankind was done violently." In a more enlightened time, Cattell continued, in those "clearly established cases, where it is obvious that the races concerned cannot hope to catch up in innate capacity (and therefore in cultural capacity) to other groups, the leading nations may attempt to reduce the numbers of the backward people by birth-control regulation, segregation, or humane sterilization"; this "repeopling," as he called it, "by more intelligent and alert peoples, of parts of the earth possessed by backward people is merely following the highest moral considerations when it is done with humane feeling for the happiness of the generation of backward peoples then existing." Horn now maintained that the accurately quoted two paragraphs containing these observations were an "instance—a particular possible extension—of the principal argument" Cattell was making but one that "does not follow necessarily from the arguments of the context." That is, because I had chosen a passage from Cattell's writings that, according to Horn, was a poor illustration of the point Cattell was attempting to make, it was further proof that I was "not being objective, and not being scholarly," and, once again, "would not be an appropriate contributor" to any subsequent debate.⁴⁷ Quite apart from the questionable notion that it was a sign of bias on my part not to have determined that Cattell's own example had been poorly chosen to make his point, this putatively inapt instance of his argument was repeated regularly for the next four decades. Cattell's 1972 discussion of Beyondism, for example, again referred to the moral obligation of "successful" groups to expand, increasing their "power, influence and size of population" at the expense of "failing" groups, which were to be "'phas[ed] out' . . . by educational and birth control measures." Aside from this one bizarre claim that I had misrepresented Cattell's beliefs by citing what he himself thought was its logical implication, none of his defenders could produce any specific example in which his ideas had not been rendered faithfully. Indeed, although she claimed that his views had since been modified, even Cattell's daughter Heather—herself a psychologist—acknowledged, shortly before his death, that her father "did write some pretty terrible stuff" before World War II.[48]

However, in response, Heather Cattell, who was also a member of the electronic discussion group assembled by McDonald, did offer a different and more interesting exculpatory claim about her father's early writings, arguing that, in the 1930s, eugenical concepts were far more in vogue among intellectuals in general than was the case after the war. Gorsuch, too, had raised a similar point in his letter to Matarazzo, noting that Cattell's early statements had been "taken out of historical and cultural context" and had appeared at a time when such eugenical issues were "being actively debated among many scientists." According to this line of reasoning, the criticisms of Cattell may have described his early thinking accurately but neglected to consider the zeitgeist of the time, resulting in the sort of misapplication of current moral standards to the interpretation of statements made by historical figures called "presentism." As the 2002 president of the American Historical Association noted, presentist thinking can encourage a feeling of self-congratulation over the moral superiority of contemporary society in comparison to previous generations.[49] In Cattell's case, of course, this concern fails to take into account the substantial similarity between his evolutionary ethics of the 1930s and his Beyondist philosophy developed decades later; in addition to the many indications in his own writing, the *Beyondist* newsletter's enthusiasm over the proposals for racial balkanization in Wilmot Robertson's *Ethnostate* strongly suggested that Cattell's opinions on race had persevered long past the termination of any influence that might have been exerted by the sociomoral views of the earlier era.

But even overlooking this continuity, the claim of presentism is unfounded for a number of reasons. First, this image of Cattell as essentially passive, his ethical beliefs blowing in the direction of the prevailing cultural wind, is in marked contrast to the bold, independent thinker who spent so much of his life telling the scientific mainstream in his field that it was hopelessly adrift, incompetent, or both. Defending Cattell against the "intolerance" and "character assassination" of his critics, one of his supporters accurately described him as an "iconoclast who valued the importance of principle . . . over popular conformity, a scholar who . . . enraged his detractors."[50] Indeed, when the scientific zeitgeist changed dramatically in the postwar period, replacing the genetic determinism underlying evolutionary development with an emphasis on environmentally influenced cultural differences as the preferred explanatory construct for the diversity of human behavior, Cattell did not hesitate to oppose this new paradigm or to support racial separation as a scientifically rational—indeed, necessary—policy, even though he was now in a tiny minority. Although mainstream scientists had abandoned the sort of eugenical thought on which Beyondism was premised, Cattell was as certain of its validity as ever; not the least bit influenced by the zeitgeist, he did not hesitate to stand firmly against the contemporary tide. The claim that Cattell's earliest eugenical pronouncements were no more than a reflection of the intellectual context of his youth is contradicted by the rest of his life.

In addition, Cattell's most unsubtle pronouncements occurred in the late 1930s, a time when the movement was in severe decline, abandoned by numerous scientists, including many leading geneticists, who had once been supportive. As early as 1927, Harvard, which had been in the forefront of the movement, offering four different courses on eugenics in the late 1910s, lost much of its interest, refusing a sixty thousand–dollar legacy from a prominent Philadelphia surgeon because his will had stipulated that the money be used to support a course in eugenics emphasizing "treatment of the defective and criminal classes by surgical procedures." And a decade after attracting hundreds of delegates from all over the world to the Second International Congress of Eugenics, the Third Congress, held in 1932, drew a paltry seventy-three participants. Also in 1932, a *New York Times* editorial called eugenics a "disguise for race prejudice, ancestor worship, and caste snobbery." Four years later, shortly before Cattell warned that England would be swamped by "sub-men," the *Times* called such claims of intellectual decline the substitution of "fear and emotion for science and reason." Many scientists, repelled by eugenics' association with the Third Reich and, in the United States, with groups such as the Ku Klux Klan, came to similar conclusions about the movement's prejudicial nature. In 1937 E. A. Hooten, for example, a Harvard professor of anthropology and former member of the Galton Society, eugenics' eminent inner circle, decided that he could no longer bring himself to play an active part in the movement because of its "vicious racial propaganda." A year later Cattell named "the negro" as one of those races that, despite their "endearing qualities," were appropriate candidates for a process of humane elimination, in which "by gradual restriction of births, and by life in adapted reserves and asylums, must the races which have served their turn be brought to euthanasia."[51] At the time, this was more the statement of someone opposed to the intellectual zeitgeist rather than in thrall to it.

The truth is that, rather than merely being a product of his times and espousing a belief in the sort of eugenics undeniably quite common among the educated classes during his youth, Cattell was a proponent of a particularly extreme form that was rejected by mainstream eugenicists at the time. Although his reliance on Hans Günther and Mathilde Ludendorff as authorities on racial differences might have been understandable in 1933, four years later, with the concentration camps already beginning to fill, the Reich was clearly heading down the slippery slope. Nevertheless, it was in 1937 that Cattell praised the Nazi government both for the involuntary sterilization law, which had been enacted immediately after its seizure of power, and for the regime's "positive emphasis on racial improvement," the most important expression of which had been the Nuremberg laws, banning Jews from various professions, depriving them of the rights of citizenship, and forbidding their marriage to Aryans. Then a year later, just after Jews had been subjected to the hideous persecution of Kristallnacht, he hailed the rise of the Nazis as a ray of hope for their encouragement of the emergence of serious religious values in an otherwise purposeless modern world—an indication that "we shall not be allowed to sink into stagnation or adopt foolish practices in fatal detachment from the stream of evolution."[52]

Yet from the beginning of the Nazi administration, these same policies, which Cattell found to be such an encouraging sign for the development of a scientifically mature religious system, had been viewed as a source of great consternation by many of his senior colleagues in the British Eugenics Society, who worried that the Reich's *politische Biologie,* based as it was on atrocious science and tyrannical methods of enforcement, would only discredit more responsible and respectable approaches to eugenics. Thus, prominent members of the society took pains to separate themselves from the Nazi eugenic policies. Early in 1933, before the passage of any legislation, there was still hope that the Reich might enact more benign measures, and in its official publication, *Eugenics Review,* the society looked forward to a German sterilization law that "will certainly command the assent of all experienced eugenicists." But even while expressing this optimistic view, the society found it "doubly deplorable that the scientific tenor of the proposals should be entirely vitiated by the inclusion of 'foreign races' among the potential sterilizees," observing that "we have not for many years had so disturbing an example of a great nation making itself ridiculous as the whole German campaign against the Jews."[53]

As soon as the Reich actually enacted its sterilization statute, however, any reason for optimism dissolved. The new law was analyzed in *Eugenics Review* by C. P. Blacker—the society's general secretary at the time and later to become director and eventually chairman—who found its provisions regrettable, especially in comparison to the proposals for sterilization supported by the society. "The German Act differs from our Bills in one important respect," wrote Blacker, "which dominates its whole intention and sense": it authorized "compulsory sterilization," meaning that the initiative "for sterilization can be taken by persons other than the candidate for sterilization himself." In addition, he continued, the Nazi legislation contained none of the precautions favored by the society "to safeguard the individual against abuses of his liberty." Finally, the fact that the Nazi act allowed for "sterilization . . . [to] be applied on penal grounds" raised for Blacker further "grounds for disquiet," especially considering the "many occupants of German prisons . . . sentenced for political reasons." Although he acknowledged that the society's council had not yet taken an official position on the Reich's new legislation, Blacker reported that the body had, however, "passed a resolution, bearing indirectly upon Nazi eugenics," declaring that "this *Society* deprecates the use of the term Eugenics to justify racial animosities." In order to assure the public that any English sterilization law would create a system far different from the one enacted by the Reich, in his official capacity as general secretary Blacker called for members of the society to "do their best to dissipate the view that to legalize sterilization necessarily implies compulsion or even the smallest infringement of individual liberty," lest the public be "led to suppose that Nazi eugenics is the only kind of eugenics." Blacker was particularly fearful of the latter possibility:

> That Nazi eugenics is the logical fulfillment of the *Society's* eugenics is doubtless sincerely believed by many people who . . . hate eugenics. Such persons will feel it their duty to give the widest publicity to such beliefs. . . . [T]hey will warn the trustful British public that in supporting the *Society's* policy it will, in fact, be unwittingly taking the first step down the slippery declivity that leads to compulsion, bureaucracy and the tyranny of racial or social majorities. Fellows and Members of this *Society* would therefore do well to seize all available opportunities of pointing out what this *Society* does stand for.[54]

Thus, at the same time that a high-ranking official in the Eugenics Society was making this fervent plea for British eugenicists to dispel the notion that their own platform had anything in common with the Nazi program, Cattell was pointing to the Reich's initiatives as a model for the democracies to follow.

Julian Huxley, another leading voice in eugenics at the time, was invited to deliver the prestigious Galton Lecture in 1936. Like Blacker, Huxley too was dedicated to the movement and optimistic about its prospects, certain that "eugenics will inevitably become part of the religion of the future, or of whatever . . . may . . . take the place of organized religion." No egalitarian, he also shared Cattell's concern that the lowest social classes, those "allegedly less well-endowed genetically," were reproducing at too high a rate and, in response, called for a "curative and remedial" program, which included teaching birth control methods to the poor and making economic assistance contingent on their successful use. Yet at the same time, Huxley denounced "Nazi racial theory . . . [as] a mere rationalization of Germanic nationalism on the one hand and anti-Semitism on the other," calling the attempt to distinguish between Aryans and others—the policy on which Cattell lavished such praise two years later—a "myth" with "no real biological meaning" and ultimately "anti-eugenic." And after one of Cattell's more outrageous predictions of precipitous national decline was reported in the press, provoking a public rebuke from another scientist and causing some embarrassment for most other eugenicists, Huxley wrote to Blacker that "our friend Cattell has been letting himself go in a rather stupid way."[55]

Contemporary scholars writing about the eugenics movement in Britain have concluded similarly that Cattell's views were far from the mainstream. Economist Adrian Wooldridge, for example—author of an influential book on the history of the relation between psychological measurement and education in Britain—called him one of "the most bigoted British intelligence testers" of the time. And in a discussion of British eugenics in the 1930s, G. R. Searle, a well-known specialist in English history, referred to Cattell as a "right-wing extremist." Neither of these scholars could be accused of liberal bias. Wooldridge, for example, opposed the critics of IQ tests, arguing that, contrary to popular opinion, early proponents of widespread testing, such as the controversial Cyril Burt, were actually educational progressives and that, "for all their inadequacies," such tests were "still the best means yet for spotting talent wherever it occurs."[56]

Thus, although it is important to avoid judging behavior from three-quarters of a century ago by contemporary standards, Cattell's pronouncements during that period cannot be explained away merely as a product of the intellectual context of the time. Indeed, not only while his fellow eugenicists were condemning the Nazi obsession with Jews but even long after the onset of war with the Reich, Cattell was continuing to make the kind of statements— for example, his observations about Jews, perseveration, and disposition rigidity—that could have fitted nicely into the literature on the *Judenfrage*. Though, to be sure, Cattell's beliefs were a derivative of the eugenics movement, they were no more a direct expression of the prevailing intellectual atmosphere in the 1930s than David Duke, the unabashed white supremacist and anti-Semite who won elected office as a Republican, could be considered a direct expression of contemporary conservatism or Weatherman, the small violent sect that splintered off from Students for a Democratic Society, a direct expression of the anti–Vietnam War movement. From the moment he first expressed them, Cattell's views were recognized as extremist.

* * *

Because there has been so little widespread, open discussion of the Cattell controversy, many psychologists who know only of his contributions to the study of personality and intelligence are still unaware of the reasons for the withdrawn Gold Medal. Of course, the Cattellians believe that their mentor's thought has been misrepresented and that, as a consequence, there is nothing to discuss. But there are also scientists who are familiar with the basis of the controversy yet, for reasons known only to themselves, wish to deny that it exists. One of the members of the e-mail discussion group assembled by Marvin McDonald in his role as guest editor of the special issue of the *History and Philosophy of Psychology Bulletin,* for example, was the distinguished University of Minnesota researcher David Lykken. Although he did not participate in the exchange, Lykken was a recipient of every message circulated to the group, the majority of which concerned the proper interpretation of Cattell's numerous statements throughout his life recommending that backward races, usually those with darker skin, be eliminated by the "more intelligent and alert peoples" in some manner—"brought to euthanasia" by control of their reproduction, "allowed to go to the wall," or in some other way subjected to the "phasing out" that he called "genthanasia."[57] Lykken received paragraph after paragraph of such exhortations taken verbatim from Cattell's writing. Also circulated to Lykken and everyone else as part of the same discussion were Cattell's observations about Jews—his claim that the inherited racial differences displayed by these "intruders into Europe" caused all sorts of conflicts and misunderstandings, provoking a natural aversion that, he insisted, was called "prejudice" only by the biologically uninformed.[58]

Then in 2004 in an APA journal—as part of his highly favorable review of a book arguing that the late twentieth-century rejection of eugenics had been misguided and that we are on the verge of an era of "new eugenics," in which biotechnologies, such as embryo selection and gene implantation, will be used by the affluent to produce genetically improved children—Lykken offered to the profession his own summary of the charges that, he claimed, had prompted postponement of Cattell's award:

> These allegations were based on work published in Britain in the 1930s reporting Cattell's empirical tests of certain assumptions of eugenics theory. Having developed a measure of intelligence that was relatively "culture-fair," Cattell showed that, indeed, average IQ levels increase as one moves from the unskilled, to

semiskilled, to skilled workers, to those in white-collar occupations, and finally to those in the professions. Another study involved comparing the measured IQs of 3,700 10–year-old children with their number of siblings, showing that, as eugenicists then supposed, the less intelligent children came from larger families. To counteract the decline in overall intelligence that these findings suggested, Cattell proposed the "provision of financial rewards for the more intelligent to have children and the more effective provision of birth control facilities for the less able."[59]

It was "this solid research and these humane proposals," according to Lykken, that resulted, "60 years later, in charges of 'racism' and 'genocide'" from the "small group of zealots" who had "threatened a protest demonstration if the award ceremony went forward." This "irrational antipathy with which eugenics has become invested," he continued, had led the "APA to . . . publicly humiliate one of the most distinguished . . . psychologists"—an illustration, he declared, of the "dangers that confront any contemporary scientist brave enough to explore" eugenic issues.[60]

This account of the reasons for concern about the award was a complete fabrication. Six decades later, Cattell's research on the interrelationships between social class, family size, and IQ score was relatively uncontroversial, certainly unoriginal—the claim that the poor are less intelligent and more prolific had been made both long before and long after his 1937 study—and in any event played no role in the controversy over his award.

One can only speculate about why a highly respected scientist who indisputably knew better decided to offer such a distorted version of the events in a widely read APA publication. For some years Lykken himself had advocated establishment of a system of parental licensure, in which the government would grant formal permission to have children only to couples who can demonstrate that they are economically independent, law abiding, mentally healthy, free of substance abuse, and married. In this plan, a child born to an unlicensed mother would be removed immediately and put up for adoption, while the biological father would be required to pay all costs associated with the birth; if either parent was involved in a second unlicensed birth, "long-lasting or permanent contraceptive treatment" would be mandatory.[61] Lykken insists that this proposal is not eugenics but rather what he calls "eumemics."[62] In contrast to the former, which focuses on increasing the proportion of good genes, the self-replicating units of *biological* transmission, the latter attempts to maximize the spread of good "memes," the self-replicating units of *cultural* transmission; a term first coined by British evolutionary biologist Richard Dawkins, memes not only are passed from one generation to another through tradition and culture but can also be spread horizontally through education and imitation. Although Lykken is correct that, strictly speaking, such requirements for parental licensure would be premised not on genotypes but on behavior, his proposal has undeniably eugenic overtones, especially in view of his explanation that the plan was developed in large part as a method for reducing the size of the "Black underclass."[63] And although Lykken's description of the proposal contained neither mention of phasing out any group nor intent to do so, perhaps he was concerned that an acknowledgment of the true reason for the Cattell controversy would remind a contemporary audience that previous proposals for state interference in individual decisions about childbearing have been informed by less benign motives—an association with potentially harmful consequences for the prospects of a plan that, even without such baggage, naturally elicited considerable opposition.[64]

Or perhaps Lykken and many others have been unwilling to discuss Cattell's views with candor out of fear that such "exposure" would have adverse consequences for the entire discipline's reputation. It has been difficult for some psychologists to acknowledge the role that prominent members of their profession have played not just in the rationalization but in the encouragement of inequality—a reluctance to confront psychology's own complicity in justifying discrimination. In an effort to avoid embarrassment for their field, some contemporary researchers have attempted to deny or revise a historical record clearly demonstrating that a number of their predecessors supported various oppressive social policies on the basis of science[65]—including racial segregation and the restriction of immigration by the "inferior" races from southern and eastern Europe—or arrived at patently absurd conclusions from their own research that nevertheless could provide such support.[66] The controversy over Cattell differs from these other cases mainly in that it began while the scientist at its center was still alive and able to issue his own denial. And the fact that the controversy was sparked by an award from the American Psychological Foundation provided an even more practical reason to be concerned about its repercussions for the rest of psychology: the APF, a nonprofit organization, depends on donations to support its many worthwhile programs—scholarships for gifted students, support for research, and recognition of major contributors. In the brief exchange in the corridor after Wiesel's keynote address, Matarazzo, the organization's president at the time, expressed concern at the possibility that an accusation of "racism" on the part of an honoree could affect the organization's ability to raise funds.

But whatever the reason for the denial and distortion of the facts, the result has been to propagate a version of the events fostering the erroneous impression that the Cattell controversy had to do with the transgression of some frivolous, politically correct boundary, a view that has prevented any consideration of the more important and thought-provoking questions emanating from his work. That more realistic discussion must begin by acknowledging the facts—that throughout a highly productive career Raymond Cattell intended that his scientific contributions eventually provide the data for implementation of an ethical system and corresponding set of policies diametrically opposed to universally accepted principles of human rights and constitutional guarantees, thus deliberately using the authority of science as a justification for racial segregation and other oppressive policies, and providing intellectual support for a host of groups with overtly Nazi sympathies. Only then can there be an informed analysis of the relation between science and ideology in Cattell's work and whether the APF—an organization dedicated to the recognition of scientists whose work "light[s] the way for what can be done to benefit humanity"—should honor a member of the profession with such a record.

A quarter century after the end of the war, Germany began the lengthy process, stretching to the present day, called *Vergangenheitsbewältigung*—the task of coming to terms with the nation's past by present-day Germans, the overwhelming majority of whom had no direct role in it. Psychology too needs to engage in a similar process of candid examination of its own past, not out of guilt or as an exercise in self-flagellation but in order to understand better how some members of the profession have become such comfortable traveling companions with the forces of bigotry and oppression. One significant step in that process would be a forthright examination of Cattell's role in this relationship.

CONCLUSION
SCIENCE, AWARDS,
AND IDEOLOGY

In response to the charges that Cattell's work had encouraged racism, many of his supporters emphasized his warmth and personal decency; this was a good person, they emphasized, who had never displayed ethnic prejudice of any kind, responding to everyone as an individual. "In conversation," recalled Richard Gorsuch—a clergyman as well as an APA fellow, who had been a civil rights activist at the same time that he apprenticed in Cattell's lab—"I . . . never heard comments from Ray that I would interpret as racist." The Web site created in Cattell's memory quickly filled with reminiscences from friends and colleagues noting, for example, that his "close friends included people of all shades of color and beliefs." One respondent, a student at the University of Illinois thirty years earlier, observed that "even as a lowly undergraduate Dr. Cattell accorded me the respect of an equal colleague," adding that he now tried "to treat younger people in the manner that Dr. Cattell treated me."[1] Moreover, as a result of the intermarriage of one of his children, near the end of his life the scientist who had once considered anti-Semitism a biologically unavoidable reaction to the presence of "outsiders" attended his grandchild's bar mitzvah.

There is no reason to doubt that Cattell was indeed a decent, thoughtful person to his friends and acquaintances, and a kindly mentor to his many students with an admirable ability to elicit from them an almost filial loyalty. There is also no reason to believe that these commendable personal characteristics are in any way relevant to a discussion of his socioreligious ideology. The issue is not Cattell's personal reactions to others; no one has claimed that he is David Duke in a psychology lab, personally spewing invective against blacks and Jews. Humans are complex beings, often composed of seemingly contradictory tendencies, and it is hardly unusual to find considerable personal charm and kindness coupled with monstrous beliefs. Two hundred years ago Goethe commented on this paradoxical nature in his almost Freudian observation that "Zwei Seelen wohnen, ach! in meiner Brust, Die eine will sich von der andern trennen" (Two souls reside alas! in my breast; the one wants to separate itself from the other).[2]

In his revealing study, *The Nazi Doctors*, Yale psychiatrist Robert J. Lifton enlarged on this notion, coining the term *doubling* for the process in which two selves were constructed, each one psychologically isolated from the other. For many of these physicians, one self was committed to National Socialist ideology, carrying out such grizzly duties as selection—the regular differentiation of those fit to work from those destined for the gas chambers—while the other self was a loving father and husband, typically characterized by friends as a dedicated and sensitive professional. A leading medical authority in the Reich and administrator of its euthanasia program, later found guilty of war crimes and executed, was described by a close colleague as "a highly ethical person, . . . one of the most idealistic physicians I have ever met," someone who had been ready earlier in his life to work with Albert Schweitzer in Africa. Some concentration camp doctors in Lifton's study displayed sensitivity and kindness toward inmates, in one case even treating Jewish prisoners who had been physicians in a "gentlemanly" manner, as if they were still members of the profession.[3] In no way is this meant to argue that Cattell was involved in or responsible for anything remotely comparable to the atrocities in the camps, but rather to suggest that, if these persons could make such a dramatic separation between the persona that faithfully executed their ideological responsibilities and the one displayed to family members and professional colleagues, then Cattell's cordiality and generosity in personal relationships can hardly be construed as evidence that his system of evolutionary ethics—which, after all, was entirely theoretical and never involved him in personally inflicting harm on anyone else—had no horrific implications.

Justifying Totalitarian Tribalism

In fact, despite his personal charm, Cattell's ideological thought—from his evolutionary ethics in the 1930s to its refinement as Beyondism four decades later—was essentially an intellectual justification for the form of fascism adopted by Nazi Germany and most precisely encapsulated by the phrase "totalitarian tribalism."[4] Although fascism does not have as clear-cut a definition as, say, democracy or even socialism, it is distinguished by a handful of core characteristics also central to the society informed by the principles of Cattell's scientifically based ethics. The most important of these characteristics is the subordination of individual freedoms to the interests of the nation or state, which, in the Nazi tribalist incarnation of fascism, was defined in the racial terms called for by Cattell. As political historian Kevin Passmore has described it, fascism "seeks to place the nation, defined in exclusive biological, cultural and/or historical terms, above all other sources of loyalty and to create a mobilized national community"; it is the pursuit of this latter goal that distinguishes fascism from more garden-variety dictatorships such as those headed by Latin American caudillos. And it was exactly the creation of this mobilized national community, its energy directed toward the society's eugenic improvement and attainment of its racial ideal, that inspired Cattell in the 1930s to lavish praise on the fascist countries for having "disciplined their indulgences as to a religious purpose."[5]

Paradoxically, however, at the same time that it attempts to foster the unity necessary for biological reification of the state, fascism is also typically contemptuous of the mass of ordinary people, believing that their inferiority makes democracy impossible and necessitates instead a system in which they must remain subservient to their betters. As Passmore put it, "Fascists . . . fear that without heroic leadership the masses will degenerate. The people are not capable of choosing a leader through the ballot box—elections simply permit the mediocre masses to choose mediocre representatives." Again, throughout his career, Cattell expressed similar views about the intelligence of the masses, though, in place of the strong man characteristic of fascism, he substituted the handful of elite scientists as the heroes to whom the inferior masses owed a level of well-being unmerited by their own meager abilities. The comforts of modern civilization, he wrote in 1933, "cannot be regarded as the rightful and hard-earned inheritance of all types and all people" but were rather "the creation of perhaps a hundred men of genius," whose accomplishments were enjoyed by "the millions whose minds are indistinguishable in quality from those of the average humans of the paleolithic ages."[6] More than six decades later, Cattell's opinion of ordinary people had not changed, although the number of their scientific benefactors had increased. The improvements in standard of living, he now observed, were due to the efforts of "perhaps 2000 people over the last 500 years who showed an intelligence, independence, dedication and selflessness quite beyond the capacity of the millions who benefited from that work." Indeed, he maintained, "in terms of toil and foresight and intelligence," the latter managed their lives no better than had their distant ancestors.[7]

Finally, in pursuit of its ultranationalist interests fascism also displays contempt for traditional moral obligations toward outsiders—those excluded from the favored race or nation—and even toward insiders if their behavior is perceived to be detrimental to the group's well-being. Thus, Cattell's own rejection of all traditional moral sources and his emphasis on a morality empirically determined by whatever actions contributed to evolutionary progress provided an ideal scientific rationale for fascist systems, and his desire to blur the line between nation and race was particularly well suited to the Nazi regime's emphasis on the creation of a *völkisch* state. Indeed, Hitler's constant focus on the Aryan roots of every aspect of German society—art, music, education, science, personality—was almost identical to the concept of the group mind, which Cattell had borrowed from his mentor and made an essential element of his own ethical system.

Personal animus on Cattell's part toward Jews or any other group was not a necessary element of this ideology. There have always been two routes to totalitarian tribalism, the emotional and the rational; whereas the former relies on hatred—in the case of the Reich, on visceral anti-Semitism—the latter appeals to a cold-blooded but biologically based logic, the premises of which, under the Nazis, were so monstrous that they could override the traditional bounds of morality and provide murder with scientific justification. As Nazi Minister of Propaganda Joseph Goebbels pointed out, some speakers were persuasive through reason and logic, others through rhetoric that came from the heart.[8] In Nazi Germany there was no shortage of either type of appeal. At the emotional extreme were propagandists such as Julius Streicher, the publisher of *Der Stürmer,* the Nazi periodical notorious for its anti-Semitic cartoons, claims of Jewish blood libel—the accusation that Jews used Christian blood in religious rituals—and the motto appearing on the front page of each issue: "Die Juden sind unser Unglück" (The Jews are our misfortune). Yet at the same time that *Der Stürmer* was inciting the masses, Nazi doctrine was being provided with a more intellectually respectable basis by numerous German scientists, most of whom were neither Nazi ideologues, compromising their science to perform a service for the party, nor academic small-fry but distinguished scholars and researchers, often with international reputations. They certainly did not subscribe to the sort of inflammatory rhetoric peddled by rabble-rousers like Streicher. Rather, they believed that the Nazi program was in fact the appropriate mechanism to attain goals that had been judged scientifically necessary, the inescapable route to a society organized according to the iron truths of biology, genetics, and anthropology. In his memoir of Germany's transition to Nazi rule, Sebastian Haffner wrote that "an entire generation of Germans had a spiritual organ removed: the organ that gives men steadfastness and balance, but also a certain inertia and stolidity. It may variously appear as conscience, reason, experience, respect for the law, morality, or the fear of God. A whole generation learned . . . to do without such ballast."[9] The removal of this organ may not have been accomplished through a medical procedure, but it was assisted to a considerable degree by some of Germany's most prestigious scientists and researchers.

These scholars too proposed a scientifically based social ideology essentially indistinguishable from Cattell's thought. University of Munich genetics professor Fritz Lenz, for example, the first German academic to hold a chair in *Rassenhygiene*, welcomed Hitler's ascent to power—and with good reason. Long before anyone heard of the führer, while still a graduate student Lenz had proposed a system of racial ethics *(Rassenethik)* strikingly similar to Cattell's preoccupation with the group mind, in which the highest value was "the people as an organism" and the purpose of the state was enforcement of a biological goal: not to defend the rights of individuals but to ensure that the individual "serves the life of the race. All rights must accord with and be subordinate to this end."[10] To improve the health of the race, in one of the most important prewar German texts on genetics Lenz called for the involuntary sterilization of "the least competent third of the population"— approximately twenty million people.[11] In the same work he also offered a Darwinian explanation for the Jews' development of the traits that made them uniquely suited for such parasitic professions as merchant, trader, money-lender, and politician, all callings in which success depended largely on the ability to exert "mental influence" over others. As a result, Lenz, like Cattell, did not judge Jews substantially less intelligent than Nordics, but thought it important to identify other ways in which the two groups differed; whereas the English psychologist concentrated on differing levels of perseverance as the key characteristic, the German geneticist concluded that the Nordic was "inclined to seek his ends by force, the Jews rather by cunning." In any event, Lenz declared, the racial differences between the groups were genetically inharmonious, and any "crossing of Teutons and Jews is likely . . . to have an unfavorable effect."[12] Soon after Lenz's genetics text was published, a movement arose, led by a politician who, Lenz was pleased to note, had read the book while in prison after a failed putsch and now had announced his determination to implement its conclusions as part of his program. Unsurprisingly, Lenz was impressed by Hitler's wisdom, praising the future führer in one of the most important German biological journals a year before the Nazi seizure of power as the first significant figure who appreciated the fact that racial purification was "a central task of all politics and is ready to campaign for it energetically."[13] And Lenz was extremely proud of his own contribution to the rise of the Nazi movement: when his 1917 discussion of racial ethics was republished just as Hitler assumed control of the state, in the foreword Lenz boasted that the essay "contained all the essential features of National Socialist ideology."[14]

Lenz was hardly the only prominent German scientist to come to the conclusion that the nation's problems were primarily eugenical—at both the individual and the racial levels—and that the Nazis had the solution. These academic authorities typically were not anti-Semites in the vulgar sense, but they could not ignore what they perceived as the scientific facts: like Cattell, they too had decided that the Jews were genetically inimical to the Germans. Otmar von Verschuer, a leading geneticist and director of the Frankfurt Institute for Rassenhygiene, explained that National Socialist policy was "rooted in the science of heredity . . . in the knowledge of the alien racial nature [Fremdrassigkeit] of the Jews," a claim echoing Cattell's observation that the Jews were "intruders" into Europe.[15] Another scientist pointed out that racial miscegenation produced disease because the offspring's various organs would degenerate at different rates;[16] Cattell too had written that mixed-race children suffered from abnormalities caused by genetically "inharmonious" glands. Long before Hitler's seizure of power, Hans F. K. Günther, the Nazi's favorite anthropologist, had argued that anti-Semitism was not culturally determined but the result of an unavoidable hostility to Jews rooted in Nordic blood;[17] on the eve of the Nazi takeover Cattell similarly complained that, because an "unbiologically-minded civilization cannot perceive or appreciate any intellectual causes" for anti-Semitic feelings, they were erroneously "branded as 'prejudice' by would-be intellectuals."[18] Neither Nazi state officials nor leading scientists in the Reich fell prey to this confusion. Both groups agreed that science had transformed anti-Semitism from an irrational, emotional reaction to a more intellectually respectable, scientific basis, one consistent with the latest teachings of biology. Thus, with ample justification the Nazis could claim merely to have designed and implemented a mechanism to attain the goals that the researchers had proclaimed to be scientifically necessary for the genetic health of the nation.

Obviously, the point here is not to hold Cattell responsible for the crimes committed by the Reich; indeed, there is no record that any German official took note of his enthusiasm for National Socialist policies. Rather, the point is to suggest that the same belief system to which Cattell was so firmly committed—at least as enthusiastically as any of the German scientists who fawned over the state's readiness to translate their conclusions into policy—led inexorably to the kind of morally intolerable result that occurred under the Nazis. In *Mein Kampf*, Hitler had called Jews "only and always a *parasite*," who, ever in search of "a new feeding ground for his race . . . had lived in the states of other peoples," imitating their host's culture rather than creating a separate state and culture of their own. Or as Cattell put it, in only slightly less inflammatory terms, the "Jewish . . . practice of living in other nations, instead of forming . . . their own . . . is not 'playing the game.'" Both the psychologist and the führer began by embracing the premise that one racial group can and should find another—because of the latter's genetic incompatibility, reluctance to play the game correctly, or any other reason—so dangerous or degraded that, as a matter of state policy, its members must be physically removed in order to prevent them from contaminating the former. As Sartre observed about the assertion that God did not exist, from such a premise "everything is . . . permitted."[19]

Indeed, a number of scholars have commented on the consistency of the dialectic that drove Hitler from this initial presumption to the Final Solution. In his essays on the Third Reich, historian James H. McRandle, for example, noted, "From insane premises to monstrous conclusions Hitler was relentlessly logical." The führer believed that, in Germany and in every other European society, the Jews were a divisive force, a "culture destroyer"; as Cattell had put it in his own discussion of the social discord caused by ethnic diversity, "Think of the Jews anywhere." Although, according to McRandle, at first Hitler hoped that the Jewish population could be "eliminated from public life" or "stripped of . . . power" without being murdered, eventually he "derived the conclusion" that if Jews were indeed the cultural and biological enemy, then "he who loves the human race must destroy the Jews." It was no doubt with this sort of reasoning in mind that the noted philosopher and political theorist Hannah Arendt commented on Hitler's tendency to refer to the "'ice coldness' *[Eiskälte]* of human logic." And in his discussion of the two different types of appeals, to reason and to emotion, Goebbels used a similar phrase—"the ice coldness of a relentless logic" (Mit der eisigen Kälte einer unerbittlich entwickelnden Logik)—probably repeating what he had heard from the führer.[20] Although the premises of the Nazi state were horrific, once accepted, there was a terrifying rationality to the outcome.

Though sharing Hitler's premises, Cattell would not have arrived at the same conclusion, believing, as he did, that it was necessary only to remove the Jews, not destroy them. But the psychologist certainly would have understood the Nazi leader's reasoning. The two men agreed on the importance of a national identity defined in racial terms, in many ways spoke the same moral language, and considered the elimination of some racial groups not a tragedy but a remedy, a sometimes brutal but nevertheless necessary step toward a world inhabited by better human beings. Hitler too believed firmly in a system of evolutionary ethics, the ultimate goal of which was biological improvement of the human species resulting from eugenic selection both within and between races. In a passage from *Mein Kampf* that could have flowed easily from Cattell's pen, the führer described a *völkisch* philosophy that

> by no means believes in an equality of the races, but along with their difference it recognizes their higher or lesser value, and feels itself obligated through this knowledge, to promote the victory of the better and stronger, and demand the subordination of the inferior and weaker in accordance with the eternal will that dominates this universe. Thus, in principle, it serves the basic aristocratic idea of Nature and believes in the validity of this law down to the last individual. It sees not only the different value of the races, but also the different value of individuals.[21]

It is true that after the war Cattell condemned the Third Reich on a number of occasions, but he never disavowed its policy of physically separating the Jews; in theory the Nuremberg laws were quite in keeping with the goals of evolutionary ethics. What was offensive to Beyondist principles about the Final Solution was certainly not the segregation of a racial minority but rather, first, the lack of more specific scientific evidence that the Jews were in fact a backward race whose "innate capacity" was hopelessly far behind that of "the more intelligent and alert peoples" and, second, the use of violence to achieve a genocidal goal when more peaceful and humane methods were clearly available.

Consider the following thought experiment: suppose that the largest minority group in Germany during the 1930s had been not Jews but "Negroes"—a "racial experiment" that Cattell judged at the time to be a failure, having "contributed practically nothing to social progress and culture"[22] and clearly constituting one of those "instances where interference is called for."[23] At the very least it would have been morally proper in Cattell's analysis to confiscate their land and property and move them onto "reservations"—that is, into concentration camps—where they would be prevented from reproducing as part of a systematic attempt to eliminate the black population. Not only would Cattell have approved of such an incarceration of all members of the race, but he would have praised the action as a reflection of "the highest moral considerations."[24] And even if, in this hypothetical case, the Nazis had decided to eschew the "humane" route for "reduc[ing] the numbers of backward people" in favor of the methods actually employed with Jews, Cattell would have harbored reservations because less uncivilized methods were preferable. But faced with the choice of violent elimination of an outmoded group or the necessity to countenance their continued existence, the scales of evolutionary morality would have come down decisively in favor of the former path.

Cattell never repeated his inflammatory observations about Jews after the fall of the Axis powers—though he never explicitly repudiated them, either—but his ethical system continued to emphasize both the negation of individual rights and the rejection of the moral sources on which they were based. His lengthy explication of Beyondism, written just as Cattell was approaching seventy, called for a number of measures that sounded like vague euphemisms for more modernized versions of policies enacted by the Reich: instead of the demand for *Lebensraum,* a call for "successful" races to "increase their power, influence and size of population" at the expense of "failing" groups; instead of the Nuremberg laws to prevent the intermarriage of particular groups, the management of "hybridization"; instead of racial purification, a program to "screen out the many defective combinations"; instead of forcibly removing those groups whose presence was deemed harmful to the society, "a regular cost-accounting for parasitisms, cultural and genetic";[25] instead of the Lebensborn project, which attempted to produce a superior race by selective breeding,[26] the bizarre proposal to control the increase in mutation rates by first creating mutations and then aborting the overwhelming majority, which could be recognized in utero as "genetic failures"[27]—a plan likely to be found repulsive by even the most ardent prochoice activist. Nor was it coincidence that a publication such as *American Renaissance*—whose own survey of its readership ranked Adolf Hitler first on the list of "Foreigners Who Have Advanced White Interests"[28]—devoted more space, in a three-part series including an interview with Cattell, to Beyondism and its originator than to any other topic since the monthly's appearance in 1990. Just as respected scientists such as Lenz and von Verschuer had refrained from anti-Semitic rhetoric, even while dignifying Nazi policy with their pronouncements, Cattell would never have engaged in *American Renaissance*'s blatant racism yet did not hesitate to lend his prestige to a publication founded on the belief that blacks should be deprived of their constitutional rights.

And despite his eleventh-hour insistence that Beyondism had been intended only for voluntary implementation, Cattell's comments on the "toleration of deviation," near the end of the 1972 book containing all the above proposals, suggested quite the contrary. The "only logical justification for 'liberal' permissiveness," he explained in that work, was ignorance of the "true moral values." But once "morality becomes a branch of science it has the authority of truth; and then should be enforced in practice as 'tightly' as the degree of approximation at that point of scientific advance of the subject permits. The objections frequently raised to authority are actually to a dogmatic, non-explanatory and unprogressive authority, and these vanish if authority itself has a built-in machinery for research movement and is more closely in touch with scientific advance than is the general public."[29]

If research demonstrated that a particular "deviation," cultural or genetic, was not compatible with a society's evolutionary development, then there would be nothing voluntary about its elimination—an ominous pronouncement from a scientist who was certain throughout his career that the interbreeding of some races produced genetically defective offspring. Nor would Beyondism tolerate public opposition to the imprimatur of science. Authority based on scientific certainty, wrote Cattell,

> connotes the possibility of censorship or restraint which, though resisted by mass media in the name of "freedom of the press" constitutes the as yet missing "frontal lobes" in the institution we call the press and T.V. Either an internal or an external censorship has as important and legitimate a role here notably in relation to misrepresentation of fact, biased choice of what is news, and pollution of young minds, as it does already in respect to other professions and other goods supplied to the public. The press has no more right to be free of democratic "quality" controls than education, medicine, the legal profession or business.[30]

It is difficult to interpret these two passages as anything but an intellectual rationale for the sort of subordination of individual rights to the state's interests characteristic of fascism, the one unique aspect of Beyondism being its reliance on science to define the latter.

Measuring Human Worth

At their heart, Nazism and Beyondism—not the 1933 version of the latter proposed by a relative youth putatively influenced by a eugenical zeitgeist but the system of ethical thought outlined in Cattell's mature years—both dismissed the notion of the sanctity of human life in favor of a view of individual and group existence as purely instrumental, the momentary link in an evolutionary chain, concern for the future quality of which had to take precedence over the rights of the living.[31] Rather than being an end in itself, life was a means to an end: evolutionary improvement. Morality thus had to be redefined to give precedence to the preservation not of life in the abstract but of demonstrably superior life, those specimens who would ensure that humanity continued to head in a progressive direction. To identify those who belonged in the latter category, in theory it was necessary to define and assess scientifically each person's inherent, biological value.

The Nazis did not shrink from this task—or so their rhetoric maintained. One German official declared that every individual should be examined for biological worth and then assigned a position according to the results; those whose genetic value did not indicate a productive assignment should be eliminated. Citing estimates as high as 20 percent for the genetically defective proportion of the German population, Reichsminister of the Interior Wilhelm Frick, who later was tried before the Nuremberg Tribunal and hanged, denounced the "exaggerated care for the single individual," which had burdened the state with so many "sick, weak and inferior." "We must have the courage," Frick told the members of the Expert Advisory Council for Population and Racial Policy, "to rate our population for its hereditary value."[32] Noting that the "treatment given a tuberculous patient is partly determined by his social worth," the head of the Tuberculosis Section of the Public Health Service explained that "we National Socialists are in duty bound to foster individuals of social and biological value."[33] Indeed, even the word *minderwertig*, which was commonly used by the Nazis to denote those "inferior" or "defective" persons who were burdening the society, meant literally "less" *(minder)* "valued" *(wertig)*. Yet despite these official commitments, the Reich displayed little interest in any attempt at individual assessment of traits, preferring to judge the worth of individuals according to physical health or racial membership.

Although he may not have approved of the fate accorded to the less valuable members of the Reich, Cattell believed firmly in the premise to which the Nazis merely paid lip service. Indeed, the prospect of rating the inherent value, in some evolutionary sense, of both individuals and races was the reason he had relinquished a promising career in the physical sciences to enter a new field of questionable status, and it was with this goal in mind that he had devoted his lifework to the identification and measurement of the basic dimensions of personality and its group analogue, "syntality." Early in his career, before turning to the use of factor analysis, Cattell had focused his attention primarily on differences in intelligence, but there was never any doubt that the underlying purpose of these studies was to provide a numerical assessment of human value that could be put to such practical uses as determining an individual's number of allowable offspring or right to exercise the franchise. Never reluctant to acknowledge this goal, in his 1937 book, *The Fight for Our National Intelligence,* Cattell excoriated what he called the "moribund morality" that produced misguided appeals for the "equal treatment of unequals" and the equally wrongheaded attempts "to dispel the notion of human worth, and the different worths of different beings." To clinch the case that persons differed in their innate value, Cattell offered an example that, in his view, was so obvious and compelling that it did not need an accompanying explanation: "as if a motorist in an unavoidable situation would hesitate to run over . . . a feebleminded in preference to a healthy, bright child."[34] A morality informed by the scientific measurement of individual traits would instruct society about differences in human worth that were not so clear-cut.

Even near the end of his life Cattell was still certain that scientifically identifiable distinctions in human value were both desirable and theoretically possible, though the more nuanced view of assessment to which he now subscribed led to a less optimistic prediction of how soon science might achieve such a goal. "We reject here the philosophical-religious basis of doubt of 'individual worth,'" he wrote in 1994,

> but we bow to the extreme unreadiness of present socio-biological science to assign value to an individual's total contribution to the viability of a culture. The values, as weights, to be assigned to personal behaviors, would be different in different countries because each group has different goals and faces a different situation from any other. Personal military valor might receive large weight in one and financial skill or scientific creativity in another. . . . But the *conception* of an assignable worth of a given individual for a given culture remains valid.[35]

It might take time to complete the project, but the calculation of human value was still the long-term goal of Cattell's research.

It is important to distinguish between these efforts on Cattell's part and the numerous attempts over the past hundred years to calculate human value in economic terms or to justify economic inequality by appeals to differences in individually measurable characteristics—usually intelligence. As early as 1901, in a lecture to the Royal Anthropological Institute, the British polymath Sir Francis Galton, who coined the word *eugenics* and founded the movement, alluded to his unsuccessful attempts "to make an approximate estimate of the worth of a child at birth" in actual monetary terms, "according to the class [of ability] he is destined to occupy when adult."[36] During the heyday of the movement, eugenicists commonly argued that remuneration should be linked to ability. H. H. Goddard, for example—one of the major developers of the IQ test and the psychologist who devised the nomenclature of "moron, imbecile, and idiot" for the various levels of "feeblemindedness," together with the test scores corresponding to each category[37]—insisted that persons with higher scores were entitled to higher pay as the economic recognition of their biological superiority: "'D' men are worth and should receive 'D' wages; C men C wages (which are higher), etc." The most well-known recent exponent of this position has been Harvard psychologist Richard J. Herrnstein, who famously argued—first, in a magazine article in 1971 and then, twenty-three years later, in the controversial book *The Bell Curve*—that it made good sense to ensure a steep differential in the distribution of resources, with those occupations demanding a high IQ for success receiving more money and prestige, as society's way of expressing "its recognition . . . of the importance and scarcity of intellectual ability."[38] And following the September 11 attack on the United States, a Victims' Compensation Fund was created, administered by a "special master," who was assigned the Solomonic task of determining the relative dollar value of the life of every deceased person from a dishwasher at Windows on the World to an executive at Cantor Fitzgerald.[39] Controversial though some of these positions or activities may be, each of them can be defended without doing violence to traditional notions of morality; all realistic economic systems recognize the necessity for differential rewards associated with different kinds of contributions to society.

Cattell's purpose, however, was never to assess personal characteristics in order to match a person to his or her appropriate material compensation, but rather to determine the "assignable worth" of a life in some more fundamental, nonmonetary sense, one that violates our deeply held beliefs about the equal value of different lives. As the editor of the *Journal of Medical Ethics*, University of Manchester professor of bioethics John Harris, has noted, it is the latter principle that underlies the "view that there are basic human rights possessed by all people in virtue of their humanity." Although naturally there are particular roles and purposes for which some people are preferable to others, the notion of equal value "in this sense," wrote Harris, is the belief "that the individual whose life is valuable is entitled to the same concern, respect and protection as that accorded to any other individual."[40] Nor was Cattell's attempt at differential valuation concerned with the sort of issues involved in cases where life that otherwise could not endure is sustained by medical technology, thus raising complex questions concerning quality of life, right to self-determination, and cost of care. In contrast, Cattell looked forward to the possibility that scientists, on the basis of psychological data, would pass judgment on the relative value of the lives of healthy, functioning, law-abiding members of society. And although his later writings were less specific about the consequences resulting from these calculations, in the context of Beyondism—a religious system that judged the tolerance of genetic shortcomings to be the greatest evil—the notion of scientifically determined differences in human value could not help but lead to the conclusion that some lives were worth saving and others not. Suppose, for example, that the "feebleminded" child that Cattell would not hesitate to run over in order to spare a "healthy, bright" child possessed healthy organs that could be harvested to save the life of a desperately ill, brilliant scientist. The same moral calculus that made the former decision so clear and obvious would have similarly ominous implications for the latter.

The "intellectual comrades" acknowledged by Cattell in his last major work on Beyondism provided additional reason for concern: Revilo Oliver, Roger Pearson, Carleton Putnam, and others whom Cattell referred to as "pioneer writers" and whose thought he pronounced consistent with "the Beyondist viewpoint"[41] were all furious opponents of extending constitutional guarantees to members of races they considered scientifically inferior and had spent much of their lives in a campaign to bring the equivalent of the Nuremberg laws to the United States. Even under the charitable assumption that Cattell's acknowledgment of his intellectual similarity to these persons should not be taken as an indication that he shared their abhorrent opinions and that he somehow envisioned only benign uses for scientific judgments of human value, there is little doubt that Beyondist principles were tailor-made to provide justification for their purposes.

In addition to judging the value of individual lives, Cattell intended for science to make similar determinations about large groups of lives—the different racial "experiments" or "racio-cultural" groups that he viewed as the fundamental elements in the evolutionary process. In this case, his candid explanations left no doubt about how such judgments would be applied. Beyondism defined the highest morality as synonymous with evolutionary progress, a goal that could be attained only by elimination of those groups that scientific measurements had demonstrated to be inferior or less fit. Once again, the logic was as chilling as it was inescapable. As Cattell frankly observed, "moribund cultures," those that had shown themselves incapable of meeting the challenges of nature or of keeping up with more advanced societies, were to be phased out through "educational and birth control measures"—the process that he called "genthanasia"—lest the earth become "a living museum" choked by "more primitive forerunners." Indeed, the provision of assistance to such a failing group or the reluctance of a more advanced race to benefit from its decline he considered the height of immorality. According to Beyondism, once science had pronounced judgment on a group's value, no spurious philanthropy should place an obstacle in the path of evolutionary progress.

Nor were these harsh-sounding views merely abstract rhetoric that might surrender to kinder, gentler impulses in the face of an actual humanitarian crisis. In the early 1990s, Somalia was ravaged by a famine that in some areas took the lives of 70 percent of the children under five years old. In the document prepared for the first meeting of the Beyondist Society, Cattell cited Somalia as an example of an "unsuccessful" society that might be left to "cultural economic failure and natural self genocide."[42] Every natural or medical disaster in a "backward" country was thus to be considered not a calamity but an opportunity—a chance to clear space, removing groups incapable of meeting the evolutionary challenge and replacing them with others more equal to the task. From the Beyondist perspective, for example, an AIDS epidemic decimating sub-Saharan Africa should not necessarily be alleviated with medications developed by more advanced cultures, and Southeast Asian nations, which had not developed the scientific sophisti-cation that would have allowed them to predict an oncoming tsunami in time to evacuate the affected population, should be left to deal with the resulting devastation entirely on their own. Charitable intervention in such cases, informed by what Beyondism considered a misguided sympathy, only perpetuated cultural and genetic defects; a society had to be forced to bear the consequences of its own shortcomings. The inability to do so was an indication that a group lacked the value necessary for evolutionary advance-ment and, provided that scientifically reliable measurements contributed the appropriate confirmation, should be subjected to genthanasia.

Ideology and Accomplishments

Of course, abhorrent ideology and extraordinary cultural contributions are not mutually exclusive. Although he died half a century before the Nazi sei-zure of power, the great composer Richard Wagner, for example, coined the term *final solution* as a euphemism for the elimination of Judaism,[43] and his viscerally anti-Semitic writing contained many of the themes that became central to Nazi thought. In his 1869 essay on Judaism in music, Wagner wrote that Germans experienced an "instinctive aversion" to Jews, an "uncontrol-lable repulsion" in response to their alien "nature and personality"—an ob-servation almost identical to the putatively more scientific formulation later offered by the factor analytic specialist himself. Yet despite these pronounce-ments Wagner is universally recognized as a musical genius, the composer of some of the masterpieces of the late nineteenth century, and although his music is generally banned in Israel, even there the rejection is based solely on a desire not to offend members of the audience, some of whom are Holocaust survivors; according to a former Israeli diplomat, the director of the Israel Philharmonic has acknowledged that "no orchestra can be a real orchestra without playing Wagner."[44]

If it is possible to evaluate artistic accomplishments independent of politics, then there would seem to be even greater reason to make a similarly independent evaluation of scientific work, especially given the objective standards by which achievements in the latter domain are supposed to be judged. Most discussions of the relation between science and politics focus on the extent to which science can be considered in some sense "pure" or "neutral," rendering it exempt from moral critique and suggesting that neither the enterprise nor its practitioners bear any responsibility for the objectionable uses that others may make of scientific results.[45] The instant case, however, involves the opposite question: how to regard the work of a researcher whose accomplishments were intended from the outset to serve a specific and morally repugnant political agenda. Science inspired by such a goal can certainly produce significant advances. Indeed, even in the Third Reich remarkably progressive, socially responsible research was conducted as a direct consequence of Nazi ideology, which called for German society to be purified of environmental toxins in the same way that it was to be purified of alien racial elements. In *The Nazi War on Cancer* historian of science Robert Proctor has described the numerous public health initiatives launched by the regime, whose scientists were far ahead of their time in recognizing the adverse effects of tobacco (including secondhand smoke), carcinogenic substances in the workplace, and excessive consumption of meat and processed foods. Some of the most ardent advocates for public health in the Reich were vicious anti-Semites. Karl Astel, for example, orchestrated the removal of Jews from their positions at the University of Jena, where he was dean and professor of medicine, and later organized their deportation to concentration camps. Nevertheless, it was under his leadership as director of the Scientific Institute for Research on the Hazards of Tobacco (Tabakgefahren) that pioneering research on the effects of nicotine was conducted, including a landmark study on "lung cancer and tobacco consumption," the first clear demonstration of smoking as a central factor in the illness. The scientific importance of this work is not vitiated by Astel's political agenda. As University of Minnesota psychologist Paul E. Meehl—well known for his contributions to philosophy of science as well as to clinical psychology, measurement, and statistical prediction—concisely observed, in an article that did not mention Cattell but was obviously motivated by the controversy over his award, "It would be odd . . . to condemn a scientist for a track record of excellent work products, free of procedural errors, because we had suspected that this 'good science' was ideologically motivated."[46]

Although the notion is certainly appealing that scientific contributions can be evaluated independently from political or religious beliefs, in Cattell's case—a researcher who maintained throughout his professional life that morality should be indistinguishable from science and that scientists should be granted the authority to make decisions about the most fundamental rights of individuals and groups—the two domains are not so easily separable; often it is not possible to place his work cleanly in one category or the other. Cattell himself adamantly insisted that his writing considered "political" by others was strictly scientific. When his 1937 book, *The Fight for National Intelligence*—which declared, inter alia, that the "sub-cultural" not be allowed to vote, that parents have their birth rate adjusted "to the magnitude of their contribution," and that blacks, though "good-natured and lovable," were incapable of functioning in modern civilization—was called "reactionary," Cattell was irate. "I am not interested in politics," he responded, but was only explaining, according to the "scientific evidence," how "the law of natural selection . . . is working out"; anyone exercised by the conclusions, he suggested, should take it up with Darwin.[47]

Indeed, before the controversy over the award, Cattell's supporters had not hesitated to acknowledge that his work elided the distinction between science and ideology. Disappointed that his mentor's work had not exerted greater influence on the field, in 1984 Cecil Gibb, the Australian psychologist who had studied and then collaborated with Cattell, pointed out with obvious annoyance that the professional literature had paid no attention to Cattell's first major statement of Beyondism, even though the book "integrate[d] Cattell's social psychological thinking into a much broader frame and must be, by anybody's standards, very provocative." And in the introductory comments to Gibb's article, John Horn, perhaps Cattell's chief defender in the controversy over the award, characterized his mentor's 1933 work on evolutionary ethics, *Psychology and Social Progress*, as "a plan for adventure that includes almost all the psychology under the heading of social psychology" and "the guide for much of Cattell's subsequent work."[48] To assert, on the one hand, that Cattell's lengthy books on ideology were scientific contributions and, indeed, that other social scientists were remiss in not recognizing their significance for the discipline while, on the other hand, insisting that it was completely inappropriate to consider anything about the contents of these works in judging whether he merited the APF's honors was, to say the least, contradictory.

In any event, the controversy over Cattell was never about whether he should be, as Meehl phrased it, "condemned"—there has been no call to remove his name from introductory textbooks—but whether he should be accorded American psychology's highest honor. In the aftermath of the withdrawn award, his supporters, even while maintaining that Cattell's thought had been misrepresented by critics, insisted that, whatever his ideology, it should have had no bearing on the APF's decision to honor him. Herbert Eber, for example, a close friend of Cattell's and the president of Psychological Resources, an Atlanta firm that specialized in the screening and assessment of public safety personnel, called the postponement "a direct negation of the most fundamental principles of the scientific enterprise."

> A scientist's advocacy of or deviation from "a politically correct" viewpoint, no matter how desirable may be the political goal, is simply irrelevant. APF and APA have undermined the shared civility without which science is impossible.
>
> Not even the most scurrilous charges have even hinted that Cattell's *science* has been in any way compromised or contaminated by his religious or political views. Indeed, Cattell has never done any work comparing intellectual, personality or other traits of *any* racial ethnic or national groups. And such charges, if based upon some reasonable grounds, would constitute the *only* legitimate basis for any "review" of Cattell's research. By its submission to threats . . . APF and APA have done serious disservice.[49]

Of course, in Cattell's early writing empirical comparisons of intelligence between racial groups had not been necessary for him to determine which ones were inferior and should be slated for (preferably nonviolent) elimination. But Eber's larger point elicited considerable sympathy, and even many scientists with no connection to Cattell were offended by the thought that his politics had been a factor in the APF's deliberations. Mark Gluck, for example, the recipient of the APA's Early Career Contributions award who organized his fellow recipients to submit a letter of protest over the postponement, also had acted out of a belief that Cattell's award should be a reflection solely of his scientific accomplishments unaffected by his political ideology no matter what form the latter might take.[50] And with apparent astonishment at what he perceived to be the outrageousness of the APA's decision, Yale University professor Robert J. Sternberg, one of the world's most influential intelligence researchers, claimed that Cattell's award actually had been "suspended pending investigation of his religious beliefs!"[51]

However, even assuming the possibility of disentangling Cattell's science from his ideology, it is naive to expect, as both Eber and Gluck apparently did, that, in determining who should receive science's highest recognitions, the principle of separation between science and ideology should have no limitations whatsoever—that there should be boundless tolerance for scientific work linked to extremist ideology. There is a world of difference between acknowledging that Karl Astel presided over important work on the effects of tobacco and naming him the recipient of some prestigious award for medical research. As Meehl noted in his insightful discussion of the "relevance of a scientist's ideology in communal recognition of scientific merit," there are conditions that clearly warrant considering the former in deciding on the latter. One instance in which, according to Meehl, ideology "may properly be taken into account as a negative factor" occurs when the scientist, "functioning in a scientific capacity, commits clear and gross violations of law or (quasi–universally accepted) ethics." Meehl offered the hypothetical example of a scientist with eugenicist inclinations who advocated in publications and lectures that "all infants born to parents with IQs below 90 should be exposed to the elements on a mountain side."[52] This is not to suggest that Cattell ever favored anything as draconian as Meehl's example. Rather, the point is that, had a scientist spearheaded a campaign to implement such a policy, it would be unrealistic to insist that a professional organization should pay no heed at all to the matter in deciding whether to bestow its honors on such a person. The separation of science and politics is an important principle, to be respected in most instances, but it is not an absolute.

Although Cattell's proposals were offered indisputably in his scientific capacity, whether they did indeed violate ethical standards that are universally accepted is not a simple determination, but there is certainly a strong case to be made for the affirmative. In the 1930s he had argued that the black population should be systematically eliminated and that, to attain this goal, all blacks should be involuntarily sterilized and confined to restricted areas. Though he was never again so specific about either the group to be eradicated or the means to be used, four decades later the larger picture remained essentially unchanged, as Cattell continued to call for the extinction of failing races as a requirement for evolutionary progress, a result now to be obtained through "newer and more humane methods."[53] It is difficult to imagine a set of policies directed toward such a goal that would not violate the United States Constitution, the Universal Declaration of Human Rights, the moral teachings of the major religions, and the common notions of social justice in a free society. Although it is true that numerous technical advances in birth control had occurred by the time Cattell offered the latter proposal, it is ludicrous to expect that people slated for elimination would use them without objection. Despite the vague language promising benign approaches, inevitably lurking behind the concept of genthanasia was once again the specter of confinement to camps and forcibly administered medical procedures.

And even if one grants the extremely charitable assumption that a plan for "phasing out" backward races could in fact be implemented without resorting to intolerable methods, there was still no doubt that Cattell believed that constitutional rights should be abrogated on the basis of scientific conclusions. Law and science, in his view, were regularly in conflict. "The lawyer plays, often ingenuously, with artificial obsolete laws," Cattell wrote in 1994, "while the scientist boldly seeks a basis in natural law." As a result, he noted, in the United States "the past is enshrined" in the Constitution, even though "science defies it at some points, e.g., in asserting the biological inequalities in mankind." Thus, what the country needed to counter its judicial dependence on an outmoded document, according to Cattell, was "a Supreme Court of scientists, expounding newly discovered scientific laws"; without such a forward-looking body, it was not possible to "advance into the future tied to a particular historical accident . . . of the past."[54] Obviously, this analysis confused the Constitution's guarantee of political equality with an assumption of biological equality, the validity of which Cattell believed could be demonstrated or disconfirmed empirically. But the confusion itself was a clear indication of his readiness—indeed, eagerness—to find scientific justification for the violation of constitutionally based, ethical principles that certainly qualify as "universally accepted."

Another condition cited by Meehl in which ideology could constitute a legitimate consideration for a scientific award occurs when "a scholarly organization . . . cherishes a mixture of aims." The American Psychological Association's Division 44, for example, the Society for the Study of Lesbian, Gay, and Bisexual Issues, which describes itself as "psychology's focal point for research, practice, and education on the lives and realities of LGBT people," presents an annual award for Distinguished Scientific Contribution to its field.[55] No one could reasonably argue that, in deciding on the recipients of this honor, the division should be precluded from ruling out a researcher, no matter his or her scientific accomplishments, who was known to support the Supreme Court decision in *Bowers v. Hardwick*, which upheld the constitutionality of antisodomy laws.[56] Indeed, if a psychologist declared his or her conviction that gays were condemned to hell, then, Sternberg's astonishment notwithstanding, Division 44 would have ample justification for considering religious belief in determining whether to honor such a person.

Similarly, if not quite as narrow in scope, the American Psychological Foundation, which named Cattell as the recipient of its Gold Medal Award, seeks not only to recognize outstanding researchers but also "to advance psychology and its impact on improving the human condition," a goal that, among other priorities, includes support for "cutting-edge research and programs . . . in areas such as . . . comprehending and eliminating prejudice."[57] As an additional indication of the latter goal's official status, embedded within the 1997 convention at which Cattell was to be honored was a special "Minicon-vention on Psychology and Racism," organized by the APA's Public Interest Directorate and featuring more than 120 presentations, many of them on how to eliminate "racism in psychology"; as part of the miniconvention, the previ-ous year's president gave a paper titled "APA's Efforts to Combat Racism."[58] Moreover, the APA has regularly issued formal resolutions opposing racial prejudice and discrimination, and published brochures encouraging members to "fight prejudice and racism."[59] In view of such an organizational emphasis, there is nothing inappropriate about considering the ideology of a scientist who, when other members of his profession first turned their attention to the study of prejudice at the beginning of the movement to end segregation in the late 1940s, opposed the entire line of research as itself "woefully unscientific bigotry," based on an inability to understand that the desire to prevent blacks from having contact with whites was rational and defensible.[60] Indeed, the expressions of outrage over the postponement of the award for political rea-sons are tinged with a certain irony in view of Cattell's insistence that anyone who used the word *prejudice* as a scientific concept should be "automatically disqualif[ied] . . . as a social scientist"—not even granted membership in the scientific community, much less be considered for recognition;[61] such a "dis-qualification" would expel from the discipline many of psychology's most illustrious researchers. The fact that well into the 1990s Cattell still maintained that racism was often a "virtue" suggests that the intervening dramatic social changes resulting in greater racial equality had exerted little effect on his views. In any event, the APF was entitled to consider its multiple objectives in decid-ing on whom to honor. As an APF spokeswoman noted in response to the Cattell controversy, "We have two critical concerns as a science organization: we want to protect science, even if it's politically unpopular science, but on the other hand, we also are very much against the inappropriate use of science to promote anti-social or destructive measures."[62] Thus, despite the general importance of separating disciplinary contributions from political ideology, in this case they were linked by the APF's and APA's organizational goals.

A final condition in Meehl's analysis that could justify the consideration of ideology as a negative factor occurs when it influences the scientist "to com-mit scientific errors which are major or numerous and unretracted despite being clearly shown." Although this concern is less applicable to Cattell's work than the other two, throughout his career he persisted, for apparently ideological reasons, in certain claims that were demonstrably false. Most glaring was his decades-long insistence that the offspring of interracial matings suffered from various genetic defects, a scientifically unfounded conclusion to which Cattell nevertheless adhered—from his prewar warnings of glandular abnormalities caused by races that were "inharmoniously adapted to each other" and claims that the "unstable governments" in some European countries were due to "mixed blood" to his 1987 observation that the "unfortunate combinations" produced in the American melting pot were "partly responsible for the higher crime and insanity rates in the U.S.A. than in the parent countries." There has never been any empirical evidence in support of these assertions. Indeed, in 1974 biologist Kenneth F. Dyer conducted an exhaustive review of the research on racial mixtures, concluding that "the whole notion of disharmony as a result of ethnic crossing is a pure myth. . . . [R]ace crossing in man has no harmful or detrimental effects in the long term or the short term, to the races involved, or indeed to man in general."[63] There has been no subsequent research that would challenge Dyer's words. Cattell's various claims of hybrid aberrations and harmful interracial combinations were all baseless—properly relegated to the same category of scientific validity as hypnotically retrieved memories of past lives or alien abduction.

Also in the face of substantial evidence to the contrary, Cattell continued to insist that the population's intelligence was systematically declining, often citing the results of his 1937 study, which had concluded that the average decrease was about one point per decade.[64] Yet one of the most well-documented conclusions in the modern study of intelligence—hinted at as early as 1948[65] but known with certainty since at least 1984—has been the "Flynn effect," discovered by New Zealand political scientist James Flynn, who found that IQ scores have been increasing throughout the world at a rate of some three points per decade.[66] Thus, at almost the exact same time that Cattell was still warning of the same decline in intelligence he had claimed to find a half century earlier,[67] the American Psychological Association, as part of its "commitment to enhance the dissemination of scientific psychological knowledge," published a volume titled *The Rising Curve: Long-Term Gains in IQ and Related Measures*. The bulk of the book was devoted to possible explanations for the established finding that, as the introduction noted, "Scores on intelligence tests are *rising*, not falling; indeed they have been going up steeply for years. This rapid rise is not confined to the United States; comparable gains have occurred all over the industrialized world."[68] Whether it was the benign effects of racial interbreeding or the increasing level of intelligence, Cattell did not hesitate to assert the exact opposite of scientific results inconvenient from the Beyondist perspective. Although it might be argued that these scientific errors, which had little to do with Cattell's own research and did not taint his contributions to the study of personality and intelligence, were minimal and should be overlooked, the other two conditions suggested by Meehl certainly apply to Cattell's work.

Because Cattell withdrew his name from consideration for the Gold Medal Award, it is not possible to know what the Blue Ribbon Panel would have decided had its members proceeded with their charge, but there is substantial evidence in his writing to justify the APA's concern over "the inappropriate use of science to promote anti-social or destructive measures." Assuming that the panel did indeed make such a determination, however, there is still a wide range of actions that it could have recommended as a consequence. Withdrawal of the award is at one end of a spectrum of possibilities. Less extreme, for example, the panel might have recommended that Cattell nevertheless be honored for some narrowly defined contribution—perhaps the distinction between fluid and crystallized intelligence or his pioneering work on the factor analysis of personality; this sort of possibility was actually suggested by Robert Sternberg.[69] Or it might have recommended that the award be conferred but accompanied by a statement in which the APF/APA formally dissociated themselves from elements of Cattell's work. But even had the panel determined that there was no reason to withhold the award, I would have had no objection: after a thorough process of examination, I was prepared to accept the results, whatever they might be. The point is that, given the record in Cattell's case, there was certainly ample reason to have such an examination. The outraged denunciations of mistreatment and claims that Cattell had done no more than transgress some meaningless boundary of political correctness emanated either from ignorance or from disingenuousness.

"The Chief Source"

Quite apart from whatever judgment the Blue Ribbon Panel might have rendered about the extent to which Cattell's science promoted antisocial or destructive measures, his belief that moral or religious values should be derived from scientific knowledge was extremely misguided. From Aristotle, who maintained that, for some people, empirically identifiable traits made "the condition of slavery . . . both just and beneficial," through the Third Reich, which proclaimed National Socialism to be "the political expression of our biological knowledge," to the campaign to preserve racial segregation in the United States on the grounds that blacks were biologically inferior, history is filled with horrible examples of the misery caused by predicating moral directions on supposedly scientific conclusions.[70] No matter how valid or profound the latter may be, they have no implications for the former, which are an expression of humanitarian ideals and notions of social justice, informed by such sources of moral thought as conscience, constitutional rights, and traditional religious beliefs. This dualism has been a fundamental concept in Western thought at least since the Enlightenment, resulting in the oft-observed truism that "ought" should not be derived from "is." In particular, Cattell's attempt to derive religion from science thus sought to interlink two domains that evolutionary biologist and popular essayist Stephen Jay Gould called "nonoverlapping magisteria," science seeking to answer questions about the lawfulness of the empirical universe and religion extending "over questions of moral meaning and value." Or as Einstein similarly and more succinctly replied, after the archbishop of Canterbury had asked him what effect the theory of relativity would have on religion, "None. Relativity is a purely scientific matter and has nothing to do with religion."[71]

Of particular irony, Cattell's contention that evolutionary science provided the basis for a religion made him a strange bedfellow of some of science's most intransigent enemies. Biblical fundamentalists have long maintained that evolution is incompatible with traditional religion, arguing that the former inevitably leads to its own (per)version of the latter, one that substitutes scientific materialism in place of a divine creator. Of course, this assertion has been, in large part, a tactic designed to provide a rationale for the introduction of creationism into science classes on an equal footing with evolution. But there is certainly no doubt that, for some scientists, the fact of evolution has rendered the rejection of a creator not only possible but indisputable; one publishing trend in the new century has been the emergence of what *Time* magazine called an "atheist literary wave," cresting with the appearance in 2006 of evolutionary biologist Richard Dawkins's succinctly titled book *The God Delusion,* an unapologetic argument that religious belief is not merely nonsense but "pernicious . . . evil" nonsense and that rearing children in the faith is tantamount to child abuse.[72] However, only Cattell among contemporary scientists took the next step, confirming the reality of the antimodernists' ultimate bogeyman by offering evolution not only as a reason to deny the existence of God but as the basis for faith's oxymoronic competitor: an atheistic religion.

The substance of that religion, the ultimate goal toward which Cattell's research was directed, is disturbing for many reasons. First of all, its scientific premise is untenable. At the core of Cattell's ethical thought is racial essentialism, first expressed in his early attempts to find specifically racial characteristics and later embodied in his use of the slightly more nuanced term *racio-cultural* group. Inherent in this point of view is the notion that culture is a genetic consequence of racial group membership—that science and technology, art, music, literature, and custom are all manifestations of, and therefore essentially inseparable from, race. This assumption misunderstands the process by which culture is acquired. A relationship to culture is established by an individual through personal engagement, not by being born into one race or another. Although culture frequently arises from the experience of a racial group, no race has a proprietary claim on its culture or an exclusive, genetically derived ability to enjoy it. As the famous intellectual and activist W. E. B. DuBois wrote in *The Souls of Black Folk,* "I sit with Shakespeare and he winces not. Across the color line I move arm in arm with Balzac and Dumas. . . . I summon Aristotle and Aurelius and what soul I will, and they come all graciously with no scorn or condescension."[73] "Sitting" with these authors, DuBois has attained a relationship with them unavailable to others who have not made the necessary effort, no matter how impeccably Anglo-Saxon their pedigree might be.

This genetic identification of race with culture on Cattell's part has become ever more anachronistic, a reminder of eras and societies with beliefs now universally considered both inane and unjust. It was under the apartheid regime, for example, that the South African Broadcasting Company barred four nonwhites from participating in a Beethoven contest on the grounds that "different races perform best in their own idioms."[74] In the same vein a book highly recommended by a reviewer in the *Mankind Quarterly* a few years before Cattell joined its editorial board declared that a "Japanese or Indian conducting Beethoven or Verdi, a Chinese playing Chopin, or . . . Negro opera singers should offend our sense of truth" because "Western music" was inevitably degraded when played by "non-Westerners."[75] And the Nazis opposed what they called the "niggerizing" *(Verniggerung)* of music and forbade Germans to play jazz.[76] Though phrased less odiously, Cattell expressed similar sentiments when he warned, for example, that "the musical beat from the jungle, or even the mood of the literature of Dostoyevsky [could] introduce incompatible elements in . . . Anglo-Saxon culture," or worried that a "borrowed" cultural element could "prove indigestible, functionally inconsistent and disruptive of the existing pattern in the borrower."[77]

Especially at the dawn of the new century the whole idea of "racio-cultural" groups is myopic. Cultures have always had what the distinguished Princeton University philosopher K. Anthony Appiah calls an "inevitably mongrel, hybrid nature," making the notion of "cultural purity . . . an oxymoron," and the degree of intermingling has become ever more extensive as the electronic era's development of a global network of information, and the instantaneous communication that it enables, has led to new connections between people, whatever their race, location, or nationality, solely on the basis of common cultural interests.[78] Moreover, the exponential growth in interracial marriage has begun to create what demographers call "the beginning of the blend," blurring definitions and boundaries, calling old categories into question, and changing the society's entire concept of race. In the academy the canon has been enlarged to include more works by non-Western authors; if Cattell was concerned that Dostoyevsky might be incompatible with Anglo-Saxon sensibilities, one can only imagine what he would have said about Chinua Achebe or Gabriel García Márquez. Indeed, the notion of an Anglo-Saxon popular culture in the United States is largely an anachronism. From the plays of August Wilson to the novels of Toni Morrison and John Edgar Wideman, from the clothing line marketed and performance poetry sponsored by hip-hop entrepreneur Russell Simmons to the film scores composed and the music CDs produced by Quincy Jones, the contributions of black citizens are not *at* the cutting edge of American culture; they *are* the cutting edge. And what Cattell contemptuously dismissed as "racial slumping" has produced some of the most interesting music in recent years: jazz vocalist Bobby McFerrin conducting major symphony orchestras and singing the music of Mendelssohn, Mozart, Bach, and Tchaikovsky, accompanied by a chamber orchestra, or Hasidic rabbi Matisyahu Miller, who grew up in Crown Heights, a community where Orthodox Jews and Rastafarians mingle, and whose singing combines spiritual lyrics with reggae and hip-hop rhythms. Naturally, there are individual differences in cultural interests that may be correlated to some extent with ethnicity. But the belief that race and culture are linked exclusively or that some sort of mismatch in compatibility makes it imperative for some races to avoid cultural areas for which they are not genetically suited and by which they are even, in some sense, endangered cannot be taken seriously.

Even more objectionable than its misguided beliefs about race and culture, Cattell's empirically derived religion is deeply immoral. Instead of viewing humanity as what one population geneticist calls "a single lineage sharing a common evolutionary fate," Beyondism requires groups to compete in a contest against both each other and the environment, the outcome of which would determine which ones should remain to populate the future and which ones, having served their purpose, would have their presence judged no longer biologically useful. There is little doubt, to use Cattell's terminology, who would be the "successes" in this sort of competition and who the "failures." Instead of leading to the end of history, the victory of one side in the East-West conflict has highlighted the more agonizing North-South conflict, pitting not one ideology against another but the prosperous against the poor. No longer propped up by one side or the other of the cold war, some societies in the global South have been left to their own devices, their inhabitants forced to scramble for survival, while the more powerful nations of the North rush to secure control of dwindling natural resources. As writer and correspondent for the *Atlantic Monthly* Robert D. Kaplan describes this "bifurcated world," part of it is "healthy, well fed, and pampered by technology," while the other larger part is condemned to a Hobbesian "life that is 'poor, nasty, brutish, and short.'" Disease, famine, drought, and environmental disasters threaten to overwhelm the latter areas and decimate their populations. In response to these humanitarian crises Beyondism would sanctify rapacity as religion. Rather than foster cooperation among groups and encourage aid from the wealthy and scientifically advanced to the impoverished and technologically backward, Cattell's system of ethics demands that the former deliberately withhold assistance from the latter and prepare to expand at their expense. Adamant in its opposition to ameliorate suffering, Beyondism labeled the provision of emergency aid in dire circumstances "immoral acts militating against evolution . . . to be avoided in the interests of the highest group morality," because, as Cattell explained, "charitable" support to a failing group either reinforced its faulty habits or postponed the elimination of its genetic defects.[79]

Indeed, in addition to forbidding such external assistance, Cattell judged it equally immoral for a group that had developed some technical or medical advance to share it with others, steadfastly maintaining that such breakthroughs should be kept the exclusive property of the racio-cultural group in which they were developed, lest some other people derive unmerited benefit from the discovery. That scientists themselves were disinclined to observe this prohibition, he wrote, "should by no means be considered evident [*sic*] of nobility of ideals or concern for all mankind," because "a child-like enthusiasm for what he is doing will render the average scientist blind to all kinds of consequences and moral obligations," and "in this state of excitement he feels nearer to a fellow scientist from some alien culture than he does to his fellow citizens." Quite apart from the apparent callousness of this reluctance to share advances that could improve or save lives, it is a violation of one of the "institutional imperatives" described in sociologist Robert Merton's canonical essay on "the ethos of science." As an "integral element" in the "complex of values and norms which is held to be binding on the man of science," Merton named "communism"—in the sense that "the substantive findings of science are a product of social collaboration and are assigned to the community," keeping "property rights . . . whittled down to a bare minimum." The scientist may claim the recognition and esteem commensurate with a significant discovery, and particular nations may take pride in the accomplishments of their scientists, but "all this," noted Merton, "does not challenge the status of scientific knowledge as common property."[80]

Moreover, Cattell's desire to make scientific improvements racially proprietary was based once again on anachronistic demographic assumptions, especially in the United States, which now includes more citizens than ever of Asian, Latin American, Middle Eastern, and African backgrounds. David Ho, *Time*'s "Man of the Year" in 1996, is a pioneering AIDS researcher and director of the Aaron Diamond AIDS Research Center in New York City, who was born in Taiwan and came to the United States as a twelve year old. Pingsha Dong was raised in the People's Republic of China and learned welding as a student before becoming a researcher at the Battelle Institute in Columbus, Ohio, where he revolutionized the field by developing a new method for measuring the strength of a welded joint. Mae Jemison, a black woman with an undergraduate degree in chemical engineering from Stanford and a medical degree from Cornell, was the science specialist on the Endeavor space mission before going on to found the Jemison Group, designed to integrate science and technology into daily life. (She also established two other organizations, both of them heresies from the Beyondist point of view: one intended to assist developing countries adopt new technologies, the other an international science camp for youth.)[81] In the global village that is the modern world, the belief that scientific and medical discoveries should be kept the exclusive possession of a specific "racio-cultural" group is not only immoral; it is meaningless.

Thus, the "branch of science" that, according to Cattell, would provide humans with "moral knowledge" and define "the finest ways to spend our lives" in fact sought to turn morality on its head, condemning the very acts that truly merit such lofty words.[82] Doctors without Borders/Médecins sans Frontières (MSF), for example, is an international humanitarian organization and recipient of the Nobel Peace Prize, composed of courageous medical workers, epidemiologists, and sanitation experts who volunteer to risk their own lives in the most dangerous and remote parts of the world in order to provide emergency care to people victimized by epidemics, natural disasters, and armed conflicts or marginalized by exclusion from medical attention, and to bear witness—to raise public awareness and speak out against the causes of the suffering. Making themselves available on short notice, members of MSF are often the first to arrive at the scene of a crisis and typically dedicate six to twelve months to an assignment, for which they receive only a modest stipend. In 2006 the organization's activities included addressing malnutrition in Niger and Katanga, responding to an epidemic of cholera in Angola, and providing medical assistance to refugees in Darfur.[83] To the rest of the world, these extraordinary people are heroes; from the Beyondist point of view, they are villains, interfering with the process of evolutionary advancement by helping to preserve moribund groups that should be phased out to clear space for their betters.

Indeed, in the topsy-turvy moral world envisioned by Cattell there is hardly any foreign aid program widely regarded as humanitarian that would not be considered unacceptable by Beyondist standards. In 2004 a panel of leading economists, including four Nobel laureates, considered proposals for the best way to advance global welfare if the resources were made available and rated, as the highest priorities, halting the spread of disease and combating malnutrition and hunger in developing countries.[84] An overwhelming majority of Americans support the use of taxpayer money for this sort of assistance,[85] which is not only a benevolent but often an extremely efficient use of resources: inexpensive vaccines can save the lives of millions of children in the third world, and an intervention as simple as providing five-dollar mosquito nets can prevent millions of deaths a year in Africa from malaria.[86] In 2005 *Time* named Bill and Melinda Gates and rock musician Bono its "Persons of the Year" for their efforts to end poverty and disease in developing countries. Instead of putting their names on a museum or a university building, these wealthy people chose a different type of philanthropy. In addition to helping organize the Live Aid concerts and persuading leaders of the G8 nations to double aid to the poorest countries, Bono cofounded an organization, one priority of which is to fight AIDS in Africa. The Gateses created the world's largest charity, which also focuses on third world poverty, contributing previously unheard-of amounts of money to support immunization and other measures for improving child health care and to respond to food shortages;[87] in a Beyondist heresy, the foundation's Web site declares, "All lives—no matter where they are being led—have equal value."[88] These are all efforts that transcend the usual political divisions: along with a long list of liberals from the entertainment world, Bono has involved well-known conservatives such as Jesse Helms, Rupert Murdoch, and Pat Robertson in his projects. Yet all these attempts to improve the quality of life for people living in grinding poverty are rejected by Beyondism as misguided social work, antithetical to true human progress. Whether or not one believes that Cattell should have received the APF's ultimate award, it is difficult to view the goal toward which he himself thought his research should be directed as anything other than repugnant.

* * *

"The chief source of man's inhumanity to man," observed the eminent theologian Reinhold Niebuhr in 1965, "seems to be the tribal limits of his sense of obligation to other men."[89] However, Niebuhr's observation tells us nothing specific about the nature of our moral obligations toward others, even if those tribal limits were to be overcome. Some contemporary ethicists have argued that people in the United States who are fortunate enough to enjoy material comfort should be giving substantial amounts of their worldly wealth to organizations such as UNICEF or OXFAM, which work to alleviate hunger and illness in developing countries.[90] To find such extreme utilitarianism inconsistent with our natural tendency to be more concerned about the welfare of family, friends, fellow citizens, and others with whom we share genetic, civic, or cultural bonds is not to dismiss our obligations to strangers with whom we have little in common beyond our shared humanity; as Appiah points out, "Each person you know about and can affect is someone to whom you have responsibilities: to say this is just to affirm the very idea of morality."[91] The force of this admonition is in no way diminished because there is disagreement over what that responsibility should entail, either individually or collectively. But the lack of consensus is no reason to adopt Cattell's belief, which would convert Niehbuhr's "chief source of inhumanity" into a cardinal rule.

In a debate with William Shockley—the Nobel laureate physicist who a generation ago conducted a campaign funded by a segregationist multimillionaire to persuade the public of the dysgenic threat posed particularly by blacks in the United States[92]—the anthropologist and author Ashley Montagu, with a straight face, told the story of a much "valued chimpanzee who escaped from the Bronx Zoo, and since he was a very amiable and intelligent character, a sedulous search was instituted. And you may find this difficult to believe," continued Montagu in his stiff English accent to an already chuckling audience,

> but where do you think he was found? In the lowermost stacks of the New York Public Library. And you may find this even more difficult to believe, but in his left hand he was holding a copy of the Bible, and in his right hand he was holding a copy of Darwin's *Origin of Species*. And when he was asked for an explanation of the meaning of this, he meekly replied, "Well, I was simply trying to discover whether I'm my brother's keeper or my keeper's brother."[93]

Raymond Cattell's undeniable contributions to psychology were, unfortunately, intertwined with an ethical system based on the odious belief that in many instances an affirmation of the latter conclusion necessarily indicated a rejection of the former. But as Montagu concluded about the chimp's dichotomy, the truth, of course, is that we are both.

NOTES

Introduction

1. L. R. Goldberg, "Explorer on the Run," *Contemporary Psychology* 13 (1968): 617. The book under review was R. B. Cattell and F. W. Warburton (with the assistance of F. L. Damarin Jr. and A. B. Sweney), *Objective Personality and Motivation Tests: A Theoretical Introduction and Practical Compendium* (Urbana: University of Illinois Press, 1967).

2. See S. J. Haggbloom et al., "The 100 Most Eminent Psychologists of the 20th Century," *Review of General Psychology* 6 (2002): 139–52.

3. A description of the Society of Multivariate Experimental Psychology's Cattell Award, together with a list of past recipients, can be found at the organization's Web site, http://www.smep.org/cattell.htm. A description of the American Educational Research Association's Raymond B. Cattell Early Career Award, together with a list of recipients, can be found at the AERA's Web site, http://www.aera.net/about/awards/ecapast.htm. The Psychology Department at the University of California–Davis also gives an internal award in Cattell's name for support of research work conducted while on sabbatical leave; see the note under "Leah Krubitzer" at http://psychology.ucdavis.edu/news/2002Spring/Sp2002.htm.

4. From the citation for "Gold Medal Award for Life Achievement in Psychological Science," *American Psychologist* 52 (1997): 797–99.

5. The "Statement of the American Psychological Foundation Concerning the 1997 Gold Medal Award for Life Achievement in Psychological Science," dated August 14, 1997, was distributed at the convention.

6. Both Barry Mehler and Abraham Foxman were quoted in P. J. Hilts, "Group Delays

Achievement Award to Psychologist Accused of Fascist and Racist Views," *New York Times,* August 15, 1997, A10.

7. Andrew Winston to Joseph Matarazzo, August 5, 1997. I am extremely grateful to Andrew Winston for providing me a copy of this letter.

8. W. H. Tucker, *The Science and Politics of Racial Research* (Urbana: University of Illinois Press, 1994), 239–49; Tucker to Rhea Farberman, August 11, 1997 (copy in my possession).

9. See "Victim of Liberalism," editorial, *Augusta (Ga.) Chronicle,* August 20, 1997; D. K. Detterman, letter to the editor, *APA Monitor,* May 1998, 5.

10. See C. Holden, "Cattell Relinquishes Psychology Award," *Science* 279 (February 6, 1998): 811. Composition of the panel is described in chapter 4.

11. R. B. Cattell, "Open Letter to the APA," December 13, 1997. A copy of the letter is available online at http://www.stthomasu.ca/~jgillis/awalifope.htm.

12. See, for example, the entries at http://www.stthomasu.ca/~jgillis/cattell.html and http://www.cattell.net/devon/rbcpers.htm.

13. D. Child, "Obituary: Raymond Bernard Cattell," *British Journal of Mathematical and Statistical Psychology* 51 (1998): 353. The obituary can also be found online at http://www.stthomasu.ca/~jgillis/triden.htm.

14. Quoted in H. E. P. Cattell and J. Horn, "Raymond Bernard Cattell (1905–1998): His Life and Scientific Contributions," http://www.cattell.net/devon/rbcbio.htm. The original observation appeared in Goldberg, "Explorer on the Run," 618. See also J. Horn, "Summing Up," *Multivariate Behavioral Research* 19 (1984): 339.

15. G. Boyle, "Remembering Raymond Bernard Cattell," http://www.cattell.net/devon/rbcpers.htm#Greg%20Boyle.

16. K. A. Schneewind, "Remembering Raymond Bernard Cattell," http://www.cattell.net/devon/rbcpers.htm#Klaus%20A.%20Schneewind; R. M. Dreger and I. A. Berg, "Psychology of the Scientist, LXXXIV: Raymond Bernard Cattell (1905–1998)," *Psychological Reports* 90 (2002): 844. The article is also available online at http://www.stthomasu.ca/~jgillis/tridre.htm.

17. J. I. Levy, "Remembering Raymond Bernard Cattell," http://www.cattell.net/devon/rbcpers.htm#John%20I.%20Levy; R. Gorsuch, "Eulogies: Raymond Bernard Cattell," February 7, 1998, http://www.cattell.net/devon/rbceul.htm#Richard%20Gorsuch.

18. A. Sweney, "Open Letter from Prof. Arthur Sweney," http://www.stthomasu.ca/~jgillis/triswe.htm; Dreger and Berg, "Psychology of the Scientist," 841.

19. Cattell published two chapter-length autobiographies: "Travels in Psychological Hyperspace," in vol. 2 of *The Psychologists,* edited by T. S. Krawiec (New York: Oxford University Press, 1974), 85–133; and "Raymond B. Cattell," in vol. 6 of *A History of Psychology in Autobiography,* edited by G. Lindzey (Englewood Cliffs, N.J.: Prentice-Hall, 1974), 59–100. The quote in this paragraph comes from the latter, p. 61.

20. Cattell, "Raymond B. Cattell," 62. The book was originally published as *Under Sail through Red Devon, Being the Log of the Voyage of the "Sandpiper"* (London: Alexander Maclehose, 1937). In 1984 it was republished in two parts: *Adventure through Red Devon* and *Under Sail through South Devon and Dartmoor* (Exeter: Obelisk, 1984).

21. Cattell, "Raymond B. Cattell," 62.

22. Ibid., 63.

23. Ibid., 64.

24. Ibid.

25. R. B. Cattell, "The Voyage of a Laboratory, 1928–1984," *Multivariate Behavioral Research* 19 (1984): 121; Cattell, "Travels in Psychological Hyperspace," 88; Cattell, "Raymond B. Cattell," 64, 82.

26. Cattell, "Travels in Psychological Hyperspace," 90. These positions included "tak[ing] on the protective coloration of an educationist" at Exeter University and advising at the progressive Dartington Hall school. See Cattell, "Raymond B. Cattell," 65; Cattell and Horn, "Raymond Bernard Cattell"; and J. Gillis, "Raymond Bernard Cattell (1905–1998): A View of His Life with Reflections," http://www.stthomasu.ca/~jgillis/bio.htm.

27. Cattell, "Travels in Psychological Hyperspace," 89. The book appeared as *Psychology and Social Progress: Mankind and Destiny from the Standpoint of a Scientist* (London: C. W. Daniel, 1933).

28. Cattell, "Voyage of a Laboratory," 123; Cattell, "Raymond B. Cattell," 67.

29. R. B. Cattell, *The Fight for Our National Intelligence* (London: P. S. King, 1937).

30. Cattell, "Raymond B. Cattell," 68. On the successes of the eugenics movement, see Tucker, *Science and Politics*, chap. 3.

31. E. L. Thorndike, *Human Nature and the Social Order* (New York: Macmillan, 1940); Cattell, "Travels in Psychological Hyperspace," 90.

32. Cattell, "Raymond B. Cattell," 70; R. B. Cattell, *Psychology and the Religious Quest: An Account of the Psychology of Religion and a Defence of Individualism* (London: Thomas Nelson, 1938).

33. Cattell's brief marriage was to Catherine Jones. See the entry in the "1938" section in http://www.ferris.edu/isar/bibliography/catbib.htm.

34. On G. Stanley Hall and Clark University, see D. Ross, *G. Stanley Hall: The Psychologist as Prophet* (Chicago: University of Chicago Press, 1972).

35. S. B. Sarason, *The Making of an American Psychologist: An Autobiography* (San Francisco: Jossey-Bass, 1988), 110; Cattell, "Travels in Psychological Hyperspace," 125; Cattell, *Psychology and Social Progress*, 353. See also Cattell, "Raymond B. Cattell," 74.

36. Cattell, "Raymond B. Cattell," 71; Cattell, "Travels in Psychological Hyperspace," 105. In his classic 1937 book that first defined the field, *Personality: A Psychological Interpretation* (London: Constable), Gordon Allport observed about the method in which Cattell specialized that "factorial techniques have value for certain types of problems. . . . But they are not qualified to pick out the elements of human personality" (248).

37. Cattell, "Raymond B. Cattell," 72; Cattell, "Travels in Psychological Hyperspace," 98. Passage of the Mental Health Act of 1946 called for the creation of the NIMH, which over the next quarter century provided a postwar infusion of federal grant money "on a scale unprecedented in American psychology," according to an APA archivist (W. Pickren, "Funds That Launched a Thousand Laboratories: NIMH and Psychological Science in the 1950s–1960s," American Psychological Society, Chicago, May 2004, quoted in P. Ciske, "All Labs Great and Small," *APA Observer* [August 2004]: 12).

38. Cattell, "Travels in Psychological Hyperspace," 98; Cattell, "Raymond B. Cattell," 73.

39. J. S. Wiggins, "Personality Structure," *Annual Review of Psychology* 19 (1968): 313. The new journal to which Wiggins referred was *Multivariate Behavioral Research*. The handbook was R. B. Cattell, ed., *Handbook of Multivariate Experimental Psychology*

(Chicago: Rand McNally, 1966). The volume of collected papers was R. B. Cattell, *Personality and Social Psychology: The Collected Papers of Raymond B. Cattell* (San Diego: Knapp, 1964).

40. Cattell, "Voyage of a Laboratory," 124.

41. Cattell, "Raymond B. Cattell," 73.

42. See the company's Web site at http://www.ipat.com/.

43. Cattell, "Travels in Psychological Hyperspace," 129. See also Cattell, "Raymond B. Cattell," 94.

44. R. B. Cattell, "The Birth of the Society of Multivariate Experimental Psychology," *Journal of the History of the Behavioral Sciences* 26 (1990): 49, 48. On the increase of membership limit, see the society's Web site, http://www.smep.org/index.html.

45. Cattell, "Birth of the Society," 49, 57. See the volume's introductory essay explaining its purpose: J. Horn, "To Set the Stage," *Multivariate Behavioral Research* 19 (1984): 115–20.

46. Cattell, "Voyage of a Laboratory," 162.

47. See Cattell and Horn, "Raymond Bernard Cattell"; and Gillis, "Raymond Bernard Cattell."

48. Two of the studies were H. Birkett and R. B. Cattell, "Diagnosis of the Dynamic Roots of a Clinical Symptom by P-Technique: A Case of Episodic Alcoholism," *Multivariate Behavioral Research* 13 (1978): 173–94; and R. B. Cattell and H. Birkett, "The Known Personality Factors Found Aligned between First Order T-Data and Second Order Q-Data Factors, with New Evidence on the Inhibitory Control, Independence, and Regression Traits," *Personality and Individual Differences* 1 (1980): 229–38. Her book was published as H. B. Cattell, *The 16 PF: Personality in Depth* (Champaign, Ill.: Institute for Personality and Ability Testing, 1989).

49. R. B. Cattell, *A New Morality from Science: Beyondism* (New York: Pergamon, 1972).

50. On the background of the *Mankind Quarterly,* see W. H. Tucker, *The Funding of Scientific Racism: Wickliffe Draper and the Pioneer Fund* (Urbana: University of Illinois Press, 2002), 78–97.

51. Dreger and Berg, "Psychology of the Scientist," 846.

52. Horn, "To Set the Stage," 119; Cattell, "Travels in Psychological Hyperspace," 87.

53. Cattell, "Raymond B. Cattell," 89, 91. See also Cattell, "Travels in Psychological Hyperspace," 120–21. In the latter, Cattell notes that "except for a few great men like Churchill it is difficult both to make history and write it," but "since my own time in the laboratory is coming to an end I shall in fact probably be able to write that overview" (115).

54. See L. S. Hearnshaw, *Cyril Burt: Psychologist* (Ithaca: Cornell University Press, 1979). Andrew Winston told me that he once objected to the language in a publication by an English philosopher, who had dismissed his intellectual opponents as "a bunch of chuckle-headed materialists," only to be told by another English academic that Americans were much too polite and that such an expression was both appropriate and desirable in intellectual exchanges.

55. R. B. Cattell, "Concepts and Methods in the Measurement of Group Syntality," *Psychological Review* 55 (1948): 48; Dreger and Berg, "Psychologist of the Scientist," 846–47; Goldberg, "Explorer on the Run," 618.

56. See, for example, R. B. Cattell, "Evaluating Therapy as Total Personality Change: Theory and Available Instruments," *American Journal of Psychotherapy* 20 (1966): 71; R. B. Cattell, S. S. Dubin, and D. R. Saunders, "Personality Structure in Psychotics by Factorization of Objective Clinical Tests," *Journal of Mental Science* 100 (1954): 154; and R. B. Cattell and H. Birkett, "Can P-Technique Diagnosis Be Practicably Shortened? Some Proposals and a Test of a 50-Day Abridgement," *Multivariate Experimental Clinical Research* 5 (1980): 1.

57. R. B. Cattell, "What's Wrong with Psychology?" *Psychologist* (1992): 10. See also Cattell, "Travels in Psychological Hyperspace," 94; and R. B. Cattell, "Personality Pinned Down," *Psychology Today* (July 1973): 41.

58. Cattell, "Travels in Psychological Hyperspace," 121; Cattell, "Raymond B. Cattell," 91, 90. This tendency to accuse others of his own excesses was also characteristic of Burt and those who looked to him as a model. The well-known psychologist Hans J. Eysenck, who also studied with Burt and adopted his mentor's furious style of academic debate, once wrote that a federal judge who had placed restrictions on the use of IQ tests had "achieved immortality by joining Hitler and Stalin" in banning such measures. Then, two paragraphs later in the same publication, he complained of smear tactics in the IQ controversy, noting that some scientists who had argued for a genetic explanation of racial differences in test scores "have been accused of following in the steps of Hitler . . . an absurd attempt to establish guilt by association" ("H. J. Eysenck vs. L. Kamin," in *The Intelligence Controversy* [New York: John Wiley, 1981], 88–89).

59. Cattell, "What's Wrong with Psychology?" 11; Cattell, "Personality Pinned Down," 42. See also Cattell, "Travels in Psychological Hyperspace," where he worries that psychology was becoming "fed largely by student escapees" from more rigorous disciplines.

60. R. B. Cattell, "On the Disuse and Misuse of P, Q, Q$_s$, and O Techniques in Clinical Psychology," *Journal of Clinical Psychology* 7 (1951): 207, 212; Cattell, "Raymond B. Cattell," 85.

61. "Interview with Raymond B. Cattell," *Eugenics Bulletin* (Spring–Summer 1984), available online at http://www.eugenics.net/papers/eb7.html. The observation that "psychology is too difficult for psychologists," which Cattell attributed originally to McDougall, appeared, among other places, in Cattell, "What's Wrong with Psychology?" 10; and in "Interview with Raymond B. Cattell."

62. Horn, "To Set the Stage," 119; A. R. Jensen, "'Revised'? Updated," *Contemporary Psychology* 34 (1989): 140, 141. The book under review was R. B. Cattell, *Intelligence: Its Structure, Growth, and Action* (Amsterdam: North-Holland, 1987). Perhaps most astonishing, the book made no mention whatsoever of any of the work done by either Howard Gardner or Robert Sternberg, the two most innovative thinkers in the field.

63. Cattell, "Raymond B. Cattell," 92, 93.

64. Goldberg, "Explorer on the Run," 618; C. Hanley, "A Factor Omnibus for Personality," *Contemporary Psychology* 3 (1958): 324. The book under review was R. B. Cattell, *Personality and Motivation Structure and Measurement* (Yonkers-on-Hudson, N.Y.: World Book, 1957).

65. See the "Editor's Note" in R. B. Cattell, "The Structured Learning Analysis of Therapeutic Change and Maintenance," in *Improving the Long-Term Effects of Psychotherapy,* edited by P. Karoly and J. J. Steffen (New York: Gardner, 1980), 163.

66. Max Frankel's observation was told to me by Robert Curvin, a member of the editorial board of the *New York Times* for six years.

67. Cattell, "Travels in Psychological Hyperspace," 114; Cattell and Horn, "Raymond Bernard Cattell."

68. Dreger and Berg, "Psychology of the Scientist," 846.

69. R. B. Cattell and A. Miller, "A Confirmation of the Ergic and Self-Sentiment Patterns among Dynamic Traits (Attitude Variables) by R-Technique," *British Journal of Psychology* 43 (1952): 292; Horn, "To Set the Stage," 120.

70. See Gillis, "Raymond Bernard Cattell." The personal papers of Cecil A. Gibb, an eminent researcher in the field of personality and leadership who worked in Cattell's lab in the late 1940s, contain his letter in support of his mentor's nomination for the Gold Medal in 1985. See the description of the papers, housed in the National Library of Australia, at http://www.nla.gov.au/ms/findaids/9231.html#des.

71. A study of seven creative giants of the twentieth century by the originator of "Multiple Intelligence" theory found that they were "marginal personalities" (H. Gardner, *Creating Minds: An Anatomy of Creativity Seen through the Lives of Freud, Einstein, Picasso, Stravinsky, Eliot, Graham, and Gandhi* [New York: Basic Books, 1994]).

Chapter 1: Factor Analysis and Its Discontents

1. H. Bloom, *Shakespeare: The Invention of the Human* (New York: Riverhead, 1998), 4; R. C. Cabot, quoted in *Inventing Personality: Gordon Allport and the Science of Selfhood*, by I. A. M. Nicholson (Washington, D.C.: American Psychological Association, 2003), 3. Although this observation pertained to psychiatry, as Nicholson noted, "Cabot could have made a similar comment about 'personality' psychology."

2. Nicholson, *Inventing Personality*, 36.

3. The observation appears in the 1957, 1978, and 1997 editions of the best-selling text, C. S. Hall and G. Lindzey, *Theories of Personality* (New York: John Wiley), 4.

4. L. J. Cronbach, "The Two Disciplines of Scientific Psychology," *American Psychologist* 12 (1957): 671–84.

5. A study of the history of textbook presentations of psychological methodology investigated the belief, accepted as "a cornerstone of psychological pedagogy," that the notion of an experiment—defined as the manipulation of an independent variable while holding other events constant in order to observe the effect on a dependent variable—was acquired "from more established sciences, particularly physics." Finding little evidence for the use of this approach in other disciplines, the study concluded that the consensus description of its background is an "origin myth" (A. S. Winston and D. J. Blais, "What Counts as an Experiment? A Transdisciplinary Analysis of Textbooks, 1930–1970," *American Journal of Psychology* 109 [1996]: 599).

6. I am grateful to Andrew Winston for explaining to me the way in which this term was used by early twentieth-century psychologists.

7. J. M. Cattell, "Mental Tests and Measurements," *Mind* 15 (1890): 373–80; Tucker, *Science and Politics*, chap. 3 (see introduction, n. 8); R. M. Yerkes, "Testing the Human Mind," *Atlantic Monthly* 131 (1923): 369; Allport, *Personality: A Psychological Interpretation*, 181 (see introduction, n. 36); P. R. McHugh, "Psychotherapy Awry," *American Scholar* 63

(1994): 17; Allport, *Personality: A Psychological Interpretation;* R. Stagner, *Psychology of Personality* (New York: McGraw-Hill, 1937); H. A. Murray, W. G. Barrett, and E. Homburger, *Explorations in Psychology* (New York: Oxford University Press, 1938).

8. The meaning of this term is most fully discussed in R. B. Cattell, *Description and Measurement of Personality* (Yonkers-on-Hudson, N.Y.: World Book, 1946), 71.

9. For example, the Eckart-Young theorem for decomposition of a matrix (C. Eckart and G. Young, "The Approximation of One Matrix by Another of Lower Rank," *Psychometrika* 1 [1936]: 211–18).

10. See, for example, R. B. Cattell, *Factor Analysis: An Introduction and Manual for the Psychologist and Social Scientist* (New York: Harper, 1952), 78, although I have changed the letters in the equation to conform more closely with most other treatments of factor analysis; Cattell uses *b*'s instead of *a*'s for the coefficients and *T*'s for the factors, both common and unique. Although the basic equation for the factor analytic model was well developed by the time Cattell began to use the procedure, its designation as the "specification" equation seems an idiosyncratic practice on his part. I have not found this term in other discussions of the topic.

11. Both factor analysis and principal components analysis are often subsumed under the former label, although there is an important distinction between them. Briefly, "true" factor analysis, the technique used by Cattell, seeks the matrix of factor loadings that best reproduces the original correlation matrix when multiplied by its transpose and is thus a model that can be tested for goodness of fit. Principal components analysis calculates the linear combination of variables that accounts for the largest amount of variance and is thus not really a model. In practical terms, principal components analysis places the number 1 in the diagonal cells of the correlation matrix, whereas factor analysis uses some estimate of the variable's communality—the proportion of its variance accounted for by the common factors. In his typically overdramatic style, Cattell maintained that the former method "of putting unity in the diagonals is, scientifically, both barbarous and deceptive" ("Extracting the Correct Number of Factors in Factor Analysis," *Educational and Psychological Measurement* 18 [1958]: 807). On the difference between the two approaches, see, for example, R. A. Reyment and K. G. Jöreskog, *Applied Factor Analysis in the Natural Sciences* (Cambridge: Cambridge University Press, 1993), 78–79.

12. Equally acceptable in the sense above that the correlation multiplied by its transpose reproduces the correlation matrix. Thus, the entry for any pair of variables in the correlation matrix should be reproduced by the sum of the products of their respective loadings on each factor. The correlation between variables p and q, for example, would be the product of their loadings on factor *I* plus the product of their loadings on factor *II* plus the product of their loadings on factor *III* and so on.

13. C. Spearman, "'General Intelligence,' Objectively Determined and Measured," *American Journal of Psychology* 15 (1904): 201–93. Although Spearman's "two factor" theory soon became untenable, many contemporary psychologists maintain that the "correct" way to factor analyze a test battery is always to begin by extracting a "general" factor accounting for the largest possible amount of the variation in scores. The most well-known exponent of this position is Arthur Jensen (for example, see *The G Factor: The Science of Mental Ability* [Westport, Conn.: Praeger, 1998]).

14. See L. L. Thurstone, *Vectors of the Mind* (Chicago: University of Chicago Press, 1935) and *Multiple Factor Analysis* (Chicago: University of Chicago Press, 1947).

15. Cattell, *Factor Analysis*, 66.

16. See C. L. Burt, *The Distribution and Relations of Educational Abilities* (London: P. S. King, 1917) and *The Factors of the Mind* (London: University of London Press, 1940). There is considerable controversy about the extent of Burt's contributions to factor analysis. His biographer concludes that although Burt was "one of the pioneers" and his work was "a most important exemplification and extension of Spearman's original theory," he attempted, after Spearman's death, to rewrite history, largely eliminating the latter's role and presenting himself as "the first factorist in psychology" (Hearnshaw, *Cyril Burt: Psychologist*, 179, chap. 9 [see introduction, n. 54]). However, a prominent psychometrician argues that Burt may have shaded history "more to his favour than is perhaps justified by the facts" but that his work in factor analysis has "had far more practical impact than Spearman's" (S. F. Blinkhorn, "Burt and the Early History of Factor Analysis," in *Cyril Burt: Fraud or Framed?* edited by N. J. Mackintosh [Oxford: Oxford University Press, 1995], 40–41).

17. Cattell, "Birth of the Society," 48 (see introduction, n. 45). There was good reason for annoyance on Cattell's part. In the same article he describes how he once submitted a multivariate study to the *Journal of Experimental Psychology*, only to have it returned by the editor with a note stating, "This is not an experiment" (56). In addition to such practical consequences, as Winston and Blais point out, the denial that Cattell's research qualified as experimental derogated it to an "epistemologically inferior role of mere description" ("What Counts as an Experiment?" 609).

18. See, for example, R. B. Cattell, "Foundations of Personality Measurement Theory in Multivariate Experiment," in *Objective Approaches to Personality Assessment*, edited by B. M. Bass and I. A. Berg (Princeton: D. Van Nostrand, 1959), 43.

19. See, for example, Cattell, "Birth of the Society," 48; and Cattell, "Travels in Psychological Hyperspace," 93 (see introduction, n. 19).

20. R. B. Cattell, "Personality Theory Growing from Multivariate Quantitative Research," in *Psychology: A Study of a Science*, vol. 3, *Formulations of the Person and the Social Context*, edited by S. Koch (New York: McGraw-Hill, 1959), 263; Cattell, "Travels in Psychological Hyperspace," 119.

21. Cattell, "Disuse and Misuse," 203 (see introduction, n. 60); R. B. Cattell, "The Measurement of the Healthy Personality and the Healthy Society," *Counseling Psychologist* 4 (1973): 13; Cattell, "Concepts and Methods," 48 (see introduction, n. 55); R. B. Cattell and M. Adelson, "The Dimensions of Social Change in the U.S.A. as Determined by P-Technique," *Social Forces* 30 (1951): 191–92.

22. For a brief history of the development of some of these instruments, see L. R. Goldberg, "A Historical Survey of Personality Scales and Inventories," in vol. 2 of *Advances in Psychological Assessment*, edited by P. McReynolds (Palo Alto, Calif.: Science and Behavior Books, 1971), 293–382.

23. Cattell, *Description and Measurement of Personality*, 3–4; R. B. Cattell, *The Scientific Analysis of Personality* (Chicago: Aldine, 1965), 55.

24. Cattell, *Scientific Analysis of Personality*, 25. See also pp. 78–81.

25. R. B. Cattell, "Temperament Tests: I. Temperament," *British Journal of Psychology* 23 (1932): 308–29; C. Burt, "The Analysis of Temperament," *British Journal of Medical Psychology* 17 (1938): 158–88; D. Howie, "Aspects of Personality in the Classroom: A Study of Ratings on Personal Qualities for a Group of Schoolboys," *British Journal of Psychology* 36 (1945): 15–29; H. E. Brogden, "A Multiple-Factor Analysis of the Character Trait Intercorrelations Published by Sister Mary McDonough," *Journal of Educational Psychology* 35 (1944): 397–410.

26. E. G. Flemming, "A Factor Analysis of the Personality of High School Leaders," *Journal of Applied Psychology* 19 (1935): 596–605.

27. H. A. Reyburn and J. G. Taylor, "Some Factors of Personality: A Further Analysis of Some of Webb's Data," *British Journal of Psychology* 30 (1939): 151–65.

28. L. L. Thurstone, "The Vectors of Mind," *Psychological Review* 41 (1933): 1–32; Burt, "The Analysis of Temperament," 163.

29. The term is used here in its technical sense of consistency or repeatability.

30. J. C. Flanagan, *Factor Analysis in the Study of Personality* (Stanford: Stanford University Press, 1935).

31. F. Galton, "Measurement of Character," *Fortnightly Review* 36 (1884): 181; G. W. Allport and H. S. Odbert, "Trait-Names: A Psycho-Lexical Study," *Psychological Monographs* 47 (1936): no. 211. Actually, Allport and Odbert compiled a list of almost eighteen thousand trait names in four categories, the first of which, composed of what they called "clearly 'real' traits of personality," provided most of the list used by Cattell (26). The other categories were temporary states of mind, such as "rejoicing" or "frantic," a few hundred of which he considered enduring characteristics and so added to the list; evaluative terms, such as "worthy" or "insignificant"; and a miscellaneous category including physical qualities, talents, and capacities and explanatory terms, such as "crazed" or "pampered."

32. For n variables there are $n(n-1)/2$ separate correlation coefficients. Thus, 200 variables, for example, would produce almost 20,000 correlations.

33. The process is described in R. B. Cattell, "The Description of Personality: Basic Traits Resolved into Clusters," *Journal of Abnormal and Social Psychology* 38 (1943): 476–506. For the complete list of 171 traits, see 493–96.

34. All the clusters, together with the individual traits of which they are composed, are listed in ibid., 500–503.

35. Ibid., 504, 500, 501.

36. Cattell refers to BR-data in his original studies using this method. See R. B. Cattell, "Confirmation and Clarification of Primary Personality Factors," *Psychometrika* 12 (1947): 197; and R. B. Cattell, "The Primary Personality Factors in Women Compared with Those in Men," *British Journal of Psychology, Statistical Section* 1 (1948): 114. Soon thereafter he changed the name; see Cattell, *Scientific Analysis of Personality*, 61, for a discussion of L-data.

37. Cattell, *Scientific Analysis of Personality*, 61. See also R. B. Cattell, "The Main Personality Factors in Questionnaire Self-Estimate Material," *Journal of Social Psychology* 31 (1950): 4.

38. See, for example, R. B. Cattell and A. R. Baggaley, "The Objective Measurement of Attitude Motivation: Development and Evaluation of Principles and Devices," *Journal*

of Personality 24 (1956): 402; and R. B. Cattell, "The Dynamic Calculus: A System of Concepts Derived from Objective Motivation Measurement," in *Assessment of Human Motives*, edited by G. Lindzey (New York: Holt, Rinehart, and Winston, 1958), 203.

39. Cattell, *Scientific Analysis of Personality*, 61.

40. The test and its scoring are described in R. B. Cattell, "An Objective Test of Character-Temperament: I," *Journal of General Psychology* 25 (1941): 59–73. The correlations are reported in R. B. Cattell, "An Objective Test of Character-Temperament: II," *Journal of Social Psychology* 19 (1944): 112. (In the reference section of this article, part 1, cited above, is inaccurately listed as also in the *Journal of Social Psychology*.) The correlations between scores derived from the test and measures of leadership and cautiousness-timidity were .85 and .95, respectively, larger than the reliability of most trait measurements; indeed, as Cattell noted, "corrected for attenuation" (that is, unreliability), these correlations "reach unity."

41. More than four hundred of these tests are described in R. B. Cattell and F. W. Warburton, *Objective Personality and Motivation Tests: A Theoretical Introduction and Practical Compendium* (Urbana: University of Illinois Press, 1967).

42. See, for example, R. B. Cattell, "Projection and the Design of Projective Tests of Personality," *Journal of Personality* 12 (1944): 177–94.

43. R. B. Cattell and D. R. Saunders, "Inter-relation and Matching of Personality Factors from Behavior Rating, Questionnaire, and Objective Test Data," *Journal of Social Psychology* 31 (1950): 243.

44. R. B. Cattell, "The Description of Personality: Principles and Findings in a Factor Analysis," *American Journal of Psychology* 58 (1945): 71.

45. Compare the list of thirty-five variables in ibid., 71–74, with the list in Cattell, "Confirmation and Clarification," 201–6.

46. O. P. John, "The 'Big Five' Factor Taxonomy: Dimensions of Personality in the Natural Language and in Questionnaires," in *Handbook of Personality: Theory and Research*, edited by L. A. Pervin (New York: Guilford, 1990), 70–71.

47. Cattell, "Description of Personality: Principles and Findings," 75. The three studies were Cattell, "Description of Personality: Principles and Findings," in which the persons being rated were soldiers; Cattell, "Confirmation and Clarification," in which the persons were male students; and Cattell, "Primary Personality Factors in Women," in which the persons were female students.

48. Cattell, "Confirmation and Clarification," 208, 212, 216; Cattell, "Primary Personality Factors in Women," 128.

49. For the loadings on this factor, see column L in the table in Cattell, "Description of Personality: Principles and Findings," 88; none of the last eight factors in this table (E through L) has a loading larger than .38. The description of factor L appears on p. 89.

50. R. B. Cattell, "Primary Personality Factors in the Realm of Objective Tests," *Journal of Personality* 16 (1948): 460.

51. Cattell, "Confirmation and Clarification," 213; Cattell, "Primary Personality Factors in Women," 124. In the third study the factor was called "Cyclothyme vs. Paranoid Schizothyme," and the defining variables are not mentioned, although from the factor-loading table they can be traced as "anti-social, schizoid" versus "outgoing, idealistic, cooperative"; "rigid, tyrannical, vindictive" versus "adaptable, friendly"; and "spiteful,

tight-fisted, superstitious" versus "natural, friendly, open" ("Description of Personality: Principles and Findings," 89, 88, 72–73).

52. Cattell, "Primary Personality Factors in the Realm of Objective Tests," 467.

53. See Cattell, "Confirmation and Clarification," 211; and Cattell, "Primary Personality Factors in Women," 124. Although a factor with the same name was identified in the third study, it was not as well defined, with only three loadings in the .30s. Again, the variables were not provided but can be traced from the table as "wise, mature, polished" versus "dependent, silly, incoherent"; "demoralized, autistic" versus "realistic, facing life"; and "strong-willed, conscientious" versus "indolent, incoherent, impulsive" (Cattell, "Description of Personality: Principles and Findings," 89, 88, 71–73).

54. Cattell, "Primary Personality Factors in the Realm of Objective Tests," 471, 485–86.

55. R. B. Cattell, "The Principal Replicated Factors Discovered in Objective Personality Tests," *Journal of Abnormal and Social Psychology* 50 (1955): 313. See also Cattell, *Personality and Motivation Structure*, 315 (see introduction, n. 64).

56. Cattell, "Main Personality Factors," 4, 3. On the same page Cattell explained that not all self-report questionnaires produced Q-data; it depended on whether the responses were taken at face value. If, for example, someone answered "Yes" to the question, "Are you a very social person?" it could be scored for sociability, or it could be considered the result of some ego defense mechanism and thus scored for shyness, hysteria, or inferiority compensation. The former would treat the response as Q-data, the latter as T-data.

57. The only exceptions were three items intended to relate to personality factors from the behavior-rating studies. All eighty items are listed in ibid., 7–15.

58. Ibid., 6, 37.

59. W. C. Becker, "The Matching of Behavior Rating and Questionnaire Personality Factors," *Psychological Bulletin* 57 (1960): 202, 203. The thesis by Cattell's student was D. R. Saunders, "The Relation of Behavior Rating, Questionnaire, and Objective Test Personality Factors" (master's thesis, University of Illinois, 1949).

60. R. B. Cattell, "Theory of Situational, Instrument, Second Order, and Refraction Factors in Personality Structure Research," *Psychological Bulletin* 58 (1961): 160; Cattell and Saunders, "Inter-relation and Matching of Personality Factors," 256. The three factors that did show some degree of correspondence across the three domains were G, "Integrated Character"; I, "Sensitive Emotionality"; and L, "Paranoid Schizothymia" (see table on p. 258).

61. The questionnaire consisted of two equivalent forms, A and B, each containing 184 items (R. B. Cattell, D. R. Saunders, and G. F. Stice, *The Sixteen Personality Trait Questionnaire* [Champaign, Ill.: Institute for Personality and Ability Testing, 1950]). A recent handbook on use and interpretation of the questionnaire gives the publication date of the first edition as 1949 (H. E. P. Cattell and J. M. Schuerger, *Essentials of 16 PF Assessment* [Hoboken, N.J.: John Wiley, 2003]).

62. See Cattell, *Personality and Motivation Structure*, 153. The document referred to was J. W. French, *The Description of Personality Measurements in Terms of Rotated Factors* (Princeton: Educational Testing Service, 1953). The study on which factor O was based is listed in the ETS document only as "Saunders, D. R., 'Relation between Questionnaire and Rating Factors,' unpublished."

63. See Cattell, "Description of Personality: Principles and Findings," 89, where C is named "Emotionally Mature, Stable Character vs. General Emotionality"; and Cattell,

"Primary Personality Factors in Women," 123, where it is named "Emotionally Mature Stable Character vs. Neurotic General Emotionality."

64. John, "'Big Five' Factor Taxonomy," 71.

65. Cattell, *Personality and Motivation Structure,* 325; R. B. Cattell, "Validation and Intensification of the *Sixteen Personality Factor Questionnaire,*" *Journal of Clinical Psychology* 12 (1956): 206.

66. Cattell, "Personality Pinned Down," 42 (see introduction, n. 57).

67. See Cattell and Schuerger, *Essentials of 16 PF Assessment,* 11. The fifth edition appeared as R. B. Cattell, A. K. Cattell, and H. E. P. Cattell, *16 Personality Factor Fifth Edition Questionnaire* (Champaign, Ill.: Institute for Personality and Ability Testing, 1993).

68. Cattell, "Voyage of a Laboratory," 151 (see introduction, n. 25).

69. As an example of the former, see Cattell, *Personality and Motivation Structure,* 326; of the latter, Cattell, "Personality Pinned Down," 40–41.

70. R. B. Cattell, "Advances in Cattellian Personality Theory," in *Handbook of Personality: Theory and Research,* 102.

71. See R. B. Cattell, "A Universal Index for Psychological Factors," *Psychologia* 1 (1957): 82, 83. For a more detailed description of the system, see Cattell, *Personality and Motivation Structure,* 827–35.

72. Cattell, *Scientific Analysis of Personality,* 105, 83.

73. R. B. Cattell and D. F. Tatro, "The Personality Factors, Objectively Measured, Which Distinguish Psychotics from Normals," *Behavior Research and Therapy* 4 (1966): 41; Cattell, "Travels in Psychological Hyperspace," 104.

74. See Cattell, "Universal Index," 82.

75. There were many versions of the battery. See, for example, R. B. Cattell and J. M. Schuerger, *Personality Theory in Action: Handbook for the O-A Test Kit* (Champaign, Ill.: Institute for Personality and Ability Testing, 1978).

76. H. J. Eysenck, review of the *Objective-Analytic (O-A) Test Battery,* in the *Fifth Mental Measurements Yearbook,* edited by O. K. Buros (Highland Park, N.J.: Gryphon Press, 1959), 171; R. B. Cattell, P. L. Price, and S. V. Patrick, "Diagnosis of Clinical Depression on Four Source Trait Dimensions—U.I. 19, U.I. 20, U.I. 25, and U.I. 30—from the O.A. Kit," *Journal of Clinical Psychology* 37 (1981): 4; H. G. Gough, review of the *Objective-Analytic (O-A) Test Battery,* in the *Ninth Mental Measurements Yearbook,* edited by J. V. Mitchell Jr. (Lincoln: University of Nebraska Press, 1985), 1074–75. This was from a battery of ten tests all designed to measure the one factor of "Anxiety." See A. L. Comrey's review in vol. 1 of *Seventh Mental Measurements Yearbook,* edited by O. K. Buros (Lincoln: University of Nebraska Press, 1972), 277.

77. See, for example, D. W. Fiske, "Consistency of the Factorial Structures of Personality Ratings from Different Sources," *Journal of Abnormal and Social Psychology* 44 (1949): 329–44; E. Howarth, "Were Cattell's 'Personality Sphere' Factors Correctly Identified in the First Instance?" *British Journal of Psychology* 67 (1976): 213–30; P. Kline and P. Barrett, "The Factors in Personality Questionnaires among Normal Subjects," *Advances in Behaviour Research and Therapy* 5 (1983): 141–202; the discussion in H. J. Eysenck and M. W. Eysenck, *Personality and Individual Differences: A Natural Science Approach* (New York: Plenum, 1985), 125; A. Byravan and N. V. Ramanaiah, "Structure of the 16PF Fifth

Edition from the Perspective of the Five-Factor Model," *Psychological Reports* 76 (1995): 555–60; and the studies in the next two footnotes.

78. See E. C. Tupes and R. E. Christal, "Recurrent Personality Factors Based on Trait Ratings," *Journal of Personality* 60 (1992): 228–30. This study was actually conducted in 1961 as part of a research project sponsored by the U.S. Air Force and published as a technical report from the personnel laboratory of the Aeronautical Systems Division at Lackland Air Force base before being reprinted in the *Journal of Personality* more than three decades later (R. R. McCrae, "Editor's Introduction to Tupes and Christal," *Journal of Personality* 60 [1992]: 217–19).

79. See Tupes and Christal, "Recurrent Personality Factors," 225–51; and J. M. Digman and N. K. Takemoto-Chock, "Factors in the Natural Language of Personality: Re-analysis, Comparison, and Interpretation of Six Major Studies," *Multivariate Behavioral Research* 16 (1981): 149–70. The discussion of Cattell's errors can be found in the latter on p. 152.

80. Cattell, "Raymond B. Cattell," 91 (see introduction, n. 19). The term *Big Five* was first introduced in L. R. Goldberg, "Language and Individual Differences: The Search for Universals in Personality Lexicons," in vol. 2 of *Review of Personality and Social Psychology*, edited by L. Wheeler (Beverly Hills: Sage, 1981), 141–65. In addition to the two studies cited above—Tupes and Christal, "Recurrent Personality Factors"; and Digman and Takemoto-Chock, "Factors in the Natural Language of Personality"—other important demonstrations of the five-factor model are Fiske, "Consistency of the Factorial Structures"; W. T. Norman, "Toward an Adequate Taxonomy of Personality Attributes: Replicated Factor Structure in Peer Nomination Personality Ratings," *Journal of Abnormal and Social Psychology* 66 (1963): 574–83; and P. Noller, H. Law, and A. L. Comrey, "Cattell, Comrey, and Eysenck Personality Factors Compared: More Evidence for the Robust Five Factors," *Journal of Personality and Social Psychology* 53 (1987): 775–82. Good histories of the model and its supporting evidence can be found in R. R. McCrae and O. P. John, "An Introduction to the Five-Factor Model and Its Applications," *Journal of Personality* 60 (1992): 175–215; John, "'Big Five' Factor Taxonomy," 66–100; L. R. Goldberg, "The Structure of Phenotypic Personality Traits," *American Psychologist* 48 (1993): 26–34; and J. M. Digman, "The Curious History of the Five-Factor Model," in *The Five-Factor Model of Personality*, edited by J. S. Wiggins (New York: Guilford, 1996).

81. P. T. Costa and R. R. McCrae, *The NEO Personality Inventory Manual* (Odessa, Fla.: Psychological Assessment Resources, 1985). The acronym was first suggested in a personal communication from McCrae to Oliver John (John, "'Big Five' Factor Taxonomy," 95–96). For a different interpretation of the five factors, see D. Peabody and L. R. Goldberg, "Some Determinants of Factor Structures from Personality-Trait Descriptors," *Journal of Personality and Social Psychology* 57 (1989): 552–67.

82. R. B. Cattell, "The Fallacy of Five Factors in the Personality Sphere," *Psychologist* (May 1995): 207, 208.

83. Cattell, *Description and Measurement of Personality*, 517–20. Cattell begins this discussion by observing that a secondary factor analysis "yielded three factors" (517), but then presents a table with five factors (518), only four of which are given names, and finally goes on to interpret all five anyway (520), the last two of which are now labeled entirely differently from what appeared in the table.

84. Cattell, *Personality and Motivation Structure,* 317–21; Cattell, "Foundations of Personality Measurement Theory," 57; Cattell, "Advances in Cattellian Personality Theory," 102; R. B. Cattell and H. E. P. Cattell, "Personality Structure and the New Fifth Edition of the 16PF," *Educational and Psychological Measurement* 55 (1995): 935.

85. This observation can be found at http://www.ipat.com/ by selecting the "Personality Assessment" tab and then "Measuring the Big 5."

86. Digman and Takemoto-Chock, "Factors in the Natural Language of Personality," 168; Howarth, "Were Cattell's 'Personality Sphere' Factors Correctly Identified?" 213.

87. Cattell, "Raymond B. Cattell," 77. See also Cattell, "Foundations of Personality Measurement Theory," 63.

88. See, for example, R. B. Cattell, A. Wagner, and M. D. Cattell, "Adolescent Personality Structure in Q-Data, Checked in the High School Personality Questionnaire," *British Journal of Psychology* 61 (1970): 39–54.

89. See the references cited in Cattell and Cattell, "Personality Structure and the New Fifth Edition," 927; and in Cattell, "Fallacy of Five Factors," 208. The quote comes from the latter.

90. See, for example, the discussion and references in Eysenck and Eysenck, *Personality and Individual Differences,* 125.

91. Ibid.; H. J. Eysenck, "Stronger Words for Gordon," *Contemporary Psychology* 11 (1966): 508.

92. A good discussion of this distinction is N. Block, "How Heritability Misleads about Race," *Boston Review* 20 (January 1996): 30–35.

93. Although this statement by Oscar Kempthorne, a recognized expert in biostatistics, was made specifically with respect to the IQ controversy, it is equally applicable to any other personality trait ("Logical, Epistemological, and Statistical Aspects of the Nature-Nurture Data Interpretation," *Biometrics* 34 [1978]: 19).

94. The model assumes, for example, that there is no correlation between the genetic and environmental components of a trait and no correlation between the environments in which the separated twins are raised.

95. See R. B. Cattell, "Contributions Concerning Mental Inheritance: I. Of Intelligence," *British Journal of Education* 8 (1938): 129–49; R. B. Cattell and E. V. Molteno, "Contributions Concerning Mental Inheritance: II. Temperament," *Journal of Genetic Psychology* 57 (1940): 31–47; and R. B. Cattell, "Research Designs in Psychological Genetics with Special Reference to the Multiple Variance Method," *American Journal of Human Genetics* 5 (1953): 76–93. See also R. B. Cattell, "The Multiple Abstract Variance Analysis Equations and Solutions: For Nature-Nurture Research on Continuous Variables," *Psychological Review* 67 (1960): 353–72.

96. See, for example, R. B. Cattell, "Unraveling Maturational and Learning Developments by the Comparative MAVA and Structured Learning Approaches," in *Life-Span Developmental Psychology: Methodological Issues,* edited by J. R. Nesselroade and H. W. Reese (New York: Academic Press, 1973), 114.

97. Ibid., 119.

98. See R. B. Cattell, D. B. Blewett, and J. R. Beloff, "The Inheritance of Personality: A Multiple Variance Analysis Determination of Approximate Nature-Nurture Ratios for Primary Personality Factors in Q-Data," *American Journal of Human Genetics* 7 (1955):

122–46; and R. B. Cattell, G. F. Stice, and N. F. Kristy, "A First Approximation to Nature-Nurture Ratios for Eleven Primary Personality Factors in Objective Tests," *Journal of Abnormal and Social Psychology* 54 (1957): 143–59. These two heritability studies—one of the objective test factors, the other of twelve of the factors from the 16 PF questionnaire—appear to be based on essentially the same subject group. Although the sample size in each relationship category varies somewhat between the two analyses, the children in both studies came from school systems and welfare or placement agencies in the same three cities: Chicago, New York, and Boston.

99. See R. B. Cattell et al., "Unitary Personality Source Traits Analyzed for Heritability," *Human Heredity* 31 (1981): 261–75; R. B. Cattell, J. M. Schuerger, and T. W. Klein, "Heritabilities of Ego Strength (Factor C), Super Ego Strength (Factor G), and Self-Sentiment (Factor Q_3) by Multiple Abstract Variance Analysis," *Journal of Clinical Psychology* 38 (1982): 769–79; R. B. Cattell et al., "Heritabilities, by the Multiple Abstract Variance Analysis (MAVA) Model and Objective Test Measures, of Personality Traits U.I. 23, Capacity to Mobilize, U.I. 24, Anxiety, U.I. Narcistic [*sic*] Ego, and U.I. 28, Asthenia, by Maximum-Likelihood Methods," *Behavior Genetics* 12 (1982): 361–78; and R. B. Cattell, D. C. Rao, and J. M. Schuerger, "Heritability in the Personality Control System: Ego Strength (C), Super Ego Strength (G), and the Self-Sentiment (Q_3), by the MAVA Model, Q-Data, and Maximum Likelihood Analyses," *Social Behavior and Personality* 13 (1985): 33–41.

100. On Graham and the repository, see A. Walmsley, "The Genius Babies," *MacLean's* (September 2, 1985): 6.

101. Cattell et al., "Heritabilities, by the Multiple Abstract Variance Analysis (MAVA) Model," 375.

102. Cattell, Schuerger, and Klein, "Heritabilities of Ego Strength," 776; Cattell, Rao, and Schuerger, "Heritability in the Personality Control System," 38. The subjects in the two studies appear to be the same: both analyses were based on a group of more than three thousand boys aged twelve to eighteen, including subgroups of identical twins, fraternal twins, ordinary siblings, and unrelated.

103. See J. L. Jinks and D. W. Fulker, "Comparison of the Biometrical Genetical, MAVA, and Classical Approaches to the Analysis of Human Behavior," *Psychological Bulletin* 73 (1970): 311–49. Jinks and Fulker suggest that there may be an error in Cattell's model (331).

104. Quoted in W. Kaempffert, "A Psychologist Develops a Method for the Appraisal of Personalities," *New York Times*, November 5, 1944, E9.

105. R. B. Cattell and G. F. Stice, "Four Formulae for Selecting Leaders on the Basis of Personality," *Human Relations* 7 (1954): 506; R. B. Cattell and J. H. Morony, "The Use of the 16 PF in Distinguishing Homosexuals, Normals, and General Criminals," *Journal of Consulting Psychology* 26 (1962): 533, 534, 537.

106. This observation was made by Harvard professor E. G. Boring, the well-known historian of psychology, in his "Lewis Madison Terman, 1877–1956," *Biographical Memoirs of the National Academy of Sciences* 33 (1959): 414.

107. L. M. Terman, "The Significance of Intelligence Tests for Mental Hygiene," *Journal of Psycho-Asthenics* 18 (1914): 124.

108. L. M. Terman, *The Measurement of Intelligence* (Cambridge, Mass.: Riverside Press, 1916), 91–92.

109. L. M. Terman et al., *Intelligence Tests and School Reorganization* (Yonkers-on-Hudson, N.Y.: World Book, 1922), 28.

110. Cattell, *Scientific Analysis of Personality,* 349. For his suggestion of the two-file system, see ibid., 344–53; and Cattell, *Factor Analysis,* 86. The specification equations appear in Cattell, "Measurement of the Healthy Personality," 16.

111. See J. E. Drevdahl and R. B. Cattell, "Personality and Creativity in Artists and Writers," *Journal of Clinical Psychology* 14 (1958): 111; R. B. Cattell and J. E. Drevdahl, "A Comparison of the Personality Profile (16 P.F.) of Eminent Researchers with That of Eminent Teachers and Administrators, and of the General Population," *British Journal of Psychology* 46 (1955): 251; and P. G. Cross, R. B. Cattell, and H. J. Butcher, "The Personality Pattern of Creative Artists," *British Journal of Educational Psychology* 37 (1967): 292–99.

112. Cattell and Drevdahl, "Comparison of the Personality Profile (16 P.F.) of Eminent Researchers," 256; Drevdahl and Cattell, "Personality and Creativity in Artists and Writers," 111 (quote).

113. Cattell and Drevdahl, "Comparison of the Personality Profile (16 P.F.) of Eminent Researchers," 248.

114. R. B. Cattell and L. R. Killian, "The Pattern of Objective Test Personality Factor Differences in Schizophrenia and the Character Disorders," *Journal of Clinical Psychology* 23 (1967): 342–48. See also Cattell and Tatro, "Personality Factors, Objectively Measured," 39–51, which adds three other factors to the diagnostic list.

115. R. B. Cattell, "The Conceptual and Test Distinction of Neuroticism and Anxiety," *Journal of Clinical Psychology* 13 (1957): 231. The names of the objective test factors often changed from one study to another. In the Cattell and Tatro study in the previous note, U.I. 23 is labeled "Mobilization vs. Regression."

116. Cattell, "Evaluating Therapy," 81, 83 (see introduction, n. 56).

117. See Cattell, *Description and Measurement of Personality,* 162.

118. Cattell, "Advances in Cattellian Personality Theory," 103.

119. See Cattell, *Scientific Analysis of Personality,* 28.

120. Cattell, "Advances in Cattellian Personality Theory," 103.

121. See Spearman, "'General Intelligence.'"

122. R. B. Cattell, "A Culture-Free Intelligence Test I," *Journal of Educational Psychology* 31 (1940): 163 (quote). See ibid., 174–75, for examples.

123. Ibid., 178.

124. Cattell, *Intelligence,* 87 (see introduction, n. 62).

125. The first published appearance of this theory was R. B. Cattell, "The Measurement of Adult Intelligence," *Psychological Bulletin* 40 (1943): 153–93. However, in later reflections Cattell cited its first description as a paper he delivered at the 1941 meeting of the American Psychological Association ("Some Theoretical Issues in Adult Intelligence Testing," *Psychological Bulletin* 38 [1941]: 592). But the referenced page in the *Bulletin* contains only a summary of the presentation with no mention of the new theory. The citation to the 1941 APA paper can be found in Cattell, *Intelligence,* 95. Cattell gives the date of the APA meeting erroneously as 1942 in R. B. Cattell, "Where Is Intelligence? Some Answers from the Triadic Theory," in *Human Cognitive Abilities in Theory and Practice,* edited by J. J. McCardle and R. W. Woodcock (Mahwah, N.J.: Lawrence Erlbaum, 1998), 30.

126. Cattell, "Measurement of Adult Intelligence," 178.

127. Cattell, *Intelligence*, 98.

128. R. B. Cattell, "Theory of Fluid and Crystallized Intelligence: A Critical Experiment," *Journal of Educational Psychology* 54 (1963): 1–22; J. L. Horn and R. B. Cattell, "Refinement and Test of the Theory of Fluid and Crystallized General Intelligences," *Journal of Educational Psychology* 57 (1966): 253–70.

129. See the factor matrices in Cattell, "Theory of Fluid and Crystallized Intelligence," 12; and Horn and Cattell, "Refinement and Test," 262.

130. The exact correlation in Cattell's study was .47. However, the same correlation in the larger Horn and Cattell study was only .16, a finding never mentioned by Cattell, who subsequently referred to the correlation between abilities as "around .4–.5" (*Intelligence*, 116) or "about .5" (R. B. Cattell, "The Structure of Intelligence in Relation to the Nature-Nurture Controversy," in *Intelligence: Genetic and Environmental Influences*, edited by R. Cancro [New York: Grune and Stratton, 1971], 10).

131. R. B. Cattell, "The Heritability of Fluid, g$_f$, and Crystallised [*sic*], g$_c$, Intelligence, Estimated by a Least Squares Use of the MAVA Method," *British Journal of Educational Psychology* 50 (1980): 262.

132. R. B. Cattell et al., "The Heritability of Fluid and Crystallized Intelligences: By the MAVA Design and OSES Analysis," *Australian Journal of Psychology* 33 (1981): 369.

133. See, for example, A. R. Jensen, "How Much Can We Boost IQ and Scholastic Achievement?" *Harvard Educational Review* 39 (1969): 50–51.

134. Ibid., 38.

135. Cattell, "Heritability Estimated by a Least Squares Use," 262. See also Cattell et al., "Heritability of Fluid and Crystallized Intelligences," 370; and Cattell, *Intelligence*, 614.

136. See Cattell, "Where Is Intelligence?" 32.

137. See, for example, R. J. Sternberg, *The Triarchic Mind: A New Theory of Human Intelligence* (New York: Viking, 1988).

138. J. B. Carroll, "Raymond B. Cattell's Contributions to the Theory of Cognitive Abilities," *Multivariate Behavioral Research* 19 (1984): 300.

139. Cattell, "Dynamic Calculus," 211.

140. See R. B. Cattell, "Sentiment or Attitude? The Core of a Terminology Problem in Personality Research," *Journal of Personality* 9 (1940): 14.

141. The definition and first use of the term in this context appears in ibid. See also R. B. Cattell, *Personality: A Systematic Theoretical and Factual Study* (New York: McGraw-Hill, 1950), 199; and R. B. Cattell, "The Ergic Theory of Attitude and Sentiment Measurement," *Educational and Psychological Measurement* 7 (1947): 222.

142. R. B. Cattell and D. Child, *Motivation and Dynamic Structure* (New York: Halsted, 1975), 5; Cattell and Miller, "Ergic and Self-Sentiment Patterns," 281 (see introduction, n. 69).

143. Cattell and Baggaley, "Objective Measurement of Attitude Motivation," 402.

144. Cattell and Miller, "Ergic and Self-Sentiment Patterns," 282.

145. See Cattell, "Dynamic Calculus," 214. Cattell once hinted that, in addition to sentiments and complexes, engrams might also include "possibly other learnt patterns not yet known," but he did not elaborate (R. B. Cattell and A. R. Baggaley, "A Confirmation of Ergic and Engram Structures in Attitudes Objectively Measured," *Australian Journal of Psychology* 10 [1958]: 287).

146. Cattell, "Ergic Theory," 226.

147. Ibid., 226, 227.

148. For an example of a dynamic lattice, see Cattell and Child, *Motivation and Dynamic Structure*, 24.

149. These tests are described in R. B. Cattell, "The Discovery of Ergic Structure in Man in Terms of Common Attitudes," *Journal of Abnormal and Social Psychology* 45 (1950): 603, 606. The fifty attitude statements used in the preference method are listed on pp. 604–5.

150. The correlation of the score from each method with the score from all the methods pooled ranged from a low of .05—statistically indistinguishable from 0.00—for the psychogalvanic response to a high of .21 for the preference test, still a very modest value (ibid., 606). Nor was this problem specific to one study. In another study using three different objective measures, the correlations between pairs of the three methods were .09, .18, and .31 (R. B. Cattell and K. P. Cross, "Comparison of the Ergic and Self-Sentiment Structures Found in Dynamic Traits by R- and P-Techniques," *Journal of Personality* 21 [1952]: 256).

151. W. McDougall, *An Introduction to Social Psychology* (London: Methuen, 1908), 17; Cattell, "Discovery of Ergic Structure in Man," 602. A list of the ergs and sentiments represented by the attitude sentiments appears on p. 603.

152. Ibid., 608–16.

153. See, for example, Cattell and Cross, "Comparison of the Ergic and Self-Sentiment Structures," 250–71; Cattell and Baggaley, "Confirmation of Ergic and Engram Structures," 287–318; and Cattell and Miller, "Ergic and Self-Sentiment Patterns," 280–94.

154. Cattell and Baggaley, "Confirmation of Ergic and Engram Structures," 311.

155. Cattell, "Discovery of Ergic Structure in Man," 603; Cattell and Child, *Motivation and Dynamic Structure*, 27. Most of the empirically identified ergs and sentiments appear on pp. 28–36.

156. R. B. Cattell, "P-Technique, a New Method for Analyzing the Structure of Personal Motivation," *Transactions of the New York Academy of Sciences* 14 (1951): 30; Allport, *Personality: A Psychological Interpretation*, 244.

157. B. R. Hergenhahn and M. H. Olson, *An Introduction to Theories of Personality*, 5th ed. (Upper Saddle River, N.J.: Prentice-Hall, 1999), 262; Cattell, "P-Technique, a New Method," 30.

158. R. B. Cattell and L. B. Luborsky, "P-Technique Demonstrated as a New Clinical Method for Determining Personality and Symptom Structure," *Journal of General Psychology* 42 (1950): 4.

159. See ibid., 3–24. Cattell also made a short-lived attempt to create yet another category in the universal index of personality traits labeled "P.U.I." for those identified by P-technique (R. B. Cattell, "The Chief Invariant Psychological and Psycho-Physical Functional Unities Found by P-Technique," *Journal of Clinical Psychology* 11 [1955]: 319–433).

160. R. B. Cattell, "Personality Structures as Learning and Motivation Patterns: A Theme for the Integration of Methodologies," in *Learning Theory, Personality Theory, and Clinical Research: The Kentucky Symposium* (New York: John Wiley, 1952), 101.

161. Cattell and Cross, "Comparison of the Ergic and Self-Sentiment Structures," 255–56. The low reliability was for "Retroactive Inhibition," a test in which each of six three-digit numbers were flashed for about a second in front of the subject, who was asked to write

down as many as he could recall. Then he had to respond at some length to two statements about a particular attitude, following which he was again asked to recall the numbers. Score on this measure was the difference in recall between before and after the interpolated task on the assumption that greater interest in the attitude would cause more retroactive inhibition.

162. Ibid., 268.

163. Cattell, "P-Technique, a New Method," 33.

164. Cattell, "Disuse and Misuse," 212.

165. R. B. Cattell, "The Dynamic Calculus: Concepts and Crucial Experiments," in vol. 7 of *Nebraska Symposium on Motivation*, edited by M. R. Jones (Lincoln: University of Nebraska Press), 98; Cattell, "Disuse and Misuse," 212; Cattell and Birkett, "Can P-Technique Diagnosis Be Practicably Shortened?" 2 (see introduction, n. 56). As the title of the latter article indicated, Cattell suggested that a shorter period of data collection might make use of the technique more feasible.

166. See Cattell and Baggaley, "Objective Measurement of Attitude Motivation," 404; Cattell, *Personality and Motivation Structure*, 446–52; Cattell and Child, *Motivation and Dynamic Structure*, 7–10.

167. Cattell, *Personality and Motivation Structure*, 457–60.

168. Cattell, "Concepts and Methods," 48.

169. Cattell acknowledges McDougall's influence in ibid., 50–52. On the concept itself, see W. McDougall, *The Group Mind: A Sketch of the Principles of Collective Psychology, with Some Attempt to Apply Them to the Interpretation of National Life and Character* (New York: G. P. Putnam, 1920).

170. See R. B. Cattell, "Determining Syntality Dimensions as a Basis for Morale and Leadership Measurement," in *Groups, Leadership, and Men: Research in Human Relations*, edited by H. Guetzkow (New York: Russell and Russell, 1963), 25–26; and R. B. Cattell, "New Concepts for Measuring Leadership, in Terms of Groups Syntality," *Human Relations* 4 (1951): 164.

171. See R. B. Cattell and L. G. Wispe, "The Dimensions of Syntality in Small Groups," *Journal of Social Psychology* 28 (1948): 57–78; and R. B. Cattell, D. R. Saunders, and G. F. Stice, "The Dimensions of Syntality in Small Groups," *Human Relations* 6 (1953): 331–56. Although these two studies have identical names, they were conducted with different subject groups and tasks. Also, in the latter study subjects were administered Cattell's *Sixteen Personality Factor Questionnaire*, the results of which were entered into the factor analysis.

172. Cattell and Wispe, "Dimensions of Syntality," 73; Cattell, Saunders, and Stice, "Dimensions of Syntality," 349.

173. See, for example, R. B. Cattell, "The Principal Culture Patterns Discoverable in the Syntal Dimensions of Existing Nations," *Journal of Social Psychology* 32 (1950): 217.

174. A list of the variables can be found in R. B. Cattell, "The Dimensions of Culture Patterns by Factorization of National Characters," *Journal of Abnormal and Social Psychology* 44 (1949): 446–49. See also the list in R. B. Cattell, R. K. Graham, and R. E. Woliver, "A Reassessment of the Factorial Cultural Dimensions of Modern Nations," *Journal of Social Psychology* 108 (1979): 255–57.

175. R. B. Cattell, H. Breul, and H. P. Hartman, "An Attempt at More Refined Definition of the Cultural Dimensions of Syntality in Modern Nations," *American Sociological*

Review 17 (1952): 414–15. See also Cattell, "Dimensions of Culture Patterns by Factorization," 460.

176. Cattell, Breul, and Hartman, "Attempt at More Refined Definition," 414. In Cattell, "Dimensions of Culture Patterns by Factorization," the same factor is called "Vigorous, Self-Willed Order vs. Unadapted Perseveration" (463).

177. R. B. Cattell and R. L. Gorsuch, "The Definition and Measurement of National Morale and Morality," *Journal of Social Psychology* 67 (1965): 77–96; Cattell and Adelson, "Dimensions of Social Change in the U.S.A.," 191, 199.

178. This refers to the conclusions of other researchers who view factor analysis as an appropriate tool for identifying the basic dimensions of personality but disagree with Cattell's specific results. There are also some scientists who believe that the method is not "an adequate basis for drawing conclusions about the real world" and warn against "the temptation to reify 'factors'" (D. T. Lykken, "Multiple Factor Analysis and Personality Research," *Journal of Experimental Research in Personality* 5 [1971]: 169).

179. C. Gibb, "The Influence of Cattell in Social Psychology and Group Dynamics," *Multivariate Behavioral Research* 19 (1984): 196. Gibb's personal papers, housed in the National Library of Australia, list his letter of support for Cattell's nomination in 1985. See the description of the papers at http://www.nla.gov.au/ms/findaids/9231.html#des.

180. On the categorization of mental activity, see E. R. Hilgard, "The Trilogy of Mind: Cognition, Affection, and Conation," *Journal of the History of the Behavioral Sciences* 16 (1980): 107–17.

181. See R. B. Cattell, "The Scree Test for the Number of Factors," *Multivariate Behavioral Research* 1 (1966): 245–76. In contrast to previous methods, which decided when to stop factoring by applying a test of statistical significance at the standard .05 level to the last factor extracted, Cattell proposed inspecting a graph of the latent roots from the correlation matrix—the eigenvalues—to see at what point the steep curve changes to a straight, negatively sloping line. This straight-end portion Cattell called the "scree," from the word for the weathered rock fragments at the base of a cliff. Everything corresponding to the roots in the scree were to be discarded as "a 'rubbish' of small error factors" (249).

182. See R. B. Cattell and J. L. Muerle, "The 'Maxplane' Program for Factor Rotation to Oblique Simple Structure," *Educational and Psychological Measurement* 3 (1960): 569–90; J. R. Hurley and R. B. Cattell, "The Procrustes Program: Producing Direct Rotation to Test a Hypothesized Factor Structure," *Behavioral Science* 7 (1962): 258–62; and R. B. Cattell and M. J. Foster, "The Rotoplot Program for Multiple Single-Plane, Visually-Guided Rotation," *Behavioral Science* 8 (1963): 156–65.

183. See, for example, R. B. Cattell, "The Three Basic Factor-Analytic Research Designs: Their Interrelations and Derivatives," *Psychological Bulletin* 49 (1952): 499–520; and Cattell, *Factor Analysis*, chaps. 7 and 8.

184. Cattell, "Raymond B. Cattell," 82.

Chapter 2: In the Name of Evolution

1. See Cattell's reflections in his two autobiographical chapters: Cattell, "Travels in Psychological Hyperspace," 87–88; and Cattell, "Raymond B. Cattell," 64 (for both, see introduction, n. 19).

2. This was an alliance that produced benefits for both sides. Although it may not have been the primary motivation for their extensive involvement in eugenics, psychologists in the United States could not help but notice the enhancement their support for the movement brought to the status of their science. As Lewis M. Terman, the most influential IQ tester of his time, observed in 1924, the psychologist had once been perceived as "just a harmless crank," but now that the discipline's results had "become the beacon light of the eugenics movement, . . . no psychologist of to-day can complain that his science is not taken seriously enough" ("The Mental Test as a Psychological Method," *Psychological Review* 31 [1924]: 105–6).

3. This observation was made in a review of two books on the history of lobotomy. See S. B. Nuland, "Killing Cures," *New York Review of Books* 52 (August 11, 2005): 23.

4. E. Huntington, *Tomorrow's Children: The Goals of Eugenics* (New York: John Wiley, 1935), 104–5.

5. A. E. Wiggam, *The New Decalogue of Science* (New York: Blue Ribbon Books, 1923), 25.

6. Cattell, *Fight for Our National Intelligence*, 146 (see introduction, n. 29).

7. C. Spearman, *The Abilities of Man: Their Nature and Measurement* (New York: Macmillan, 1927), 8.

8. C. Burt, "Experimental Tests of General Intelligence," *British Journal of Psychology* 3 (1909): 94–177; C. Burt, "The Inheritance of General Intelligence," *American Psychologist* 27 (1972): 175–90. The flaws in Burt's data were first noted in L. J. Kamin, "Heredity, Intelligence, Politics, and Society," invited address, Eastern Psychological Association (Washington, D.C., 1973). The first accusation of fraud appeared in O. Gillie, "Pioneer of IQ Faked His Research Findings," *Sunday Times (London)*, October 24, 1976, 1; and was apparently confirmed by Burt's biographer, L. S. Hearnshaw, in *Cyril Burt: Psychologist* (see introduction, n. 54). Hearnshaw's verdict has since been challenged in R. Joynson, *The Burt Affair* (London: Routledge, 1989); and R. Fletcher, *Science, Ideology, and the Media* (New Brunswick, N.J.: Transaction, 1991). New data strengthening the case against Burt are presented in W. H. Tucker, "Re-reconsidering Burt: Beyond a Reasonable Doubt," *Journal of the History of the Behavioral Sciences* 33 (1997): 145–62.

9. See Mackintosh, *Cyril Burt: Fraud or Framed?* (see chap. 1, n. 16), which contains a detailed discussion of the various charges against Burt.

10. See, for example, C. Burt, "Individual Psychology and Social Work," *Charity Organization Review* 43 (1918): 11.

11. C. Burt, "Psychological Tests for Scholarship and Promotion," *School* 13 (1925): 741.

12. Quoted in Hearnshaw, *Cyril Burt: Psychologist*, 111. The observation comes from one of the three Hadow reports, *The Primary School*, published in 1931. As Hearnshaw points out, the findings of the other official documents that shaped the British educational system in the 1920s and '30s—the other two Hadow reports and the Spens report—were also based largely on evidence supplied by Burt, and their recommendations reflected his influence.

13. See Tucker, "Re-reconsidering Burt."

14. R. B. Cattell, "Some Changes in Social Life in a Community with a Falling Intelligence Quotient," *British Journal of Psychology* 28 (1938): 430.

15. See R. B. Cattell and J. L. Willson, "Contributions Concerning Mental Inheritance," *British Journal of Educational Psychology* 8 (1938): 129–48.

16. Sarason, *Making of an American Psychologist*, 117, 118 (see introduction, n. 35).

17. W. McDougall, "William McDougall," in vol. 1 of *A History of Psychology in Auto-biography*, edited by C. Murchison (Worcester, Mass.: Clark University Press, 1930), 194, 195, 196, 200.

18. According to one historian, McDougall signed on to the expedition "because of a failed romance" (F. W. Rudmin, "William McDougall in Colonial Borneo: An Early Applied Social Psychology of Peace," *Cross-Cultural Psychology Bulletin* 26 [1992]: 10). However, McDougall states that his only motivation was eagerness to be involved in research ("William McDougall," 201).

19. Nicholson, *Inventing Personality*, 165 (see chap. 1, n. 1).

20. The reasons for McDougall's "rapid decline in influence and credibility" are discussed in R. A. Jones, "Psychology, History, and the Press: The Case of William McDougall and the *New York Times*," *American Psychologist* 42 (1987): 931–40. Along with McDougall's extreme eugenic views and opposition to then popular behaviorist notions, Jones cites his interest in such "not-quite-respectable topics" (938) as drugs and extrasensory perception for contributing to the media's depiction of him in unflattering terms. No doubt his extremely sarcastic and sometimes outright insulting style of argument played some role in the hostility. In a famous debate with the founder of behaviorism, John Watson, for example, McDougall began by acknowledging his own "unfair" advantage: everyone with "common-sense will of necessity" be on his side and everyone attracted to the "bizarre, paradoxical, preposterous, and outrageous . . . will inevitably" side with his opponent. And when forced to acknowledge that his forecast of behaviorism's rapid demise was "too optimistic," he blamed the failure of this prediction "upon a too generous estimate of the intelligence of the American public" (W. McDougall, "Fundamentals of Psychology" Behaviorism Explained," in *The Battle of Behaviorism*, by J. B. Watson and W. McDougall [New York: W. W. Norton, 1929], 40–41, 86). Although McDougall claimed to have been "very happy in America," he resigned from the American Psychological Association and later acknowledged, "The more I write, the more antagonism I seem to provoke" (McDougall, "William McDougall," 213, 223).

21. J. C. Flugel, "Obituary Notice: Professor William McDougall, 1871–1938," *British Journal of Psychology* 29 (1938–1939): 323. The book was W. McDougall, *Physiological Psychology* (London: Richard Clay, 1905).

22. McDougall, *Introduction to Social Psychology* (see chap. 1, n. 151). Over the next sixty years the book was reprinted more than thirty times. In chapter 3 McDougall defines the seven "principal" instincts as flight, repulsion, curiosity, pugnacity, subjection, self-assertion, and the parental instinct, although he also acknowledges the significance of four others—the instincts for sex, gregariousness, acquisition, and construction.

23. F. Rudmin, "William McDougall in the History of Social Psychology," *British Journal of Social Psychology* 24 (1985): 75; McDougall, *Group Mind* (see chap. 1, n. 169). In the preface McDougall states that *Group Mind* is a "sequel" to *Introduction to Social Psychology*, noting that "it builds upon that book and assumes that the reader is acquainted with it" (xi).

24. W. McDougall, *Ethics and Some Modern World Problems* (London: Methuen, 1925), xiv; W. McDougall, *Is America Safe for Democracy?* (New York: Charles Scribner's Sons,

1921), vi; W. McDougall, *The Indestructible Union: Rudiments of Political Science for the American Citizen* (Boston: Little, Brown, 1925); W. McDougall, *World Chaos: The Responsibility of Science* (London: Kegan, Paul, Trench, Trubner, 1931).

25. McDougall, *Is America Safe?* 146, 115, 106, 69–70, 82, 81, 83, 118–19.

26. McDougall, *Indestructible Union*, 137–38; McDougall, *Is America Safe?* 147–48, 132.

27. McDougall, *Ethics and World Problems*, 12–17.

28. Ibid., 20.

29. See I. Zangwill, *The Melting Pot: Drama in Four Acts* (1932; reprint, New York: Arno Press, 1975). The work was first published in 1909.

30. McDougall, *Indestructible Union*, 135, 136, 144.

31. Ibid., 145, 138, 130. See also the discussion of racial differences in personality and artistic style in McDougall, *Is America Safe?* 72–83.

32. McDougall, *Is America Safe?* 102.

33. McDougall, *Indestructible Union*, 150, 151.

34. McDougall, *World Chaos*, 35. See also ibid., 35–36.

35. McDougall, *Indestructible Union*, 140. Shortly before publication of this work, the Immigration Restriction Act of 1924—the so-called National Origins Act—was passed, enacting nationally selective quotas in proportion to a country's residents in the United States according to the 1890 census, that is, just before the shift from northern to southern and eastern Europe as the major source of immigrants, and thus severely reducing newcomers from the latter areas. Immigration from Italy, for example, decreased from approximately two hundred thousand per year to about four thousand. See Public Law 139, Chapter 190, 43 Stat.

36. McDougall, *Group Mind*, 176.

37. McDougall, *Indestructible Union*, 133–34, 160–65.

38. McDougall, *Ethics and World Problems*, 65.

39. Ibid., 125–26, 60, 38.

40. Ibid., 80.

41. W. McDougall, "Philosophy and the Social Sciences," in *Human Affairs*, edited by R. B. Cattell, J. Cohen, and R. M. W. Travers (1937; reprint, Freeport, N.Y.: Books for Libraries Press, 1970), 345.

42. McDougall, *World Chaos*, 23; McDougall, *Ethics and World Problems*, 82, 74.

43. Quoted as an observation by Lord Bryce with which McDougall enthusiastically agrees (McDougall, *Ethics and World Problems*, xi).

44. Ibid., 168, 95, 90, 169.

45. The plan is described in detail in ibid., 156–65. See also J. Allett, "Crowd Psychology and the Theory of Democratic Elitism: The Contribution of William McDougall," *Political Psychology* 17 (1996): 213–27. Although Allett makes neither mention of nor reference to the plan for reorganizing the political system, he nevertheless calls McDougall "a founding theorist of the modern doctrine of democratic elitism" (213).

46. Flugel, "Obituary Notice," 328; Cattell, Cohen, and Travers, *Human Affairs*, 6, vii.

47. Cattell, *Psychology and Social Progress* (see introduction, n. 27). See the foreword, dated September 1931, in which Cattell states that the "tentative outline of this work was written nearly eight years ago" (10).

48. Ibid., 25.

49. Ibid., 20, 140; S. J. Gould, *Wonderful Life: The Burgess Shale and the Nature of History* (New York: W. W. Norton, 1989), 25.

50. Though used in later editions of *Origin of Species,* the phrase was coined by Spencer, first in his 1851 book *Social Statics* (reprint, New York: A. M. Kelley, 1969) as a description of competition in the marketplace and then as a synonym for "natural selection" in *Principles of Biology* (New York: Appleton, 1864), where it was picked up by Darwin.

51. See, for example, Spencer, *Social Statics.*

52. C. Darwin, *The Origin of Species* (New York: Mentor, 1958), 75; K. Pearson, *National Life from the Standpoint of Science* (London: Adam and Charles Black, 1905), 21.

53. H. Spencer, *Social Statics,* 322–26.

54. W. B. Smith, *The Color Line* (1905; reprint, New York: Negro Universities Press, 1969), 192.

55. See F. L. Hoffman, *Race Traits and Tendencies of the American Negro* (New York: American Economic Association, 1896), 328, 176 (quote).

56. C. S. Bacon, "The Race Problem," *Medicine* 9 (1903): 342.

57. Cattell, *Psychology and Social Progress,* 305. The four groups were southern Ireland, Wales and Cornwall, England and the Scottish Lowlands, and the Scottish Highlands.

58. Ibid., 35, 69.

59. Ibid., 69–70.

60. Ibid., 70.

61. Ibid., 345, 71.

62. Ibid., 65, 66.

63. Ibid., 299.

64. For the discussion of racial differences in "inborn dispositions," see ibid., 40–48.

65. Ibid., 299–300.

66. C. B. Davenport, "The Effects of Race Intermingling," *Proceedings of the American Philosophical Society* 56 (1917): 366; Cattell, *Psychology and Social Progress,* 63.

67. Cattell, *Psychology and Social Progress,* 63, 61–62, 300; W. Faulkner, *Light in August* (1932; reprint, New York: Modern Library, 1950), 393.

68. Cattell, *Psychology and Social Progress,* 47, 75, 81.

69. Ibid., 10.

70. Ibid., 322, 314, 315, 317, 323.

71. Ibid., 319, 335, 326.

72. Ibid., 103.

73. Ibid., 31–32, 298, 324–25, 76.

74. Ibid., 333, 341, 339–40.

75. Ibid., 358.

76. Ibid., 299, 358, 359, 360.

77. Ibid., 360.

78. Francis Bacon's brief piece of utopian fiction describing a land organized according to the results of empirical research is contained in F. Bacon, *Advancement of Learning and New Atlantis* (London: Oxford University Press, 1960).

79. Cattell, *Psychology and Social Progress,* 364.

80. R. B. Cattell, "The Place of Religion and Ethics in a Civilization Based on Science," in *A Revaluation of Our Civilization,* by F. R. Wulsin et al. (Albany, N.Y.: Argus, 1944), 46.

81. Cattell, *Psychology and Social Progress*, 364, 365–66; Cattell, "Place of Religion and Ethics," 46.

82. Cattell, *Psychology and Social Progress*, 175, 146, 28. Richard L. Gorsuch, one of Cattell's close friends and strongest supporters, is also an ordained minister in the Disciples of Christ. Although he has written specifically about Cattell's system of ethics, citing *Psychology and Social Progress*, Gorsuch made no mention of this conflict between traditional religion and evolutionary morality ("R. B. Cattell: An Integration of Psychology and Ethics," *Multivariate Behavioral Research* 19 [1984]: 209–20).

83. Cattell, *Psychology and the Religious Quest* (see introduction, n. 32).

84. Although the word *eugenics* was not coined until eighteen years later, the idea of a systematic plan for the encouragement of marriage between the best young men and their female counterparts first appeared in F. Galton, "Hereditary Talent and Character," *Macmillan's Magazine* 12 (1865): 157–66. Galton settled on the name for this concept in his book *Inquiries into Human Faculty and Its Development* (London: Macmillan, 1883).

85. Galton was the grandchild of poet and physician Erasmus Darwin and his second wife; Charles Darwin was the grandchild of Erasmus Darwin and wife number one.

86. See, for example, F. Galton, *Hereditary Genius* (1892; reprint, London: Macmillan, 1925), 249.

87. F. Galton, "Hereditary Improvement," *Fraser's Magazine* 7 (1873): 119.

88. A possible exception was Nathaniel Hirsch, whose 1924 doctoral dissertation in psychology at Harvard, written not coincidentally under the supervision of William McDougall, concluded with a chapter advocating that eugenics be adopted as a religion (N. B. Barenbaum, "Diversifying the Discipline: Jews and Academic Psychology in the U.S., 1900–1940," paper presented at the annual meeting of Cheiron, the International Society for the History of Behavioral and Social Sciences, Akron, Ohio, June 2004).

89. C. Rosen, *Preaching Eugenics: Religious Leaders and the American Eugenics Movement* (Oxford: Oxford University Press, 2004), esp. chaps. 2 and 4; Wiggam, *New Decalogue of Science*, 110–11.

90. Cattell, *Psychology and the Religious Quest*, 29, 30, 39, 40, 55, 58, 59.

91. Ibid., 59, 61, 77.

92. Ibid., 147.

93. Ibid., 84, 88–89, 91.

94. Ibid., 91, 92, 93, 95, 94, 147.

95. Ibid., 145, 147, 94.

96. Cattell, *Fight for Our National Intelligence*, 56.

97. Cattell, *Psychology and the Religious Quest*, 145, 94.

98. Ibid., 147.

99. Faced with opposition from the League of Nations to its invasion, a year later Italy formed an alliance with Germany, which had withdrawn from the league after the Nazis took power in 1933.

100. Cattell, *Fight for Our National Intelligence*, 68.

101. Cattell, *Psychology and Social Progress*, 313; Cattell, *Fight for Our National Intelligence*, 88–89, 141.

102. On the Nazi exhibit of "degenerate art," see P. Adam, *Art of the Third Reich* (New

York: Harry N. Abrams, 1992), 120–27; and J. Petropoulos, *Art as Politics in the Third Reich* (Chapel Hill: University of North Carolina Press, 1996), chap. 2.

103. Technically, Japan was not yet a part of the Axis, becoming a member formally as a result of the Three-Power Pact, signed by representatives of Germany, Italy, and Japan in 1940.

104. Cattell, *Psychology and the Religious Quest*, 149–50.

105. Cattell, *Psychology and Social Progress*, 328.

106. Announcement of the award was made in "Notes of the Quarter," *Eugenics Review* 27 (1935): 186.

107. Cattell, *Fight for Our National Intelligence*, 9, 16, 2, 43, 3. These projections were based on some rather simplistic assumptions about what Cattell called "mental capacity as an inborn gift of the individual" (26). Interestingly, however, in this work he also stated that, in contrast to "inherited" mental ability, "character, emotional reactions, habits and skills are largely matters of environment" (35)—the opposite of what he had argued five years earlier in *Psychology and Social Progress*.

108. Ibid., 111–12.

109. Ibid., 112–18 (for the discussion of ways to encourage intelligent parents to have more children), 156.

110. Ibid., 82.

111. Ibid., 106–9, 58–59, 93, 89–90.

112. See, for example, R. B. Cattell, "Is National Intelligence Declining?" *Eugenics Review* 28 (1936–1937): 181–203; R. B. Cattell, "Intelligence and Citizenship: A Prospect," *New Era in Home and School* 18 (1937): 136–40; and R. B. Cattell, "A Study of the National Reserves of Intelligence," *Human Factors* 11 (1937): 127–37.

113. See, for example, J. L. Gray, "Influence of Environment on Mental Capacity: Comparative Intelligence of the Poor and Well-to-Do," *Manchester Guardian*, January 7, 1936, 18, which called Cattell's opinion "so irresponsible and so little based on scientific evidence."

114. "Peril of Race Deterioration," *London Times*, January 2, 1936, 15; "English Children Getting More and More Stupid," quoted in A. M. Paul, *The Cult of Personality: How Personality Tests Are Leading Us to Miseducate Our Children, Mismanage Our Companies, and Misunderstand Ourselves* (New York: Free Press, 2004), 180; "Ban Balmy Babies" quoted in A. Woolridge, *Measuring the Mind: Education and Psychology in England, c. 1860–c. 1990* (Cambridge: Cambridge University Press, 1994), 145.

115. Cattell, "Is National Intelligence Declining?" 190. In Cattell, "Intelligence and Citizenship" (137), he repeated this statistic but converted the approximation implied by "about" to the lower bound of "at least" 75 percent.

116. J. B. S. Haldane, letter to the editor, *Eugenics Review* 28 (1937): 333; R. B. Cattell, letter to the editor, *Eugenics Review* 28 (1937): 334. For Haldane's reply further skewering Cattell, see his letter to the editor, *Eugenics Review* 29 (1937): 81.

117. See, for example, P. Moshinsky, "A Gloomy Prophecy," *New Statesman and Nation* 14 (1937): 190–92, which, among other criticisms, argues that no proof of the inheritance of intelligence could be "forthcoming until a more equalized society renders possible the standardization of environmental influences"; and the anonymous review, "National Intelligence," *British Medical Journal*, no. 3991 (July 3, 1937): 15–16, which remarks on Cattell's tendency "to find only what he sought and to square conclusions with his preconceptions."

118. Letter from Julian Huxley to C. P. Blacker, January 9, 1936, Eugenics Society Archives, posted on the Institute for the Study of Academic Racism's Raymond Cattell bibliography, http://www.ferris.edu/isar/bibliography/catbib.htm; letter from Leonard Darwin to C. P. Blacker, March 23, 1937, Carlos P. Blacker Papers, also posted on the Institute for the Study of Academic Racism's Raymond Cattell bibliography.

119. Cattell, *Fight for Our National Intelligence*, 5; Cattell, *Psychology and Social Progress*, 252, 262, 282, 134, 373.

120. R. B. Cattell, "The Fate of National Intelligence: Test of a Thirteen-Year Prediction," *Eugenics Review* 42 (1950): 140; R. B. Cattell, "Differential Fertility and Normal Selection for IQ: Some Required Conditions in Their Investigation," *Social Biology* 21 (1974): 170, 171, 176.

121. The story of Graham's Hermann J. Muller Repository for Germinal Choice—known as the "Nobel Prize sperm bank" after Nobel laureate William Shockley announced that he had made a number of contributions—is engagingly told in D. Plotz, *The Genius Factory: The Curious History of the Nobel Prize Sperm Bank* (New York: Random House, 2005); see p. 32 for the reference to Cattell's membership on the advisory board. According to Plotz (personal conversation), Cattell was involved at the inception of the bank in 1963, arranging a meeting between Graham and the geneticist after whom it was named— Hermann Muller, also a proponent of "germinal choice."

122. R. K. Graham, *The Future of Man* (North Quincy, Mass.: Christopher Publishing, 1970), 50; see also 77–78. Graham acknowledges Cattell's "generous counsel" on the page before the table of contents.

123. R. B. Cattell, *Beyondism: Religion from Science* (New York: Praeger, 1987), 121.

124. Cattell, *New Morality*, 406, 47 (see introduction, n. 49).

125. Ibid., 262. See also Cattell, "Structure of Intelligence," 5 (see chap. 1, n. 130).

Chapter 3: Beyondism and the Necessity for "Genthanasia"

1. Cattell, *Psychology and the Religious Quest*, 148 (see introduction, n. 32).

2. C. Rangachar, "Differences in Perseveration among Jewish and English Boys," *British Journal of Educational Psychology* 2 (1932): 199–211; Cattell, *Psychology and Social Progress*, 53 (see introduction, n. 27).

3. R. B. Cattell, "Temperament Tests: II. Tests," *British Journal of Psychology* 24 (1934): 29, 32–33; R. B. Cattell, "Perseveration and Personality: Some Experiments and a Hypothesis," *Journal of Mental Science* 81 (1935): 165–66.

4. Cattell, "Temperament Tests: II. Tests," 46.

5. Cattell, "Perseveration and Personality," 162–63.

6. Cattell and Molteno, "Contributions Concerning Mental Inheritance: II. Temperament," 39, 41 (see chap. 1, n. 95).

7. R. B. Cattell, "The Riddle of Perseveration: II. Solution in Terms of Personality Structure," *Journal of Personality* 14 (1946): 244–47, 253, 264.

8. R. B. Cattell, "Ethics and the Social Sciences," *American Psychologist* 3 (1948): 195.

9. R. B. Cattell, "The Integration of Psychology with Moral Values," *British Journal of Psychology* 41 (1950): 27.

10. Cattell, "Ethics and the Social Sciences," 198. Cattell never relinquished the notion that what was called "prejudice" could in fact be a rational attitude "substantiated by fact,"

and that to assume otherwise was itself prejudicial. Even in 1984, two decades after passage of the landmark civil rights legislation, he characterized the famous "Authoritarian Personality" study on the psychodynamic roots of racial prejudice as research "combined . . . with propaganda" (Cattell, "Voyage of a Laboratory," 174, 163 [see introduction, n. 25]).

11. For the role of social scientists in the *Brown* case, see J. P. Jackson, *Social Scientists for Social Justice: Making the Case against Segregation* (New York: New York University Press, 2001); and Tucker, *Science and Politics*, chap 4 (see introduction, n. 8).

12. R. B. Cattell, "The Scientific Ethics of 'Beyond,'" *Journal of Social Issues* 6 (1950): 26.

13. R. Lynn, *Eugenics: A Reassessment* (Westport, Conn.: Praeger, 2001), vii, 39. See also Plotz, *Genius Factory* (see chap. 2, n. 121).

14. L. L. King, "The Traveling Carnival of Racism," *New Times* (December 28, 1973): 36. On Shockley, see Tucker, *Science and Politics*, 183–95; and Tucker, *Funding of Scientific Racism*, 140–55 (see introduction, n. 50). Shockley's contribution to the sperm bank and public endorsement of the project are described in Plotz, *Genius Factory*, chap. 6.

15. On Pearson, see Tucker, *Funding of Scientific Racism*, 159–79. Pearson is discussed at greater length in the description of Cattell's participation with the *Mankind Quarterly*, described later in this chapter.

16. Cattell, *New Morality* (see introduction, n. 49); R. B. Cattell, *Beyondism: Religion from Science* (see chap. 2, n. 123).

17. Cattell, *Beyondism: Religion from Science*, 88.

18. Cattell, *New Morality*, 411.

19. Cattell, *Beyondism: Religion from Science*, 130, 83.

20. Cattell, *New Morality*, xiii, 38.

21. Cattell, "Structure of Intelligence," 5 (see chap. 1, n. 130).

22. Cattell, *Beyondism: Religion from Science*, 20, 8.

23. Cattell, *New Morality*, 175.

24. Cattell, *Beyondism: Religion from Science*, 103.

25. Cattell, *New Morality*, 98, 102.

26. Cattell, "Structure of Intelligence," 5.

27. Cattell, *Beyondism: Religion from Science*, 137. For a discussion of evolutionary biology's rejection of group selection as a mechanism for change, see U. Segerstrale, *Defenders of the Truth: The Battle for Science in the Sociobiology Debate and Beyond* (Oxford: Oxford University Press), esp. chap. 4.

28. This quatrain comes from "Clifton Chapel" by the English poet Sir Henry Newbolt. Cattell quotes all four lines in *Psychology and the Religious Quest*, 96; and in *New Morality*, 102. In *Beyondism: Religion from Science* he quotes only the last two (137).

29. Cattell, *Beyondism: Religion from Science*, 136.

30. Cattell, *Psychology and Social Progress*, 300.

31. Cattell, *Beyondism: Religion from Science*, 68, 202.

32. Cattell, *New Morality*, 146, 172.

33. Ibid., 298; Cattell, *Beyondism: Religion from Science*, 261, 210, 189.

34. Cattell, *Psychology and Social Progress*, 70.

35. Cattell, *New Morality*, 153–54.

36. The gene for sickle cell anemia is a mutation on the eleventh chromosome, causing

red blood cells to cluster together in the shape of a sickle, thereby leading to blockages that deprive the tissues of oxygen. Although there is no doubt that this example was intended to suggest blacks as the group immune to malaria, in fact a high incidence of sickle cell disease is also found in a number of Mediterranean regions, including Greece and Italy, and the misdiagnosis of non–African Americans is not uncommon, even when there are clear symptoms of sickle cell disease (A. H. McGowan, "Genes and Race in the Classroom," *Journal of College Science Teaching* 34 [2005]: 32).

37. Cattell, *New Morality*, 154.

38. For example, Cattell, *Beyondism: Religion from Science*, 29.

39. Cattell, *Fight for Our National Intelligence*, 56 (see introduction, n. 29).

40. Cattell, *Beyondism: Religion from Science*, 43, 40–41.

41. Cattell, *Psychology and Social Progress*, 60, 65, 66.

42. Cattell, *New Morality*, 211; Cattell, *Beyondism: Religion from Science*, 65, 31.

43. Cattell, *Beyondism: Religion from Science*, 47, 280. This figurative characterization of the poor is remarkably similar to Richard Herrnstein's observation in a highly controversial 1971 article that in a wealthy society "there will be precipitated out of the mass of humanity a low-capacity residue . . . unable to master the common occupations." Herrnstein, however, was trying to make the point that equality of opportunity inevitably led to genetic stratification, because by reducing arbitrary barriers, hereditary differences are left as the only reason for differences in outcomes ("IQ," *Atlantic Monthly* [September 1971]: 43–64).

44. Cattell, *New Morality*, 160, 161.

45. Cattell, *Beyondism: Religion from Science*, 129, 351.

46. See, for example, J. R. Flynn, "The Mean IQ of Americans: Massive Gains 1932 to 1978," *Psychological Bulletin* 95 (1984): 29–51; J. R. Flynn, "Massive IQ Gains in 14 Nations: What IQ Tests Really Measure," *Psychological Bulletin* 101 (1987): 171–91.

47. Cattell, *Beyondism: Religion from Science*, 211.

48. Ibid., 113, 251, 224, 114.

49. Cattell, *New Morality*, 343.

50. Cattell, *Beyondism: Religion from Science*, 244.

51. Ibid., 223, x; R. P. Oliver, *Christianity and the Survival of the West* (Cape Canaveral: Howard Allen, 1973), 75.

52. Cattell, "The Scientific Ethics of 'Beyond,'" 25.

53. Cattell, *New Morality*, 103, 407, 180.

54. Cattell, *Beyondism: Religion from Science*, 91, 100.

55. Cattell, *New Morality*, 445. A "factorial experiment" is one in which each group in the study is matched with each culture so that all possible combinations of race and culture are included.

56. Cattell, *Beyondism: Religion from Science*, 231–32. See also Cattell, *New Morality*, 445, in which Cattell raises additional objections to UNESCO as a research institute.

57. Cattell, *New Morality*, 421.

58. Ibid., 95.

59. Ibid., 187, 216.

60. Ibid., 234.

61. Ibid., 220–21. Eschewing any of the contemporary examples of systematic attempts

to wipe out an entire group, Cattell turned again to the Old Testament, where, he wrote, there had been "several instances" of genocide.

62. Ibid., 452–53, 430, 451, 441. Cattell was particularly exercised that the courts had just allowed publication of questionably obtained government files on the Vietnam War. He saw censorship as playing a role "in relation to misrepresentation of fact, biased choice of what is news, and pollution of young minds" (441).

63. Ibid., 441, 128.

64. See, for example, Cattell, "Measurement of the Healthy Personality," 17 (see chap. 1, n. 21), where, in the last paragraph of an article on the prediction of performance from information on drives and personality dimensions, Cattell briefly summarizes the thesis of his 1972 book introducing the concept of Beyondism.

65. Draper had previously supported Ernest Sevier Cox's repatriation campaign (Tucker, *Funding of Scientific Racism*, chap. 1).

66. Letter from R. Gayre to N. Weyl, May 31, 1965, Box 12, Nathaniel Weyl Papers, Hoover Institution Archives, Stanford University.

67. Gayre boasted of his acquaintanceship in the course of praising an English translation of Günther's writing on "Aryan religion." See R. Gayre of Gayre, "Review of *The Religious Attitudes of the Indo-Europeans*," *Mankind Quarterly* 9 (1969): 143.

68. The geneticist was the British scientist R. Ruggles Gates. For the citation to his work, see N. A. Thompson, letter to the editor, *Eugenics Review* 27 (1936): 351. For more on Gates, see Tucker, *Funding of Scientific Racism*, 92–93.

69. This associate editor was psychologist Henry E. Garrett, who had been chair of the department at Columbia before returning to his native Virginia to lead the scientific opposition to the *Brown* decision (Tucker, *Funding of Scientific Racism*, chap. 3). The quote comes from H. E. Garrett to W. C. George, March 1, 1961, Wesley Critz George Papers, no. 3822, Southern Historical Collection, Wilson Library, University of North Carolina at Chapel Hill.

70. H. E. Garrett, letter to the editor, *Science* 135 (1962): 984.

71. H. E. Garrett, "Racial Mixing Could Be Catastrophic" (interview), *U.S. News and World Report*, November 18, 1963, 93.

72. D. Purves, "The Evolutionary Basis of Race Consciousness," *Mankind Quarterly* 1 (1960): 51, 53–54; W. A. Massey, "The New Fanatics," *Mankind Quarterly* 3 (1962): 79–81; G. Young, *Two Worlds—Not One: Race and Civilization* (London: Ad Hoc Publications, 1969), 28, 44, 126, 127. The review was by H. B. I. [H. B. Isherwood], *Mankind Quarterly* 11 (1970): 61.

73. Gayre's financial setback as the reason for giving up the journal is mentioned in letters from N. Weyl to Cattell, May 15 and December 4, 1978, box 12, Weyl Papers.

74. See T. Swenson, "The Works of Professor Hans F. K. Guenther," *Northern World* 5 (Winter 1960–1961): 7. Pearson was the editor of the journal and wrote many of its articles under pseudonyms. On his attempt to pay for reprinting Günther's work, see the letter from Pearson to E. S. Cox, July 15, 1958, Ernest Sevier Cox Papers, Special Collections Library, Duke University.

75. See the editorials in *Western Destiny* 10 (November 1965): 3; and 9 (June 1964): 5. Pearson acknowledged that he was the editor of *Western Destiny* in a letter to E. S. Cox, September 17, 1965, Cox Papers.

76. In a letter to General Pedro del Valle, Pearson called himself the "registered publisher and proprietor" of the *New Patriot* (Pearson to del Valle, March 30, 1966, Pedro A. del Valle Papers, Division of Special Collections and University Archives, University of Oregon, Eugene). He also acknowledged using the pseudonym "Stephen Langton" in a sworn deposition in *Hirsch v. Pearson, Humphreys and Scott-Townsend Publishers,* Champaign County, Ill., June 23, 1994. A typical article in the journal claimed that the Jews had carried out a "full scale . . . onslaught on Germany," demanding the complete "extermination or genocide of the German nation" (R. Bevan [in all likelihood, another Pearson pseudonym], "Analysis of the Hate-Germany Campaign," *New Patriot* 8 [December 1966], 48, 47, 51).

77. R. Pearson, *Eugenics and Race* (Los Angeles: Noontide Press, 1966), 26. The pamphlet was originally published in 1959.

78. In chronological order, see R. Pearson, "Ecology Adaptation and Speciation," *Mankind Quarterly* 19 (1978): 103–18; A. McGregor, "Group Conflict: An Evolutionary Residual?" *Mankind Quarterly* 22 (1981): 43–48; A. McGregor, "The Evolutionary Function of Prejudice," *Mankind Quarterly* 26 (1986): 277–84; A. McGregor, "The Double Nature of Prejudice," *Mankind Quarterly* 33 (1993): 423–32; and J. W. Jamieson, "Biological Diversity and Ethnic Identity: Changing Patterns in the Modern World," *Mankind Quarterly* 36 (1995): 193–99. Essentially the same article also appeared in another publication edited by Pearson, again authored by one of his pseudonyms, as J. W. Jamieson, "Evolution and the Future of Humankind," *Journal of Social, Political, and Economic Studies* 23 (1998): 291–301.

79. See in particular the three articles by McGregor cited in the previous note, in which the quoted observations appear more than once.

80. R. B. Cattell, "Virtue in 'Racism'?" *Mankind Quarterly* 32 (1992): 283, 284; R. B. Cattell et al., "The Relation of Blood Types to Primary and Secondary Personality Traits," *Mankind Quarterly* 21 (1980): 35–51 (the study also appeared in a collection of articles edited by Pearson, *Essays in Medical Anthropology,* Mankind Quarterly Monograph, no. 2 [Washington, D.C.: Cliveden Press, 1979], 66–82; R. B. Cattell, H. B. Young, and J. D. Hundleby, "Blood Groups and Personality Traits," *American Journal of Human Genetics* 16 (1964): 397–402; A. S. Wiener, letter to the editor, *American Journal of Human Genetics* 17 (1965): 370; H. W. Norton, letter to the editor, *American Journal of Human Genetics* 23 (1971): 225. Cattell responded that he could have answered the criticisms by a reanalysis but had not preserved the data (R. B. Cattell, letter to the editor, *American Journal of Human Genetics* 24 [1972]: 485).

81. Cattell, "Some Changes in Social Life," 323–44 (see chap. 2, n. 14); R. B. Cattell, "Some Changes in Social Life in a Community with a Falling Intelligence Quotient," in *Intelligence and National Achievement,* edited by R. B. Cattell (Washington, D.C.: Cliveden Press, 1983), 156–76.

82. Cattell, "Some Changes in Social Life" (1938), 323, 341.

83. R. B. Cattell, "Ethics and the Social Sciences: The 'Beyondist' Solution," *Mankind Quarterly* 19 (1979): 304, 308, 305. For the original observation of "anvil and hammer," see Cattell, *Psychology and Social Progress,* 303.

84. Cattell, "Concepts and Methods," 58 (see introduction, n. 55); Cattell and Gorsuch, "National Morale and Morality," 91–92 (see chap. 1, n. 177).

85. In "Voyage of a Laboratory," Cattell writes that it was "25 years later" that he was able to return to the work on syntality (135); this is probably a typographical error, as it was actually closer to fifteen years. See the footnote in ibid., 173, for Cattell's acknowledgment of support from Graham, who himself participated in the research and is listed as a coauthor in Cattell, Graham, and Woliver, "Reassessment of the Factorial Cultural Dimensions," 241–58 (see chap. 1, n. 174).

86. R. B. Cattell and J. M. Brennan, "Population Intelligence and National Syntality Dimensions," *Mankind Quarterly* 21 (1981): 338.

87. R. B. Cattell, *How Good Is Your Country? What You Should Know,* Mankind Quarterly Monograph, no. 5 (Washington, D.C.: Institute for the Study of Man, 1994). In fact, though courteous on Cattell's part, his gratitude for Pearson's/Andrews's editorial assistance was hardly justified: large chunks of prose appeared twice within pages of each other (compare pp. 77–78 with 79–80), there were numerous typographical errors, and some references in the text did not appear in the bibliography (for example, Van Court [1985] on p. 65).

88. Ibid., 95, 20, 107.

89. Ibid., 108, 93.

90. Ibid., 94.

91. See, for example, Cattell, *Psychology and Social Progress,* 46–48, 73, 87. Gobineau's thought was popularized in Germany largely through the work of Houston Stewart Chamberlain, an Englishman with German citizenship, whose book arguing that Germans were the purest Aryans, *Grundlagen des neunzehnten Jahrhunderts* (*Foundations of the Nineteenth Century,* translated by J. Lees [Munich: F. Bruckmann, 1912]), was reprinted numerous times under the Nazis.

92. On Gobineau, see *Gobineau: Selected Political Writings,* edited by M. D. Bidiss (New York: Harper and Row, 1970); and J.-A. de Gobineau, *The Inequality of Human Races* (1915; reprint, New York: Howard Fertig, 1967).

93. See, for example, Cattell, *Psychology and Social Progress,* 46, 194.

94. M. Ludendorff, *Deutscher Gottglaube* (Leipzig: Theodor Weicher, 1928); K. P. Tauber, *Beyond Eagle and Swastika: German Nationalism since 1945* (Middletown, Conn.: Wesleyan University Press, 1967), 1:672–73. On the Ludendorffs, see also R. Steigmann-Gall, "Rethinking Nazism and Religion: How Anti-Christian Were the 'Pagans'?" *Central European History* 36 (2003): 75–106 (esp. 79–85).

95. Cattell, *Psychology and Social Progress,* 196.

96. Cattell, *Beyondism: Religion from Science,* viii.

97. See Tucker, *Funding of Scientific Racism,* 113, 156–58.

98. C. Putnam quoted in *New York Times,* December 2, 1961, 47. On Putnam's campaign to stop the civil rights movement on the basis of blacks' racial inferiority, see Tucker, *Funding of Scientific Racism,* 101–11. The same publication includes the details of Draper's support for the *Mankind Quarterly* and the Foundation for Human Understanding (156–79).

99. C. Putnam, *Race and Reason: A Yankee View* (Washington, D.C.: Public Affairs Press, 1961), 94; C. Putnam, *Race and Reality* (Washington, D.C.: Public Affairs Press, 1967), 172.

100. On *Western Destiny,* see Tucker, *Funding of Scientific Racism,* 80, 162–63. On GRECE,

see I. R. Barnes, "The Pedigree of GRECE," pts. 1 and 2, *Patterns of Prejudice* 14 (1980): 14–24, 29–39; and M. McDonald, "Le nouveau Nazism," *Saturday Review* (February 1980): 13–16.

101. T. Sheehan, "Paris: Moses and Polytheism," *New York Review of Books* (January 24, 1980): 15; P. W. Valentine, "The Fascist Specter behind the World Anti-Red League," *Washington Post*, May 28, 1978, C1. Valentine referred to GRECE, incorrectly, as Nouvelle Ecole, the name of the group's journal.

102. Cattell, *Beyondism: Religion from Science*, vii, x; letter from R. Pearson to N. Weyl, May 5, 1967, Box 13, Weyl Papers.

103. B. R. Epstein and A. Forster, *The Radical Right: Report on the John Birch Society and Its Allies* (New York: Vintage Books, 1967), 113; R. P. Oliver, *America's Decline: The Education of a Conservative* (London: Londinium Press, 1982), 334, 75, 19, 30, 99, 16.

104. According to the Web sites of the Barnes Review and the American Nationalist Union—both neo-Nazi groups—Robertson's real name was Humphrey Ireland. See the entry for *The Dispossessed Majority* at http://www.barnesreview.org/books2004l.htm and the discussion forum at http://www.anu.org/forum/forum_posts.asp?TID=479&PN=1.

105. Oliver's review was never published but was circulated privately among far rightists. See the copy in the Albert C. Wedemeyer Papers, Box 57, Hoover Institution Archives, Stanford University.

106. W. Robertson, *The Dispossessed Majority* (Cape Canaveral: Howard Allen, 1981), 505, 301.

107. W. Robertson, *Ventilations* (Cape Canaveral: Howard Allen, 1974), 76.

108. "Rational Anti-Semitism," in *Best of "Instauration," 1978*, edited by W. Robertson (Cape Canaveral: Howard Allen, 1986), 14.

109. Robertson, *The Dispossessed Majority*, 189–98, 365, 200–201.

110. Cattell, "Voyage of a Laboratory," 164; B. Mehler, "Beyondism: Raymond B. Cattell and the New Eugenics," *Genetica* 99 (1997): 157; Robertson, *The Dispossessed Majority*, 556.

111. "Books That Speak for the Majority," n.d., newsprint brochure circulated by Howard Allen, P.O. Box 76, Cape Canaveral, Fla.

112. Cattell and his book were featured on the cover of *Instauration* 14 (June 1989). The two-part review of *Beyondism: Religion from Science* appeared in this issue and the next, July 1989.

113. W. Robertson, *The Ethnostate: An Unblinkered Prospectus for an Advanced Statecraft* (Cape Canaveral: Howard Allen, 1992), ix, 23, 223–24.

114. Ibid., 163, 178, 193, 211, 179, 194, 120.

115. Ibid., 76, 40, 41, 9, 36, 153.

116. Cattell, *Beyondism: Religion from Science*, 255; "The Beyondist Society: First Annual Meeting," n.d. I am grateful to Barry Mehler, director of the Institute for the Study of Academic Racism at Ferris State University, for providing me with a copy of this document and those cited in the following two endnotes.

117. Memo to members of the Executive Committee of the Beyondism Foundation from John Horn, September 29, 1993. Copy provided by Barry Mehler, director of the Institute for the Study of Academic Racism.

118. *Beyondist: The Quarterly Organ of the Beyondist Foundation* 1 (November 1994): 4. Apparently, the *Beyondist* was distributed primarily to a small circle of sympathizers.

No copies of the publication can be found in any major research library, including the Library of Congress. I was provided a copy by Barry Mehler, director of the Institute for the Study of Academic Racism.

119. Ibid., 2. Cattell's daughter later claimed (e-mail from Heather Cattell to the persons on the discussion list described in the next chapter, September 13, 1998) that her father had nothing to do with this favorable review; with Robertson himself, whom she characterized as a "rabid racist"; or even with what she called "this obscure 'Beyondist' newsletter," a publication in which, she claimed, other people had tried to involve her father. Although the evidence is overwhelming that the newsletter was Cattell's project from beginning to end, even assuming *arguendo* that she was correct, in his own writing Cattell had earlier emphasized a scientist's obligation to "make a thorough moral examination of the use being made of his results" by others (Cattell, "Integration of Psychology with Moral Values," 30) and object to misapplication; ironically, at the time he was exercised that some psychological research was cited as support for the integration of subsidized housing. Applying his own principle to the use of his work as a scientific justification for Robertson's proposal, presumably Cattell would have spoken out if he had any objections.

120. See the editor's comment at the end of T. Wansley, "Beltaine: I Investigate an Ancient European Ritual," posted on the National Vanguard Web site, http://www.nationalvanguard .org/story.php?id=1328.

121. See the "National Alliance Goals" at http://www.natall.com/what-is-na/na2.html and the "Program of the National Alliance" at http://www.natall.com/what-is-na/na3 .html.

122. "Dividing the Race," editorial, *National Vanguard Magazine*, no. 115 (November–December 1995), reprinted online at http://www.natall.com/national-vanguard/115/ dividing.html; "The Objective Ethics of Raymond Cattell and Jacques Monod: The IS and the OUGHT," *Heritage and Destiny* 1 (1980): 14.

123. J. Taylor, "The Myth of Diversity," *American Renaissance* 8 (July–August 1997): 8. Taylor was quoting a biologist, but only to indicate his enthusiastic agreement with the observation.

124. The excerpts from oral histories appeared in G. Braun, "Forgotten Black Voices," *American Renaissance* 4 (September–October 1993): 10–12.

125. S. Francis, "Prospects for Racial and Cultural Survival," *American Renaissance* 6 (March 1995): 7. See also S. Francis, "Race and the American Identity (Part II)," *American Renaissance* 10 (January 1999): 6.

126. J. Taylor, "The Racial Revolution," *American Renaissance* 10 (May 1999): 3.

127. The attack on political correctness was D. D'Souza, *Illiberal Education: The Politics of Race and Sex on Campus* (New York: Free Press, 1991). The proposal to repeal the Civil Rights Act appeared in D. D'Souza, *The End of Racism* (New York: Free Press, 1995), 545. D'Souza characterizes *American Renaissance* as "racist" in the latter book (396) and in D. D'Souza, "Racism: It's a White (and Black) Thing," *Washington Post*, September 24, 1995, C1.

128. The three-part review of Cattell's 1972 book, *A New Morality from Science: Beyondism*, appeared as T. Jackson, "What Can Replace Religion (Part I)," *American Renaissance* 2 (February 1991): 7–8; T. Jackson, "The Folly of the Welfare State (Part II)," *American Renaissance* 2 (March 1991): 5–7; and T. Jackson, "The Importance of Group Evolution

(Part III)," *American Renaissance* 2 (April 1991): 4–6. The special section, "Uses and Misuses of Altruism," appeared in part 3; the statement that it was "wrong to tell a man to love his neighbor as himself" appeared in both parts 1 and 2.

129. J. Taylor, "A Conversation with a Pioneer: Prof. Raymond Cattell Reflects on His Career," *American Renaissance* 6 (October 1995): 7, 6.

Chapter 4: The Cattell Convention

1. See the APF Web site, including its history at http://www.apa.org/apf/history.html and its "Mission Statement" at http://www.apa.org/apf/missionstatement.html.

2. The Gold Medal Awards are described by the APF at http://www.apa.org/apf/gold .html; a list of all the recipients is available at http://www.apa.org/apf/goldmedal.html.

3. "APF Recognizes Psychologists for Lifetime Achievement," *APA Monitor* (July 1997): 48. Matarazzo was interviewed by phone by Barry Mehler on July 31, 1997. I am grateful to Mehler for sharing with me the notes of his interview. At the time Matarazzo actually said that there were "five or six" other nominees; in an e-mail, the APF director, Lisa Strauss, confirmed that the exact number was "six," although in her account of the process there was a "Foundation Committee" that selected Cattell from among the nominees and then recommended him to the full board. The list of the members of the APF Board of Trustees at the time is provided in the editorial introduction preceding the formal statement of the award in "Gold Medal Award for Life Achievement," 797 (see introduction, n. 4).

4. The Cecil Gibb Papers, housed in the National Library of Australia, contain correspondence related to the nomination of Cattell for the Gold Medal Award in 1985. Gibb was one of Cattell's first doctoral students at the University of Illinois and went on to conduct studies on leadership based in part on the work done with his mentor. See the description of Gibb's papers on the Web site for the National Library of Australia at http://nla.gov.au/nla.ms-ms9231.

5. Cattell, *Beyondism: Religion from Science*, 255 (see chap. 2, n. 123); Horn quoted in Mehler, "Beyondism," 161 (see chap. 3, n. 110).

6. Gibb, "Influence of Cattell," 194 (see chap. 1, n. 179); Gorsuch, "R. B. Cattell: An Integration," 209–20 (see chap. 2, n. 82).

7. The article was Mehler, "Beyondism," 153–63.

8. Interview with Mehler.

9. "Gold Medal Award for Life Achievement," 799; interview with Mehler.

10. Personal communication with Andrew Winston.

11. I am grateful to Barry Mehler for providing me a copy of the press release and information about the recipients. In addition to the press release, Mehler also sent a large folder of materials on Cattell to the ADL, leading Abraham Foxman, its director, to protest the award formally in a letter to the APF. Personally, I would have preferred to leave this essentially political organization and its highly provocative leader (see, for example, J. Traub, "Does Abe Foxman Have an Anti-Anti-Semite Problem?" *New York Times Magazine*, January 14, 2007, 30–35) out of the controversy and let the academics who had studied Cattell's work make the case for his involvement with extremists, but there is no doubt that Foxman was well informed about Cattell's work. Nevertheless, soon after the Cattell flap, Kevin MacDonald—a psychologist popular among anti-Semitic groups

for his theory that Judaism is not a religion but rather an evolutionary strategy designed to further Jewish goals by disrupting the "host" societies in which they reside—cited the Anti-Defamation League's pressure on the APA as an example of "Jewish organizations . . . us[ing] their power to make the discussion of Jewish interests off limits" (*Separation and Its Discontents: Toward an Evolutionary Theory of Anti-Semitism* [Westport, Conn.: Praeger, 1998], 190).

12. Winston to Matarazzo, August 5, 1997 (see introduction, n. 7). Winston also sent a copy to Martin Seligman, president of the APA at the time.

13. E-mail, Fowler to Winston, August 8, 1997. I am grateful to Andrew Winston for sharing this communication with me.

14. Tucker, *Science and Politics,* 239–49 (see introduction, n. 8); Tucker to Farberman, August 11, 1997 (copy in my possession).

15. Cattell, *Psychology and Social Progress,* 70 (see introduction, n. 27).

16. See H. Saeman, "The Cattell Convention," *National Psychologist* 6 (September–October 1997): 2.

17. Brief summaries of Wiesel's address appeared in S. Sleek, "Wiesel Emphasizes Need to Thank the Elderly," *APA Monitor* 28 (October 1997): 23; and in Saeman, "The Cattell Convention," 2.

18. S. Sleek, "Lifetime Achievement Award Is Questioned," *APA Monitor* 28 (October 1997): 23; Wiesel to Tucker, September 29, 1997 (original in my possession).

19. "Statement of the American Psychological Foundation" (see introduction, n. 5); copy in my possession.

20. See Hilts, "Group Delays Achievement Award," A10 (see introduction, n. 6).

21. Ibid.

22. Tucker to Farberman, August 21, 1997 (copy in my possession); e-mail from Elisabeth Straus to me, September 5, 1997.

23. Smith testified in *Davis v. School Board of Prince Edward County [Virginia],* 103 F. Supp 337 (1952).

24. The composition of the panel was announced on November 4, 1997, in a statement released by the APA. In addition to Smith and Caplan, the other members named were Gwyneth M. Boodoo, a senior research scientist at the Educational Testing Service specializing in psychometrics; Lyle E. Bourne, an experimental psychologist at the University of Colorado specializing in human learning, memory, and cognitive processes; and Douglas N. Jackson, a clinical psychologist with expertise in measurement and multivariate techniques. Bourne had once chaired the Board of Scientific Affairs, and Jackson had been a past president of both the Society for Multivariate Experimental Psychology and the APA's Division 5 on Evaluation, Measurement, and Statistics.

25. "Statement of the American Psychological Foundation."

26. Phone call with Fowler, January 22, 1998; Cattell, "An Open Letter to the APA," available online at http://www.cattell.net/devon/openletter.htm.

27. Cattell, *New Morality,* xii, xiii, xiv (see introduction, n. 49); Cattell, *Beyondism: Religion from Science,* 1; Cattell, "Raymond B. Cattell," 88 (see introduction, n. 19).

28. Cattell, "An Open Letter to the APA"; Cattell, "Virtue in 'Racism'?" 283–84 (see chap. 3, n. 80).

29. Cattell, "An Open Letter to the APA"; R. J. Herrnstein and C. Murray, *The Bell Curve: Intelligence and Class Structure in American Life* (New York: Free Press, 1994), 315.

30. Cattell, "An Open Letter to the APA."

31. See *Loving v. Virginia*, 388 U.S. 1–14 (1967).

32. Dreger and Berg, "Psychology of the Scientist," 848 (see introduction, n. 16).

33. See "Scientists, Colleagues Defend Cattell," *National Psychologist 7* (January–February 1998): 9. Gluck and the other three awardees—Rutgers University social psychologist Lee Jussim, Iowa State University multivariate specialist David Lubinski, and Ohio State University cognitive psychologist Caroline Palmer—were named in ibid.; in a personal communication Gluck told me of his attempt to have the awards returned.

34. Winston to Matarazzo, August 5, 1997.

35. G. Whitney, "Raymond B. Cattell and the Fourth Inquisition," *Mankind Quarterly* 38 (1997): 99, 103–5, 111.

36. G. Whitney, "On the Races of Man," *Mankind Quarterly* 39 (1999): 330.

37. G. Whitney, foreword to *My Awakening,* by D. Duke (Covington, La.: Free Speech Press, 1998). Whitney's speech to the 2000 meeting of the Institute for Historical Review can be heard at http://www.ihr.org/conference/13thconf/schedule.html.

38. Detterman, letter to the editor, 5 (see introduction, n. 9); Dreger and Berg, "Psychology of the Scientist," 848; D. Lykken, "The New Eugenics," review of *Eugenics: A Reassessment,* by Richard Lynn, *Contemporary Psychology* 49 (2004): 670. In 1990 Lykken received the APA Award for Distinguished Contributions to Psychology in the Public Interest, and in 2001 he received the Award for Distinguished Scientific Applications of Psychology.

39. Comments from the reviewers were attached to the form letter announcing acceptance of the panel at the 1998 convention; D. Pope-Davis and H. L. K. Coleman (co-program chairs, Division 45) to "Presenter," March 4, 1998.

40. E-mail communication, McDonald to Earl Hunt, November 9, 1998.

41. In addition to Horn, Dreger, Gorsuch, Winston, Mehler (together with Keith Hurt, the researcher for his institute), and myself, the list of invitees included Frederick Weizmann (York University), Michael Kral (University of Windsor), Douglas Wahlsten (University of Alberta), Raymond Fancher (York University), Jack Block (University of California–Berkeley), Earl Hunt (University of Washington), David T. Lykken (University of Minnesota), Paul E. Meehl (University of Minnesota), Leo Mos (University of Alberta), John Gillis (St. Thomas University), John McArdle (University of Virginia), Heather Cattell (member of the Board of Directors of the Institute for Personality and Ability Testing and an expert on use of the *Sixteen Personality Factor Questionnaire*), Herbert W. Eber (president of Psychological Resources, a firm specializing in the psychological assessment of public safety personnel), and John Nesselroade (University of Virginia). The last six names, along with Horn and Dreger, were all outspoken supporters or collaborators of Cattell's.

42. Gorsuch to Matarazzo, n.d., available online as "Prof. Gorsuch's Letter to the APF," http://www.stthomasu.ca/~jgillis/awalifgor.htm; Dreger and Berg, "Psychology of the Scientist," 848; "Scientists, Colleagues Defend Cattell," 9.

43. E-mail communication, Horn to McDonald and the twenty persons who had been

invited to contribute to the special issue (hereinafter referred to as "the list"), September 9, 1998.

44. E-mail communication, McDonald to Horn and the list, September 9, 1998.

45. W. H. Tucker, "Does Science Offer Support for Racial Separation?" *History and Philosophy of Psychology Bulletin* 10 (1998): 19–21; the quote appears on p. 20. The other contributors to the issue were McDonald, Winston, Mehler, Wahlsten, Hunt, and Weizmann.

46. E-mail communication, Tucker to the list, September 10, 1998.

47. Cattell, *Psychology and Social Progress*, 359–60; e-mail communication, Horn to the list, September 16, 1998. Strangely, Horn changed the "subject" line of this e-mail, which had been "HPPB Special Issue" in the exchange so far, to "Note to Tucker and those to whom he mails"—as if I had initiated communication with the twenty persons on the list. In fact, after receiving Horn's initial attack on Mehler and myself, which was sent to the entire list, all I did was click "Reply all."

48. Cattell, *New Morality*, 95, 178, 220–21; Heather Cattell quoted in Holden, "Cattell Relinquishes Psychology Award," 811 (see introduction, n. 10).

49. E-mail communication, Heather Cattell to the list, September 10, 1998; Gorsuch to Matarazzo; president's column, L. Hunt, "Against Presentism," *Perspectives: Newsletter of the American Historical Association* 40 (May 2002), online version available at http://www.historians.org/Perspectives/issues/2002/0205/0205pre1.cfm.

50. K. Lamb, "Modern McCarthyism: A Case Study," *Right Now!* (October–December 1998): 13.

51. "College Courses in Genetics and Eugenics," *Eugenical News* 1 (1916): 26, 34; "Harvard Declines a Legacy to Found Eugenics Course," *New York Times*, May 8, 1927, 1; Rosen, *Preaching Eugenics*, 166 (see chap. 2, n. 89); "Genes and Eugenics," *New York Times*, August 24, 1932, 16; "Against Sterilization," *New York Times*, January 26, 1936, sec. 4, p. 8; E. A. Hooten, *Apes, Men, and Morons* (New York: G. P. Putnam's Sons, 1937), 230; Cattell, *Psychology and the Religious Quest*, 94 (see introduction, n. 32).

52. Cattell, *Fight for Our National Intelligence*, 141 (see introduction, n. 29); Cattell, *Psychology and the Religious Quest*, 150. Kristallnacht took place on November 9, and *Psychology and the Religious Quest* was dedicated to William McDougall, who died on November 28.

53. "Notes of the Quarter," *Eugenics Review* 25 (1933): 77.

54. C. P. Blacker, "Eugenics in Germany," *Eugenics Review* 25 (1933): 157, 158–59.

55. J. S. Huxley, Galton Lecture, delivered before the Eugenics Society, February 17, 1936, published as "Eugenics and Society," *Eugenics Review* 28 (1936): 11, 24, 17–18, 27; Huxley to Blacker, January 9, 1936 (see chap. 2, n. 118).

56. A. Wooldridge, *Measuring the Mind: Education and Psychology in England, c. 1860–1990* (Cambridge: Cambridge University Press, 1994); A. Wooldridge, "Bell Curve Liberals," *New Republic* (February 27, 1995): 24; G. R. Searle, "Eugenics and Politics in Britain in the 1930s," *Annals of Science* 36 (1979): 169; Wooldridge, "Bell Curve Liberals," 24.

57. Cattell, *Psychology and Social Progress*, 360; Cattell, *Psychology and the Religious Quest*, 94; Cattell, *New Morality*, 95, 220–21.

58. Cattell, *Psychology and Social Progress*, 47, 70.

59. Lykken, "The New Eugenics," 670–71. The book being reviewed was R. Lynn, *Eugenics: A Reassessment* (see chap. 3, n. 13).

60. Lykken, "The New Eugenics," 670–71.

61. The proposal originally appeared as D. T. Lykken, "The Causes and Costs of Crime and a Controversial Cure," *Journal of Personality* 68 (2000): 559–605. The requirement of birth control in response to a second unlicensed pregnancy was added in Lykken's invited address after receiving the APA's Award for Distinguished Applications of Psychology ("Parental Licensure," *American Psychologist* 56 [2001]: 892). See also D. Lykken, "Licensing Parents: A Response to Critics," *Journal of Personality* 68 (2000): 639–49.

62. Lykken, "Causes and Costs," 598. In a footnote Lykken cites a letter from the anthropologist Vincent Sarich to the June 1993 *Scientific American* as the first use of the term *eumemics*, though no such letter actually appears in that issue of the magazine.

63. R. Dawkins, *The Selfish Gene*, 2d ed. (New York: Oxford University Press, 1989), esp. chap. 11; Lykken, "Causes and Costs," 596.

64. See, for example, the responses to Lykken's proposal by R. J. Sampson, "Crime, Criminals, and Cures: Medical Model Revisited," *Journal of Personality* 68 (2000): 607–13; S. Scarr, "Toward Voluntary Parenthood," *Journal of Personality* 68 (2000): 615–23; and J. R. Harris, "The Outcome of Parenting: What Do We Really Know?" *Journal of Personality* 68 (2000): 625–37.

65. See, for example, Rushton, letter to the editor, *Society* 34 (July–August 1997): 4, in which he defends the "scholarly" work of Henry Garrett as "objective in tone and backed by standard social science evidence." Garrett, once president of the American Psychological Association, spent the last fifteen years of his life spearheading the campaign to preserve Jim Crow laws on the grounds that blacks were genetically inferior; his activities are described in Tucker, *Funding of Scientific Racism*, chap. 3 (see introduction, n. 50).

66. See, for example, M. Snyderman and R. J. Herrnstein, "Intelligence Tests and the Immigration Act of 1924," *American Psychologist* 38 (1983): 986–95, which revises H. H. Goddard's 1917 conclusion that large percentages of immigrants from southern and eastern Europe were "feeble-minded" to make it sound less unreasonable. The controversy is described in W. H. Tucker, "'A Scientific Result of Apparent Absurdity': The Attempt to Revise Goddard," *Ethnic and Racial Studies* 22 (1999): 162–71.

Conclusion

1. Gorsuch to Matarazzo, available at http://www.stthomasu.ca/~jgillis/awalifgor.htm. The memorial's home page is http://www.cattell.net/devon/rbcmain.htm; the reminiscences appear under the link "Remembering." The two quotes come from Kim Iannetta and John I. Levy, respectively.

2. Both the original and a translation appear in J. Goethe, *Faust*, translated by W. Kaufmann (Garden City, N.Y.: Doubleday, 1961), pt. 1, ll. 1112–13. Kaufmann translates the German, more poetically, as "Two souls, alas, are dwelling in my breast / And one is striving to forsake its brother."

3. R. J. Lifton, *The Nazi Doctors: Medical Killing and the Psychology of Genocide* (New

York: Basic Books, 1986), 113–14, 439. The executed leader of the euthanasia program was Hitler's personal physician, Karl Brandt.

4. This apt phrase was used to describe the Nazi government by Jonathan Ree, an expert in the history of philosophy, in "In Her Mind's Eye" (an essay review of three collections of works by Hannah Arendt), *Nation* (January 30, 2006): 28–34.

5. K. Passmore, *Fascism: A Very Short Introduction* (Oxford: Oxford University Press, 2002), 31; Cattell, *Psychology and the Religious Quest*, 150 (see introduction, n. 32).

6. Passmore, *Fascism*, 29; Cattell, *Psychology and Social Progress*, 345 (see introduction, n. 27). According to Cattell, the latter observation had been made originally by Aldous Huxley in *Jesting Pilate*.

7. Cattell, *How Good Is Your Country?* 52 (see chap. 3, n. 87).

8. See J. Goebbels, "Der Führer als Redner," in *Adolf Hitler: Bilder aus dem Leben des Führers* (Hamburg: Cigaretten/Bilderdienst, 1936), 27–34. A translation of Goebbels's article can be found online at http://www.calvin.edu/academic/cas/gpa/ahspeak.htm.

9. S. Haffner, *Defying Hitler: A Memoir*, translated by O. Pretzel (New York: Picador, 2003), 52. Haffner was the pseudonym used by German historian Raimund Pretzel, whose son translated the book.

10. F. Lenz, *Die Rasse als Wertprinzip: Zur Erneuerung der Ethik* (Munich: J. F. Lehmanns, 1934), 15, 44. This was a republication of an essay that had appeared originally in 1917.

11. F. Lenz, *Menschliche Auslese und Rassenhygiene (Eugenik)*, vol. 2 of *Menschliche Erbleichkeitslehre und Rassenhygiene (Eugenik)*, by E. Baur, E. Fischer, and F. Lenz, 4th ed. (Munich: J. F. Lehmanns, 1932), 272–92.

12. See the section by Lenz in E. Baur, E. Fischer, and F. Lenz, *Human Heredity*, translated by E. Paul and C. Paul (New York: Macmillan, 1931). This is the translation of the first volume of *Menschliche Erbleichkeitslehre und Rassenhygiene (Eugenik)*, the second volume of which is cited above but was never translated.

13. F. Lenz, "Die Stellung des Nationalsozialismus zur Rassenhygiene," *Archiv für Rassen- und Gesellschaftsbiologie* 25 (1931): 308.

14. Lenz, *Die Rasse als Wertprinzip*, 7.

15. O. F. von Verschuer, "Was kann der Historiker, der Genealoge und der Statistiker zur Erforschung des biologischen Problems der Judenfrage beitragen?" *Forschungen zur Judenfrage* 2 (1937): 218.

16. See R. Proctor, *Racial Hygiene: Medicine under the Nazis* (Cambridge: Harvard University Press, 1988), 197.

17. See the discussion of Judaism in H. F. K. Günther, *Rassenkunde des deutschen Volkes* (Munich: J. F. Lehmanns, 1928), 395–96.

18. Cattell, *Psychology and Social Progress*, 70.

19. A. Hitler, *Mein Kampf*, translated by R. Manheim (Boston: Houghton Mifflin, 1971), 304–5, 303; Cattell, *Psychology and Social Progress*, 70; J.-P. Sartre, "Existentialism Is a Humanism," in *Existentialism from Dostoevsky to Sartre*, edited by W. Kaufmann (New York: Meridian, 1960), 295.

20. J. H. McRandle, *The Track of the Wolf: Essays on National Socialism and Its Leader Adolf Hitler* (Evanston, Ill.: Northwestern University Press, 1965), 125; Cattell, *Psychology and Social Progress*, 300; McRandle, *Track of the Wolf*, 125; H. Arendt, "Ideologie und

Terror," in *Offener Horizont: Festschrift für Karl Jaspers*, edited by K. Piper (Munich: R. Piper, 1953), 244; Goebbels, "Der Führer als Redner," 27.

21. Hitler, *Mein Kampf*, 383.

22. Cattell, *Fight for Our National Intelligence*, 56 (see introduction, n. 29).

23. Cattell, *Psychology and Social Progress*, 360.

24. Ibid.

25. Cattell, *New Morality*, 146, 172, 154 (see introduction, n. 49).

26. See C. Clay and M. Leapman, *Master Race: The Lebensborn Experiment in Nazi Germany* (London: Hodder and Stoughton, 1995).

27. Cattell, *New Morality*, 160–61.

28. The survey was published as J. Taylor, "Who Reads *American Renaissance*?" *American Renaissance* 8 (July–August 1997): 8–11. No doubt because the führer has been such a public relations disaster for racists and neo-Nazis, Hitler also ranked first on the survey's list of "Foreigners Who Have Damaged White Interests."

29. Cattell, *New Morality*, 440–41.

30. Ibid., 441.

31. For a detailed discussion of the triumph of evolutionary ethics over traditional beliefs in the sanctity of life, see R. Weikart, *From Darwin to Hitler: Evolutionary Ethics, Eugenics, and Racism in German* (New York: Palgrave Macmillan, 2004), esp. chap. 4.

32. "Ansprache des Herrn Reichsministers des Innern Dr. Wilhelm Frick auf der ersten Sitzung des Sachverständigenbeirats für Bevölkerungs- und Rassenpolitik" [Speech of the Reichminister of the Interior at the First Meeting of the Expert Advisory Council for Population and Race Policy], *Archiv für Rassen- und Gesellschaftsbiologie* 27 (1933): 413, 415, 419.

33. Quoted in L. Stoddard, *Into the Darkness: Nazi Germany Today* (New York: Duell, Sloan, and Pearce, 1940), 179.

34. Cattell, *Fight for Our National Intelligence*, 67–68.

35. Cattell, *How Good Is Your Country?* 43; emphasis in the original.

36. The lecture was published as F. Galton, "The Possible Improvement of the Human Breed under the Existing Conditions of Law and Sentiment," *Nature* 60 (1902): 659–65; the quote appears on 661.

37. See "Report of Committee on Classification of Feeble-Minded," *Journal of Psycho-Asthenics* 15 (1910): 61–61. Goddard was chair of the committee.

38. H. H. Goddard, *Human Efficiency and Levels of Intelligence* (Princeton: Princeton University Press, 1920), vi; Herrnstein, "IQ" (see chap. 3, n. 43); Herrnstein and Murray, *Bell Curve* (see chap. 3, n. 29); Herrnstein, "IQ," 51 (quote).

39. Washington attorney Kenneth R. Feinberg, who was named as the special master, provides an account of his deliberations in his book, *What Is Life Worth? The Unprecedented Effort to Compensate the Victims of 9/11* (New York: Public Affairs Press, 2005).

40. J. Harris, *The Value of Life: An Introduction to Medical Ethics* (London: Routledge and Kegan Paul, 1985), 8–9.

41. Cattell, *Beyondism: Religion from Science*, vii, viii (see chap. 2, n. 123).

42. See J. Perlez, "Mission to Somalia: Somalia Famine No Different; Children Are the First to Die," *New York Times*, December 8, 1992, A1; "The Beyondist Society: First Annual Meeting," n.d. (copy provided by Barry Mehler, director of the Institute for the

Study of Academic Racism); B. Mehler, "The Natural Self-Genocide of Raymond Cattell," *Searchlight*, no. 283 (January 1999): 17. According to Mehler, the draft was circulated by John Horn to a number of Cattell's close friends and associates, including Herbert Eber, Robert Graham, and Richard Gorsuch.

43. See L. Eylon, "The Controversy over Richard Wagner," available from the Jewish Virtual Library, http://www.jewishvirtuallibrary.org/jsource/anti-semitism/Wagner.html.

44. R. Wagner, *Das Judenthum in der Musik* (Leipzig: J. J. Weber, 1869), 10; Reuven Dafani, the former diplomat, is quoted in Eylon, "Controversy over Richard Wagner." The director whose sentiments he related was Zubin Mehta. In the same article, a violinist with the Jerusalem Symphony Orchestra calls Wagner's *Tristan und Isolde* a "masterpiece," while also noting that he cannot enjoy it because Wagner's writing "will always overshadow my life."

45. See, for example, R. N. Proctor, *Value-Free Science? Purity and Power in Modern Knowledge* (Cambridge: Harvard University Press, 1991).

46. R. N. Proctor, *The Nazi War on Cancer* (Princeton: Princeton University Press, 1999), 209–17. See also S. Zimmermann, M. Egger, and U. Hossfeld, "Pioneering Research into Smoking and Health in Nazi Germany: The 'Wissenschaftliches Institut zur Erforschung der Tabakgefahren' in Jena," *International Journal of Epidemiology* 30 (2001): 35–37; P. E. Meehl, "Psychology of the Scientist, LXXVII: Relevance of a Scientist's Ideology in Communal Recognition of Scientific Merit," *Psychological Reports* 83 (1998): 1127.

47. Cattell's response, published originally in the *Psychologists' League Journal* 2 (September–October 1938), is reprinted in "On the Battlefield of Intelligence (1938)," *Social Action: Newsletter of Psychologists for Social Action* 7 (July 1974): 2.

48. Gibb, "Influence of Cattell," 204 (see chap. 1, n. 179); "The Sociological Framework," editor's introductory comments to ibid., 191.

49. Eber was quoted in "Scientists, Colleagues Defend Cattell," 9 (see chap. 4, n. 33).

50. The letter from the recipients of the Early Career Contribution award is mentioned in ibid. I am grateful to Mark Gluck for elaborating on his views in a personal communication and permitting me to cite them.

51. R. J. Sternberg, "Costs and Benefits of Defying the Crowd in Science," *Intelligence* 26 (1998): 210.

52. Meehl, "Psychology of the Scientist," 1137, 1128–29.

53. Cattell, *New Morality*, 220.

54. Cattell, *How Good Is Your Country?* 67.

55. The division's home page containing its description is http://www.apadivision44 .org/. For a description of the division's award for Distinguished Scientific Contribution, see http://www.apadivision44.org/honors/scientific.php.

56. See *Bowers v. Hardwick*, 478 U.S. 186 (1986). The decision was overturned seventeen years later in *Lawrence v. Texas*, 539 U.S. 558 (2003).

57. See the APF mission statement at http://www.apa.org/apf/missionstatement.html.

58. D. W. Cantor, "APA's Efforts to Combat Racism" (paper at the Annual Convention of the American Psychological Association, Chicago, August 18, 1997). The program for the miniconvention was published by the APA as *Abstracts: Papers Presented at American Psychological Association's Public Interest Directorate Miniconvention on Psychology and Racism* (1997).

59. See, for example, M. Feinberg, *Racism and Psychology* (Washington, D.C.: "written at the request of the American Psychological Association Public Interest Directorate," 1999). Along with its critical analysis, the publication offers a list of "Ten Things You Can Do to Fight Prejudice and Racism."

60. Cattell, "Integration of Psychology with Moral Values," 27 (see chap. 3, n. 9).

61. Cattell, "Ethics and the Social Sciences," 195, 198 (see chap. 3, n. 8).

62. See Cattell, "Virtue in 'Racism'?" 281–84 (see chap. 3, n. 80); Farberman, quoted in J. Basinger, "Psychology Association Postpones Award to Scholar Accused of Racist Writings," *Chronicle of Higher Education* (September 5, 1997): A14.

63. Meehl, "Psychology of the Scientist," 1137; Cattell, *Psychology and Social Progress*, 63; Cattell, *Beyondism: Religion from Science*, 202; K. F. Dyer, *The Biology of Racial Integration* (Bristol, England: Scientechnica, 1974), 369.

64. See Cattell, *Fight for Our National Intelligence*, 42–43.

65. The average intelligence test scores of World War II draftees were considerably higher than those of recruits during World War I. The median raw score for the latter group—that is, the 50th percentile—corresponded only to the 22nd percentile for the former; the median score for the former group was equivalent to the 83rd percentile for the latter. See R. Tuddenham, "Soldier Intelligence in World Wars I and II," *American Psychologist* 3 (1948): 54–56.

66. See J. R. Flynn, "Mean IQ of Americans," 29–51; and J. R. Flynn, "Massive IQ Gains in 14 Nations," 171–91 (for both, see chap. 3, n. 46).

67. The claim of a point per decade decline was repeated in Cattell, "Where Is Intelligence?" 36 (see chap. 1, n. 125).

68. U. Neisser, "Introduction: Rising Test Scores and What They Mean," in *The Rising Curve: Long Term Gains in IQ and Related Measures*, edited by U. Neisser (Washington, D.C.: American Psychological Association, 1998), 3.

69. See Sternberg, "Costs and Benefits," 214.

70. See E. Barker, *The Politics of Aristotle* (London: Oxford University Press, 1950), 17; T. Lang, "Der Nationalsozialismus als politischer Ausdruck unserer biologischen Kenntnis," *Nationalsozialistische Monatshefte* 1 (December 1930): 393; Tucker, *Science and Politics*, chap. 4 (see introduction, n. 8); and Tucker, *Funding of Scientific Racism*, chap. 3 (see introduction, n. 50).

71. S. J. Gould, "Nonoverlapping Magisteria," *Natural History* 106 (March 1997): 19; G. Holton, *Einstein, History, and Other Passions: The Rebellion against Science at the End of the Twentieth Century* (Reading, Mass.: Addison-Wesley, 1996), 129.

72. D. van Biema, "God vs. Science," *Time*, November 13, 2006, 50; R. Dawkins, *The God Delusion* (Boston: Houghton Mifflin, 2006). Other recent attacks on religious belief include D. Dennett, *Breaking the Spell: Religion as a Natural Phenomenon* (New York: Viking, 2006); and S. Harris, *The End of Faith: Religion, Terror, and the Future of Reason* (New York: W. W. Norton, 2004).

73. W. E. B. DuBois, *The Souls of Black Folk* (Boston: Bedford, 1997), 102.

74. Quoted in C. C. Aronsfeld, "The Theory of Prejudice," *Patterns of Prejudice* 5 (1971): 26.

75. Young, *Two Worlds—Not One*, 73 (see chap. 3, n. 72). See also the quote in Aronsfeld, "The Theory of Prejudice," 26.

76. See Adam, *Art of the Third Reich,* 127 (see chap. 2, n. 102), which reproduces a photograph from the Nazi exhibit of "degenerate art" with a placard referring to "die Verniggerung der Musik und des Theaters"; and the online essay B. Ostendorf, "Liberating Modernism, Degenerate Art, or Subversive Reeducation? The Impact of Jazz on European Culture," available at http://www.ejournal.at/Essay/impact.html.

77. Cattell, *New Morality,* 211; Cattell, *Beyondism: Religion from Science,* 31.

78. K. A. Appiah, *Cosmopolitanism: Ethics in a World of Strangers* (New York: W. W. Norton, 2006), 129, 113.

79. A. Templeton, "Human Races: A Genetic and Evolutionary Perspective," *American Anthropologist* 100 (1999): 632; R. D. Kaplan, "The Coming Anarchy," *Atlantic Monthly* 273 (February 1994): 60; Cattell, *New Morality,* 178.

80. Cattell, *New Morality,* 234; R. K. Merton, "The Normative Structure of Science," in *The Sociology of Science* (Chicago: University of Chicago Press, 1973), 267–78.

81. See H. Chua-Eoan, "The Tao of Ho," *Time,* December 30, 1996, 69, and in the same issue P. Elmer-Dewitt, "*Time* Man of the Year," 52–56; "A Perfect Weld," *Time,* September 12, 2005, unnumbered insert on "Innovators." On Jemison, see her biography at http://quest.nasa.gov/women/TODTWD/jemison.bio.html.

82. Cattell, *New Morality,* 38.

83. See the organization's Web site at http://www.doctorswithoutborders.org/.

84. See B. Lomborg, ed., *How to Spend $50 Billion to Make the World a Better Place* (New York: Cambridge University Press, 2006).

85. See T. Rosenberg, "How to Fight Poverty: 8 Programs That Work," *New York Times,* November 16, 2006, a Web-only editorial at http://select.nytimes.com/2006/11/16/opinion/15talkingpoints.html.

86. Ibid. See also, J. D. Sachs, *The End of Poverty: Economic Possibilities for Our Time* (New York: Penguin, 2005).

87. See J. Kelly, "The Good Samaritans," *Time,* December 26, 2005, 8; and in the same issue N. Gibbs, "Persons of the Year," 38–45. The Gates Foundation Web site is http://www.gatesfoundation.org/default.htm; the address for Bono's organization, DATA (Debt, AIDS, Trade, Africa), is http://www.data.org/.

88. The observation appears under "Our Values" at http://www.gatesfoundation.org/AboutUs/OurValues/default.htm.

89. R. Niebuhr, *Man's Nature and His Communities: Essays on the Dynamics and Enigmas of Man's Personal and Social Existence* (New York: Charles Scribner's Sons, 1965), 84.

90. See, for example, P. Unger, *Living High and Letting Die: Our Illusion of Innocence* (New York: Oxford University Press, 1996); and P. Singer, "Famine, Affluence, and Morality," *Philosophy and Public Affairs* 1 (1972): 229–43.

91. Appiah, *Cosmopolitanism,* xiii.

92. The financier was Wickliffe Preston Draper (Tucker, *Funding of Scientific Racism,* chap. 1).

93. From the debate between Shockley and Montagu, Princeton University, December 4, 1973. Audiotape in my possession.

INDEX

ability traits (Cattell), 50, 53
abortion, 115, 149, 175
Abyssinia, 95
Achebe, Chinua, 192
Africa: Negro race (McDougall) and, 74–75; ranking of people in, 78, 181, 195; repatriation of blacks to, 121
African Americans. *See* blacks
agencies (Cattell), 53
AIDS, 181, 194, 195
Allport, Gordon, 11, 21–22, 24, 32, 57, 199n36
Alpines: Cattell and, 105, 106–7, 134; McDougall and, 72, 84
altruism: dangers of, 80–81; toward one's own group, 93
American Bantustans, 133–34
American Educational Research Association, Raymond B. Cattell Early Career Award, 2, 197n3
American Historical Association (AHA), 158

American Jewish Committee, 142
American Journal of Human Genetics, 124
American Journal of Psychology, 10
American Nazi Party, 131
American Political Science Association, Ralph J. Bunche Award, 155
American Psychological Association (APA): annual convention, 139–40; awards offered by, 2, 139–40, 184, 186; convention of 1997, 2–6, 140–46, 186–87; convention of 1998, 152–53; Division 44 (Society for the Study of Lesbian, Gay, and Bisexual Issues), 186; experimental versus differential psychology, 22–24; origins of, 10; Public Interest Directorate, 144; Society for the History of Psychology, 142. *See also* American Psychological Foundation Gold Medal Award for Life Achievement in Psychological Science

American Psychological Foundation
Gold Medal Award for Life Achievement in Psychological Science: aftermath of Cattell withdrawal, 150–53;
Blue Ribbon Panel, 3, 4, 144–46, 153,
189; Cattell nominated to receive,
2–6, 18–19, 61, 140–42, 186–87; Cattell
withdraws name from consideration,
4, 146–49, 189; controversy concerning, 2–6, 18–19, 62, 142–66, 182–89;
described, 139–40; "Open Letter to
the APA" (Cattell), 4, 146–49; postponement of award to Cattell, 2–6,
62, 144–46, 149, 163–64, 184, 187
American Psychologist (journal), 141, 145
American Renaissance (periodical),
137–38, 148, 175–76
America's Decline (Oliver), 131
Anglo-Saxons, 78, 79, 114, 191
Annual Review of Psychology, 12, 15
antiaphrodisiac, 115
Anti-Defamation League of B'nai
B'rith, 3, 142
antimiscegenation laws, 149
anti-Semitism, 137; Cattell and, 3, 95–
96, 142, 143–44, 161, 170; Nordics and,
172–73; rational, 132–34; Wagner and,
181–82. *See also* Nazism
Appiah, K. Anthony, 191, 196
Arendt, Hannah, 173
Aristotle, 189
artificial insemination, 47, 100
Aryans, 95–96, 101, 116, 128, 160, 162,
170
assessment, as basis of eugenics, 85–90
Astel, Karl, 182, 185
attitude: dynamic lattice (Cattell) in
measuring, 55–59; motivation and,
54–59; nature of, 54
Augusta (Ga.) Chronicle, 4

Bacon, Francis, 89
Balkan block, Cattell and, 127

Behavior Genetics Association Annual
Dobzhansky Memorial Award, 2
behaviorism, 68
Bell Curve, The (Herrnstein and Murray), 148, 179
benign neglect, in social Darwinism,
78–79
Benoist, Alain de, 130–31
Berg, Irwin, 152
Beyond Eagle and Swastika (Tauber),
129
Beyondism, 3, 103–38; "brotherhood"
in, 110; Cattell and, 141–42, 145, 147,
157; culture as derivative of race and,
114; Evolutionary Principle and, 110,
180; failing groups and, 118–19, 157–
58, 174–75, 181, 185–86, 192–93; Final
Solution and, 174; genetic management and, 111–12, 149; genetic shortcomings and, 180; human worth and,
176–81; influences on development
of, 103–8, 116; *Mankind Quarterly*
(journal) and, 14–15, 120–27, 130, 131,
142–43, 148, 151, 191; Nazi ideology
and, 116; origins of, 108–20; racial
separation and, 111–14; scientific improvement within groups and, 114–17,
160; spread of gospel of, 125; successful groups and, 118–20; supporters
of Cattell and, 108, 122–26, 128–38;
tenets of, 109; totalitarian tribalism
and, 169–76; world federal government and, 117–18
Beyondism (Cattell), 109, 141
Beyondist (newsletter), 136, 158
Beyondist Foundation, 15, 152
Beyondist Society, 135–36
bigotry, 107
Birkett, Heather, 14
birth control, 149, 157, 162, 185, 235n61
Blacker, C. P., 160–61
blacks: arts and, 191–92; birth rate and,
112–13; Cattell on, 94–95, 148, 159,

246   *Index*

WILLIAM H. TUCKER is a professor of psychology at Rutgers University in Camden. He is the author of *The Science and Politics of Racial Research* and *The Funding of Scientific Racism: Wickliffe Draper and the Pioneer Fund*.

The University of Illinois Press
is a founding member of the
Association of American University Presses.

———————————————————————

Composed in 10.5/13 Adobe Minion Pro
by Celia Shapland
at the University of Illinois Press
Manufactured by Thomson-Shore, Inc.

University of Illinois Press
1325 South Oak Street
Champaign, IL 61820-6903
www.press.uillinois.edu